Just A Couple Of Chickens

Corinne Tippett

Westchester Press

JUST A COUPLE OF CHICKENS

Published by Westchester Press
Santa Fe, New Mexico
www.thewestchesterpress.com

Library of Congress Control Number: 2009942739

ISBN 978-0-9843611-0-6

To my family and friends,
And to all these creatures who have passed
through our hearts.

Chapter One

$\mathcal{I}$n the spring of 2004, my husband Andrew announced that he was going to get a couple of chickens for our young daughters.

"To help them learn about the cycle of life," he said. I was against the idea, already overwhelmed by the cycle of life.

Andrew pursued his plan and brought home a hatchery catalog. He and the girls ordered a couple of chickens. I ordered fifteen ducks, nine geese, twenty more chickens, thirty-five partridge, and thirty pheasant.

"I have an idea," I said to my horrified husband, as I looked at the hatchery catalog. "We could have eggs ranging from large to small if I ordered these different birds. I think I could sell the eggs on the Internet and earn some money."

Andrew looked at the minimum chick order on each of the birds I was proposing.

"Hey now!" he protested. "This is going to be over a

hundred birds!"

"Not all of them are going to survive childhood," I said confidently. "There's got to be a mortality rate, and we could really use the income."

"How much do you know about raising those kinds of chicks or selling eggs on the Internet?" he continued.

"What I don't know, I can look up," I said. "After all, it's just a couple of chickens, how hard can it be?"

As it turns out, it is not only hard, but there are few things funnier than watching an urban transplant try to figure out the business end of a goose. We had a two-acre parcel of rocky land forty-five minutes east of Santa Fe, New Mexico with a small house surrounded by piñon and juniper trees. We bought the property ten years earlier because we wanted to live somewhere outside of the city to grow our souls, get back to nature, and because it was all we could afford. Our families were far away, in California and Nevada, wondering why we felt we had to move all the way to New Mexico to accomplish these goals. There were days, after I had children, when I wondered about it too.

We had few neighbors, but plenty of wilderness, beauty, and fresh air. Our souls were growing like weeds. We'd gotten back to Mother Nature and found her to be an uncompromising bitch who rarely gave second chances. We spent a lot of time fending her off with a stick.

At the time of Andrew's chicken proposal, our family finances were parched. Six years earlier, I had left my full-time job in town to come home with our first baby and Andrew branched out as an independent door installer. I had intended to keep working after our first baby was born, but my plan for expressing breast milk and eschewing baby formula was threatened by reality once I returned to work after maternity leave. I just couldn't keep up with the growing baby by pumping. Two months after going back to work, I gave my employer notice — in ounces.

"I have to quit eighty-seven ounces from now," I told my boss six years ago.

"Eighty-seven ounces of what?" he unfortunately asked.

"Breast milk," I said and watched him wince. Sensitivity training had taken hold in our workplace, and the word "breast" jangled nerves on the job.

"Boob milk?" I offered helpfully.

"I'm sure I have something to do far away from this conversation," he said and fled. Eighty-seven ounces translated into very little time; certainly none to plan or save. I'd been trying everything I could think of to earn money at home since then. Now we had a second baby, a toddler, so when Andrew suggested getting a couple of chickens, I cringed at the idea of more lives to care for, but I also had an idea.

A long time ago I had taken an egg art class and I knew that egg art was a crafty hobby with a following on the Internet. I thought that I could blow out the contents of the eggs these birds would lay, then sell the decorative shells. I had some other ideas for the eggs, but with the blank looks I got when sharing my first idea, I kept them to myself.

Our patch of land was part of the old San Miguel Del Bado land grant, established in 1794, on the steep banks of the Pecos River in the stretch between the town of Pecos and the State of Texas. It wasn't quite the middle of nowhere; the original Santa Fe Trail ran within a mile of our western property line — but it was close. The Pecos River lay sixty-five vertical feet off a cliff on our northern property line, but we didn't have water rights to anything other than our own well. This would be plenty, as it was a productive well with an electric pump. We got to work making a chicken house and fenced chicken run.

River rocks permeated the soil underfoot. Postholes for the chicken pen yielded rocks. Trenches for the sunken wire yielded more rocks. Because we had predators in addition to rocks, we piled rocks jack hammered out of the earth against the base of the sunken wire for additional protection around the perimeter of the pen. More than 223,000 acres of the Pecos Wilderness lay less than twenty miles to our north. There would be no free ranging for our birds, not if we wanted them to last more than a week.

The hatchery shipped our order of day-old chicks through the U.S. Postal Service. The address label contained our phone number, and the post office was supposed to call us when the box arrived. Depending on the attitude of the postal workers, this could be within business hours, or in the middle of the night when the truck actually unloaded at the dock. That spring, the post office night shift was dedicated. My phone rang at one o'clock in the morning with the pick up call for the ducklings. I left my family sleeping and drove to town, narrowly missing one fox and two coyotes on the empty, starlit road.

The loading dock at the central post office had a steel door with a huge red button. I pressed it and a cheerful man in a neatly pressed uniform popped out with my chick box in his hands. The shipping label clearly stated that the insurance policy on the chicks would be void if the box wasn't opened at the post office for verification, so together we dutifully lifted off the lid and peered inside. He verified that there were no dead chicks.

Every one of the ducklings (fifteen being the minimum order) was alive, well, and trying to climb out. The box was difficult to close properly with so many agitated ducklings pushing the lid up from underneath. On my drive back, as ducklings happily ran along the back seat of the car and snuggled down under the accelerator pedal, I realized that I indeed hadn't closed the lid properly.

Arriving home, I sifted through gum wrappers and plastic toys in the back seat to collect all of my little ducks. I felt very un-farmer-ish, sure that real farmers didn't have to pick cheerios off their day-old ducklings before putting them in the brooder. It was when I snagged a sixteenth duckling from the passenger foot well that I realized that I didn't actually know how many ducklings had been in the box in the first place, and how many more might still be stuck in the car. The consequences of a duckling perishing in my car would scar both my soul and my environment and it became clear that I was actually going to have to clean it out. This was my first introduction to the hatchery convention of including a few extra chicks with each order to cover loss, and my realization that my plan of counting on the mortality rate to compensate for our minimum-order-driven-chick-overload might not be effective.

The chicken pen wasn't complete, but the chicken house inside the pen was ready to serve as a brooder; a draft-free indoor space equipped with a heat lamp, chick food, chick waterers and wood shavings covered with newspaper for their first two days. Once safely transferred from the car to the brooder, the ducklings immediately jumped into the waterer and began gleefully paddling around, diving, and getting as wet as was possible in the half-inch deep pan. The duckling chapter in the 1950s-era book I had borrowed from the library had emphasized how important it was to protect ducklings from moisture, because they didn't have their mother's protective oils to coat their down. So I watched in dismay as the ducklings drained their waterer, soaked their newspaper, and threw themselves under the heat lamp to sleep.

It wasn't a great farming start, but by morning they were all alive, well, and still wet. All of my efforts to keep the little birds from immersing themselves were overridden by their instincts and enthusiasm. A duckling can die if it doesn't have sufficient water available to moisten the food, and a duckling can also die if the food becomes too moist. A duckling also seemed able to saturate its entire body given only enough water to drink. In the end, probably because I was accidentally overheating them with a too-powerful heat lamp, the ducklings were just fine.

Andrew was transitioning his custom door installation business to custom home building, and most days he was out at a job site. Any time he was home, or working for a client in his workshop, I encouraged him to put in several hours work on the new chicken pen. We had a deadline now, since the ducklings were in the brooder and the other chicks were on the way. I saw building the infrastructure we needed to execute my grand plan as his part of the job, as well as earning the ready cash to build the pens, buy the chicks, and feed all of us. As a stay-at-home mom, I was supposed to be in charge of the meals, home, and childcare. Even though I had not planned on becoming a full time stay-at-home mom when I was pregnant with our first child, I still recognized that the majority of the domestic duties were going to rest in my hands.

Our eldest daughter, Blue, had turned six and would start kindergarten in the fall, but this was May and my schedule was completely my own to fill with obsessive visits to the brooders to check on the ducklings and mostly ineffectual work on the pens. Time that I should have spent doing dishes I used to teach the girls the proper way to hold a duckling. Two-year-old Juno carefully scooped the wriggling little creature into her lap and protested as its sharp claws made furrows on her tender skin. Andrew came home to dinners of macaroni and cheese, from a box, and band-aid covered children with straw in their hair.

Now Blue and Juno were unsuccessfully trying to name a brooder full of indistinguishable ducklings. Two days after the ducklings arrived, the post office called at 2 a.m. to report the arrival of my box of goslings. Once again, I left my sleeping family and made the drive to town. This time, the postman handed me the box with extra tape on the lid.

"They're all alive," he said. "I've been lookin' in the holes, so you don't have to open the box."

"Okay," I said, having harbored no intention of opening the box this time.

"I think one of 'em has a power tool in there," he said. "They've almost got out a couple of times."

I peeked through one of the holes and almost lost an eye for my effort. Goslings are significantly larger than ducklings. These were also stronger and more agitated. I'd never seen a gosling before ordering my own through the mail, but I had checked out another book at the library to help me raise them.

Off to the brooder I went, driving back home in the dead of night. I admired my new babies with red-rimmed eyes. The goslings were beautiful, soft and fuzzy, but one of them was weak, and she died within hours. Another was not doing well and perhaps I could have saved her if I knew anything about goslings, but I was busy overheating them and she died the next day. The girls and I were sad, and I was beginning to realize that book farming, with tidy printed directions specifying temperature and other helpful data, was very different than real farming. The three-dimensional complications of providing the right temperature in an un-insulated chicken house in spring under a temperamental sky were overwhelming. Temperature was only one of the factors. Food, water, and surface litter all had their own complications.

My seven (down from nine) girl goslings were clad in goose down, one of the most insulating substances on earth. Although they had the ninety-degree zone in their brooder, which the book insisted that they needed, they were overheating and too often seemed in great distress. I struggled with the brooder the second night until the sun came up. The chicken pen was now complete and to cool down the goslings, I left the chicken house door open a small amount while I went to the house for coffee. When I returned, the ducklings were drying off under their heat lamp in their own brooder space, and the goslings had staged a prison break. They were happily paddling around in the dirt and weeds of the enclosed chicken yard, enjoying the early morning sun. My book said nothing about day-old goslings being outside, but at least they weren't dying, so I went to get the family to celebrate – thinking we'd better do it quickly.

I brought my little girls into the pen and we sat down in the sun each with a gosling in our lap. Blue held one by herself, and Juno shared my lap with the yellow gosling. Just that scene alone, my little girls cradling baby geese, brought me a rush of satisfaction. Even if I wasn't doing it right, I had already achieved one goal. My girls were hands-on with creatures that had a practical purpose in our lives. This wasn't just a crazy hamster, destined for a bitter end after a nocturnally frenetic life. This was the beginning of something bigger, something fundamentally real. I knew I might not be able to avoid the bitter end part, but along the way we were all going to get in touch with the forces that drove our everyday lives. At least that was my plan. I suspected the geese might have a plan of their own.

The goslings had red paint blotches on their foreheads, which was the identifying mark the goose sexer had plunked on them at the hatchery to declare them female. It looked like a belly dancer's bindi, and combined with their long lashes to give them an exotic air.

I had struggled with the decision to raise geese. Everyone I talked to was wary of them. Even people who could be open-minded about having a pit bull were wary of raising geese. I talked about it with the clerk at the local feed store.

"If I raise the goslings from chicks, won't I be part of the flock when they grow up?" I said, "and therefore, be immune from attack?"

"Nope," said the feed store man.

"But what if I spend time with them and feed them by hand?" I asked.

"Nope," said the feed store man.

"But..."

"Nope."

"But if...."

"Let me put it this way," he said. "My wife has raised geese for years. She raises 'em up from chicks and cuddles them and talks to them. When they get big, they bite every bit of her they can. She comes in sometimes with bruises all over her arms."

"Oh," I said, "so what do you do?"

"When we get sick of it, we eat 'em," he said. "Then she gets to wanting them again and it starts all over."

"Oh," I said.

Once the goslings had arrived, I belatedly researched the chick imprinting process on the Internet. These day-old chicks were bonding to each other while they traversed the postal system inside a cardboard box. I would have to be there at the moment of hatching if I wanted them to imprint on me. By the time they were in my care, they had reviewed their inborn instruction manual that listed me as enemy number one.

With the ducklings in the brooder and the goslings spending their days in the dirt, the poultry pen had come alive. The girls and I went up there every morning for chick chores; this consisted mainly of the girls playing with the chicks and the mom doing all the cleaning, water refreshing, temperature fiddling, and wood chip replacing. We were all out in the fresh air, under deep blue skies, with hands on living creatures, and it was nice. It was costing a bundle, but it was nice.

I had grown up in the big city, adopting every living creature around me as my own. None of my family heritage could be traced to a farm, no matter how hard I tried. Andrew's red-haired ancestors had come across the country in covered wagons, and he had plenty of family farming genes, but all his recent family history was urban. Neither of us had any experience to draw on, nor any wise resource nearby. But we both had an education and the desire to get our hands dirty. We wanted to experience raising our own food with our daughters as well. As I watched a duckling pinch Juno's nose hard enough to make it bleed, I decided that we certainly were getting to the close and personal part of the experience.

The chickens (minimum order twenty-five) were our third species to arrive, four days after the goslings and almost a week later than the ducklings. This time, Blue wanted to be part of the pick-up. Fortunately, this call was within regular business hours and instead of ringing the buzzer at the loading dock, we were directed to go to the normal post office service desk. Blue and I took a number from the ticket machine, and stood in line with all the morning people holding neatly labeled envelopes and packages. I wasn't wearing all of my underwear, and Blue's shirt was inside out. The nights of running up to the brooder to watch happy chicks sleeping peacefully were starting to erode my ability to do basic daily tasks, such as dressing appropriately.

Blue waited patiently, holding her ticket and watching the glowing red number on the wall until it was finally her turn. She stepped up and did a Kilroy at the high countertop.

"May I please have my package?" she said, politely.

The postman disappeared into the back, and returned with a noisy cardboard box, peppered with holes. Blue held it reverently with both hands against her chest.

"Mommy," she said with a huge grin. "It's a peeping package!"

"You going to open that here?" asked the postman.

"No," I said firmly.

"But the insurance..." said the postman.

"I'll pass," I said, and pushed down the edges of the box more firmly. We now had the full attention of everyone in the post office. The woman behind me leaned forward to look at the box in Blue's hands.

"Are those live birds?" she asked in amazement (or horror).

"Yes," I said. "Chickens. Chicks actually, from the hatchery."

"In the mail?" she said. "You can get live birds in the mail?"

"You'd be amazed what you can get in the mail," said the postman, punching the number button. "Next!"

A separate portion of the chicken house brooder was ready and warm. Blue and I took the chicks out of the shipping box one at a time, while Juno watched, and dipped their beaks in the water as the books had instructed. This was supposed to help the chicks figure out where the water was and trigger their instinct to drink. We smoothly transferred all twenty-seven chicks to the brooder and watched as they started to eat and drink and do their chick thing. The chicks had survived the journey in excellent health, even though we had placed the shipping box under the heat lamp as we made the transfer and some of the black chicks toppled over from the heat. They recovered quickly, thankfully, but it was the first of many small not-so-obvious errors we would make over the next year.

Andrew's work sometimes required him to bring his crew to our site. They were all family men, friendly, and Mexican (legal immigrants). My Spanish was awful despite two of my teenage years spent growing up in Buenos Aires, Argentina (Dad was a geologist, searching the world for gold and potash), but Andrew's was getting pretty good in a weird, colloquial, builder-specific kind of way. The crew was fascinated with our poultry and enjoyed watching the progress. They had pitched in during their workday to finish the pen, and since then were also often busy building last-minute amenities that we hadn't realized we would need when we made our poultry plans.

Now they were stringing cables over the pen to hang the netting that was required to contain the soon-to-arrive partridge which, it turned out, could fly. The crew's expense, which seemed all right when it was on an invoice to a customer, seemed high when it was on the bill for my poultry project. But my plans for selling eggs would recoup this expense, I was sure of it. And anyway, it was time to go pick up the partridge chicks.

"You're gettin' more boxes than the feed store," said the night shift postal worker, greeting me again at the back door.

"I have a big plan," I said.

"What are these, anyway?" he said. "If you don't mind me asking."

"These are Chukar Partridge," I said, peeking in the holes of the cheeping box.

"What's that?" he asked.

"I don't know, actually," I admitted. "I've never seen one live."

I was now practically professional at transferring chicks from a shipping box to a brooder. The partridge chicks were tiny and looked like little owls with their huge eyes and sharp beaks. They had a wild smell to them, different from the warm wheat smell of the chickens. I dipped their beaks in water, and placed them near the food, and forgot to count them. I'd ordered the minimum thirty-five chicks, but future Chukar Partridge counts were anywhere from thirty-eight to forty-five, depending on how much they were running around.

The girls came up to the brooder with me in the morning. We paused outside the closed door of the brooder house to enjoy the fresh spring air. As the day heated up, the air would smell of piñon, but in the early morning it depended on the wind direction. Sometimes, we could smell the sea, direct from the Gulf of Mexico, but most mornings it was a unique tonic of clean trees and heating earth. Once we opened the brooder door, all we smelled was poultry pong, which was much less pleasant.

That morning, we discovered that one chukar chick was dead and another had an eye wound – probably suffered at the hands of its flockmates. The girls struggled to see into the chukar brooder, which was separate from the other brooder spaces because chicks of different species and different ages were not supposed to be mixed. The chukar section of the brooder house was elevated to table height in the chicken house to leave space below for the other chicks. I lifted out the dead chick and Blue stared wide-eyed at it from her taller perspective. Juno wailed from the floor about being too short to see, so I lifted her up to sit on the table and she gently stroked the tiny body with her finger. Then she lifted it carefully into her little hand.

"How do you know that it's dead?" Blue asked.

"It isn't breathing, and it isn't moving," I said.

"But how can you be sure?" Blue persisted. "Maybe it's just sleeping really hard, or knocked out."

"It will get stiff," I said, thinking *gross*.

But this was the very reason we had started this adventure. To give our girls hands-on experience of life at an early age, before they had a chance to become sentimental about the truths of Mother Nature and her harsh side. This juxtaposition of new life and sudden death was exactly the kind of truth we were looking for, and here it was already, lying limp and pathetic in my baby's rosy little hand. Juno was now leaning precariously over the edge of the table, peering at the floor.

"Dwopped it," she said.

"Well I guess it's dead *now*," Blue said.

We marched in procession out to the pile of soft dirt and compost behind the pens, site of our future garden, which would be enriched by future poultry manure but was destined to lie stagnant and unappreciated for a good many months before completing its own cycle. After we dug the tiny grave and selected a rock for a headstone, we buried the little chick next to the other miniature mounds that were the gosling's graves.

"Can we check it every day?" Blue asked. "See how it goes?"

"Gross," I said supportively.

"Gwoss," Juno echoed.

May in Northern New Mexico is a pageant of weather systems. It can still freeze, or it can reach ninety degrees during the day with the sun blazing from open skies that perfectly showcase enormous cumulous clouds. Thunderstorms and winds are common, as are idyllic calm days. The freeze-thaw cycle of this region made rocks in the earth move as if they were a growing crop. We pulled rocks out of the pens and paths in the summer, and at the end of the following spring, new rocks had risen to the surface to take their place. The range of temperatures played havoc with my brooder environments and I found it difficult to keep ideal conditions in the chicken house. I was constantly erring on the side of being too hot, since cold is a major chick killer.

The goslings were now free in the pen all the time, with the bottom part of the chicken house set up so that they could come in and out as they pleased. The ducklings were beginning to dive over the walls of their brooder, landing in the gosling's part and therefore coming and going as they pleased. Between the chickens and the partridge, the brooder was stuffed to capacity. But I was still thumbing through the hatchery catalog.

Pheasant hens laid an egg that was smaller than a chicken egg but larger than a partridge egg. It would make a perfect addition to the egg collection I was planning, which would range from large eggs to small. Pheasant eggs were also supposed to be a lovely deep green color, which would add texture and variety to my grand egg plan. We had recently made a road trip to House, New Mexico to see the wind energy farm newly installed outside of Clovis, and stopped off at the tiny Clovis zoo. Andrew had fallen in love with a Lady Amherst pheasant rooster he had seen on the grounds of the zoo, and since his birthday was coming up, I wanted to get some pheasant as a surprise. Also for the eggs and the stunning feathers.

But the hatchery didn't sell Lady Amherst pheasant chicks the same way they sold chickens, partridge, ducks, and geese. I would have to buy the Ornamental Pheasant Collection, as day-old chicks, and there was no guarantee that the selection would include Lady Amherst. There was only the chance of it. But it was my best shot, and I had a reserve on the last shipment for the season.

An additional complication was that the girls and I were scheduled to drive to Arizona to see my sister and her girls right at the time the pheasant shipment was due to arrive, in early June. The hatchery said that the mortality rate on pheasant chicks was high, and it would be a good idea to go get them as soon as the call from the post office came in. I had to ask Andrew to keep his cell phone handy.

"All night long?" he said incredulously.

"Of course," I said, nonchalantly, "maybe I'll need to call you."

"In the middle of the night?" he persisted.

"Probably more towards morning," I said.

"And why is there this new separation in the brooder space?" he asked. "I thought we were going to let the other chicks have more room now that the ducks and geese are out."

"I'm... cleaning it," I said. "It has to rest a bit before the birds can go back in, like a fallow field."

Andrew just stared at me.

"It's a bird thing," I said.

"Wait a minute...!" Andrew exclaimed.

"Gotta go!" I said.

"You didn't!" he cried, as I backed my car out. "We already have more than a hundred birds!"

"Wave to Daddy!" I told the girls, as we accelerated away.

So Andrew had the opportunity to pick up a peeping package from the back dock of the post office at two o'clock in the morning on a workday. Happy Birthday, Honey! He put the chicks into the mysteriously ready brooder and they started eating and drinking just fine. I got to see them on the second day after their arrival and was impressed at their variety of sizes and colors. We didn't know what we had, but they were definitely different from chickens. They had long legs and huge eyes. They also were already feathering out at two days old, and once again, we had zero chick mortality with their shipment. Overall, the mortality rate was extremely low, less than three percent. The hatchery and post office were doing a fine job getting these chicks to their destination in good condition, and I was doing a basically okay job keeping them that way. But the result was significantly many more chicks than we had planned for, both in cost projection for feed and in square footage in the pen. Andrew started work on a new pen extension as summer began to heat up. I had time to reflect on what I had started and suffered a moment of reality panic. I had to have enough personal fortitude to follow through with my project because it involved living creatures. This wasn't a case of overbuying art supplies, which I was also guilty of at times. I was going to have to follow through all the way with this one.

Chapter Two

That June in New Mexico was not the hottest month. Mornings were still cool and pleasant, especially early, and I enjoyed my dawn walk to the chicken house to check the growing birds. It was my quiet time to watch the sun hit the edges of nearby Rowe Mesa and color the tops of the piñon and juniper trees that crowded our two acres. Since we had moved in here, ten years earlier, the trees had grown tremendously, helped by our profligate water use. The septic system was a source, but we had also dug pits, filled them with rocks, and covered them with dirt to handle rain runoff from the sometimes-violent summer storms. Now, because of the trees, we couldn't see from one side of the property to the other unless we were up on the deck of our little two-story house.

We loved the property so much that we had stayed on it when we probably should have given up our Wild West lives and moved closer to family. I thought that if we had been in a larger metropolitan area, Andrew would be having better success with his business by now. I also thought that

I should probably get a job, but both Andrew and I wanted our children to have a full-time mom at home with them. My challenge was to make some money while being that mom, at home, in this beautiful place.

I fiddled with brooder lights and reflected on our financial stresses. My plan to make money with the eggs these chicks would one day lay was not an immediate fix to our situation. Our debt had been mounting even before I added the expense of my grand egg business plan to our balance sheet. The missing income of my working days was seen in rising balances on credit cards. Although the benefits and savings of my career as a stay-home mom were not showing up on our bank account's bottom line, they were manifesting beautifully in the children. Our babies were looking happy and proving healthy but our living expenses were outpacing our reduced income despite my efforts to spend less. I scaled back Blue's pre-school attendance to save money and started some home schooling, thinking that since it was pre-K anyway, I could handle the curriculum. The girls' vocabulary expanded to include the profane and they learned the physics of vacuuming.

I had faith in my unwritten business plan, but we were still months away from any egg laying and already racking up feed and equipment costs well beyond what I had carefully calculated in an afternoon of scribbling on the back of the hatchery catalog. I looked into applying for some of the state and county aid programs that my neighbors were on, but our income was too high for those. We were too wealthy to qualify for help and too poor to make ends meet at our current level of spending. While I planned ways to reduce our expenses,

I went to the bank to apply for overdraft protection on my checking account which could also act as a credit line.

"I'm sorry, Mrs. Tippett," the bank officer said. "But you have no income and your husband is self-employed. Your credit balance is very high, and this makes you ineligible for a credit line."

"What do you mean, I have no income?" I said, "as a stay-home mom I'm a high level, multi-tasking, responsibility-laden, critically participating member of society – raising a future generation of taxpaying, law-abiding, wage-earning, potential banking customers! I am a key partner in my husband's ability to bring home an income while we raise a family, therefore I *have* some of that income!"

"Be that as it may…" the bank officer began.

"And recent income analysis has rated my stay-home mom occupation worthy of triple digit compensation!" I continued.

"I'm sure that's true," replied the bank officer, "but since you don't actually get paid, you have no income, and with no income there is no credit line."

"So what you are saying," I said angrily, "is that as a primary nurturer, I don't rate with you bankers. But if I were something like a prostitute, a hooker, a streetwalker, lady of the night! You'd be tripping over yourself to offer me accounts because I would have an income?"

"Well," said the bank officer, "we prefer the term sex-worker."

I had to take real action to reduce our expenses or to find another income source that didn't take five months to mature and start laying. Andrew had a hobby of reading business and finance books, which seemed to fuel his eternal optimism as an entrepreneurial builder. I preferred science fiction, which I imagined made me a realist. Andrew pulled out a book about property development and suggested we stand out on our deck and cast our eyes over our rural two acres in a brainstorming session.

"The book says we are supposed to be more creative in our approach to life," I said, thumbing past the opening chapter that said something about not doing anything on credit, and the value of constantly replenishing savings accounts as bulwarks against hard times.

"More creative is my middle name!" said Andrew Gordon Hunt.

"What if we installed a trailer to live in and rented out the house?" I said, after skimming the chapter on rental property titled "Passive Income."

"I think we should rent the trailer and live in the house," he said.

"We would get more rent for the house," I said.

"But then we'd have to *live* in the trailer," he said. "So we should rent it out and keep the house for ourselves."

"Nobody in their right mind is going to want to live in the kind of trailer we can afford," I said.

"Exactly my point," he said.

"We'll be a new kind of slum lord," I said.

"The kind who lives in the slum instead of renting it out," Andrew said.

"Exactly," I said.

"Oh, Lord," Andrew groaned.

There was almost enough room on the two acres to fit a singlewide trailer and another septic field, if the trailer snuggled in close to the road. The trees were tall enough so that our target trailer site was not visible from the house, giving both areas deep privacy. Our house and an empty two-acre parcel in front of us accessed the driveway, so we were the only traffic on the road. The well could possibly support two households, if the twenty-year-old well pump held up. It was looking like a feasible plan. We just needed to find a singlewide trailer that would do the job.

We began to look for the trailer on weekly trips to Santa Fe. We knew we'd have to do some work on it, maybe a little rehabilitation, so we started with the older mobile home parks. None of them permitted the kind of trailer we were looking for to even enter their parks. Some of those park trailers, while suitably debilitated, were horribly expensive to our impoverished eyes. We moved our search to the empty lots and abandoned fields in the rougher parts of town. One nice-looking trailer had a new paint job covering the entire interior ceiling.

"No leaks," assured the owner, eyes darting everywhere but me.

"Right," I said, and kept searching.

On our next trip to town, we went deeper into the outer neighborhoods and saw a singlewide in a weedy lot with a "for sale" sign in the window. The owner lived in a new mobile home, three feet off the port side of the old one. He let us in and showed us around. I pushed at the walls, and Andrew poked at the baseboards. I gingerly opened the cupboards, and Andrew peered at the fuse box. I looked closely at the unpainted ceiling.

"No leaky," assured the owner.

"What about *ratones*?" asked Andrew, in marginal Spanish.

"No *ratones*," the owner replied, his Spanish thick with a regional dialect. "I have a cat."

"Do you think the cat is responsible for the mess in the closet?" I asked Andrew quietly.

"We can only hope so," Andrew replied.

There were no windows in the bathroom, and no power in the trailer. It would have been difficult to inspect the room without the light streaming up through the holes in the floor. After a thorough tour, we climbed down from the trailer and sat in our car to discuss our inspection.

"It looks like a refrigerator from the outside," observed Andrew.

"One that fell over a long time ago," I added.

"And rolled," said Andrew.

"Into oncoming traffic," I agreed.

"I think I need a cootie shot!" said Andrew, shuddering.

"Yes," I agreed. "It's perfect, isn't it?"

I pushed Andrew over to the hopeful owner, who was hovering next to one of the dented side panels. Andrew stood tall and looked the owner straight in his remaining eye.

"Is there anything I should know about this trailer?" he said in Spanish.

"No leaky!" assured the owner. "Everything work! Except maybe a few thing, but you can fix, you got tools!"

Andrew made him an offer and with a grin wide enough to show both of his teeth, the owner sealed the deal with a handshake. On the drive home, we discussed the finer points of the work needed on our new home.

"We aren't going to impress anyone with our financial creativity if we wake up dead of carbon monoxide poisoning," I said.

"Or go up like a Roman candle," agreed Andrew, "but ventilation is not a problem right now with that original 1975 flooring."

"We are probably going to have to fix that," I said.

"By the time we're done, we'll know a lot about mobile homes," said Andrew.

"Just think of the investment possibilities!" I mused, as we drove by a procession of abandoned mobile homes on our way out of town.

"I do wonder one thing," said Andrew. "Why aren't Warren Buffet and his team of mega-investors elbowing us out of the way to get to this gem of a bent mobile home?"

"Our genius is rare," I responded.

Buying the trailer was one thing. Preparing the site to receive it was another situation entirely. We left our trailer listing in the weedy lot while we hired a backhoe to dig the required trenches on our property for power, water, and septic. They had to be four feet deep to meet local code. Most of the trenching could be done up the middle of the driveway, but at least two trench lines had to go through the trees. We couldn't bring ourselves to bulldoze the trees, so those trenches had to be hand dug. Andrew brought his crew to the property and they set to work, an out-of-pocket expense we hadn't planned for.

It felt like major surgery and had a similar cost. The ground again proved to be mostly rocks, with a scattering of clay-like dirt, and the backhoe broke a tooth. We dug up a Tiger Salamander, native to New Mexico but seldom seen in the wild. The girls tenderly put it in a doll's bed so it could keep sleeping. It was a battle to convince them to let us take it down to the river's edge, where the soft moist soil would be better accommodation.

"We should put water to the dog pen while the trenches are open," Andrew said.

"It would be good not to have to haul buckets anymore," I agreed, and the cost went up.

"We should put water to the workshop," Andrew said.

"Yes," I said uncertainly, and the cost went up again.

"We could bootleg power to the dog pen using that trench," Andrew said.

"So that the dog can read in bed?" I asked.

"No," Andrew said, offended, "so we can plug in a heater in the winter!"

"Uh huh," I said nervously, watching the cost redline.

"Unfortunately, we have to repair a rock drain that was ripped up accidentally by the backhoe," Andrew said. I just looked at him.

"The backhoe ripped up the phone line too," he continued. "But I repaired it myself, and we really should put water and power to this site out here because then we could do something with it in the future."

"While the trenches are open," I said.

"Exactly," Andrew said.

I stopped sleeping well somewhere around this time, and was relieved when the digging finally stopped. Now we could lay the pipes, cords, cables, and various lines. We were getting closer to closing the trenches, something I was desperately looking forward to, but somehow at the close of each day, work remained to be done. A professional plumber was doing the most critical plumbing joints and gas lines.

"The plumber walked through the repaired phone line," Andrew said, "so we have to fix it again."

"Before we can fill the trenches," I said.

"That's right," he said, "and a rock fell and cracked one of the pipes – but luckily we caught it before we closed the trenches."

I said nothing.

"And we really should take this opportunity to put a phone line to the shop and put in a new electric wire to the well for the day it craps out," he continued, then he paused, looking around. I wasn't there anymore.

When it was over, we stood on the scars of the closed trenches surveying our new utilities. We had redefined the term "over budget," but we were on our way to putting in the trailer and renting out the house. The planned new income source was clear: the rent from the house. However, I was a little confused on the reducing expenses part of the idea. It had looked much better on paper before the backhoe rolled in. We didn't talk much, just looked at the completed work and the preserved trees. We could hear the well pump cycling on and off more frequently than it used to.

"What's up with the well pump?" I asked.

"It's trying to keep the pressure up in the new lines," Andrew said.

"But why does it have to keep pumping to do that?" I asked. "It would only do that if there was a..."

"Leak," Andrew said, and looked very interested in his boots.

Andrew and his crew had prepared the trailer for transport while it was still in the weedy lot in Santa Fe. They ripped out the nasty insulation underneath, busted out the rotten parts of the floor, and tore out the old fixtures. The previous owner happily packed off with the evicted fixtures after learning that they were destined for the dump.

Andrew had become intimate with our new trailer-house and wanted to revisit our idea of living in the trailer ourselves and renting out the house to someone else. He said it gave him the heebies. I accused him of chickening out, but our plan was skittering around like ice on a hot plate. It changed every day, from abandoning the whole idea, to building a guesthouse on the prepared site, to going forward with it. I accused him of being a prince, and he offered to show me an example of something that had died in the walls, but the work went on and finally the trailer was ready for transport. We called a trailer transport company from the yellow pages and began our education in the art of moving a seriously dilapidated trailer thirty-five miles over freeways and private roads.

"Your off-ramp access isn't big enough for my rig," said Ed, of the Sunburst Trailer Transport Company. "You're goin' to have to cut the fence off the freeway."

"Is that legal?" Andrew asked, aghast.

"It is once you get them State Police boys to stand by and help you," said Sunburst Ed.

"How do I do that?" said Andrew.

"Not my problem," Ed said. "Call me back when you got it set up."

The state police were not as unapproachable as we had feared on the issue of cutting the fence off the highway to move our trailer. We were not the first in our area with the requirement, but they did insist that the trailer's legal documentation had to be up to date, and that meant Andrew had to take the previous owner in person to the motor vehicle department to transfer the ownership.

"What's this line about back taxes on this DMV printout?" Andrew asked the previous owner.

"No comprendo," he muttered, and turned away. After more than an hour, Andrew was finally the proud owner-of-record of a 1975 West Chester. He was handed a shiny new license plate.

"Put this in the window of your new house," the clerk said, deadpan.

Sunburst Ed met with Andrew in the weedy lot in town to review the trailer for transport. Unlit cigarette in the corner of his weathered mouth, Ed walked around the trailer while telling Andrew Nam stories.

"So Ed," said Andrew, "can you move it?"

"You sure you want me to?" said Ed.

"Well, yeah!" exclaimed Andrew

"Well, supposing the whole chassis don't jerk out from under the walls, she'll roll," said Ed.

"Does that happen?" worried Andrew.

"You goin' to want to screw down everything that flaps in the wind," Ed squinted at the trailer. "Which looks like about everything."

Andrew screwed down everything, notified the two neighbors on our route of a potential trailer roadblock, and coordinated with the state police who vowed to show up on time to stop highway traffic and open the fence. The trailer began to move. It was a momentous event, but the girls and I went on a mini road trip to avoid having to watch it.

We drove to the nearby town of Ribera and down to the historic ford where the Santa Fe Trail crossed the Pecos River. It was such an important place two hundred years ago that Catholic leaders had built a cathedral instead of a small village church. This was the place, around 1825, where the United States ended and Mexican territory began. Mexico had only recently gained independence from Spain and declared that everyone crossing the Pecos from the east had to pay an enormous tax. Covered wagons, foot traffic, people on horseback; everyone had to pay. Many people didn't have the money and had to set up camp here for years before they earned enough to continue their journey westward.

I imagined that this had been the site of all kinds of entrepreneurial activities in those times. Perhaps a pioneer woman had stood at the banks of the river and, although it was hundreds of years ago, the river looked much the same. Willow and cottonwood trees lined the bank and the water ran milk chocolate with mud suspended in the waters. I pictured her in the same place I was now standing. Dressed in homespun, with two small daughters of her own, she wrung her hands over their financial worries. Maybe her husband was busy somewhere nearby putting up their temporary housing, a stick frame tent, or a little log lean-to, while she and the children hauled water for washing or cooking. I imagined that it was summer for her too, and she was worried how it would be to pass a winter here, where cold could be so bitter at night in her makeshift home. All the worries that preoccupied me, I shared with her, over the gulf of two hundred years. So much had changed, and so much had not.

I looked around now and saw cottonwood trees, clear running water, and adobe ruins. Beyond the slumping clay walls were mobile homes, some occupied and some derelict. There were houses in various stages of repair and the church was well kept, but it was a no more than a wide spot in the road now, no longer a center of politics, finance, and commerce. It helped me to see that times change and hard times pass the same way good times do. I also saw that there were a surprising number of mobile homes scattered under the cottonwoods, and plenty of them were in need of rehabilitation. I made a note of where some of the unoccupied ones were, just in case this whole experiment turned out well.

On our return home, we stood back to appreciate the trailer transport accomplishment and listen to Andrew's war stories about the journey. There had been some hairy moments, including one unexpected last minute backhoe rental to accommodate a right hand turn that Sunburst Ed hadn't planned for, but it was done and the trailer was in place on our property.

"It looks a little precarious on those cinderblocks," I said.

"They sit under the steel chassis," Andrew said. "They have to, or they'd just punch through the floor."

"What are the chances of it falling off the blocks?" I said.

"Well," Andrew mused. "If a whole bunch of people started running from one side of the trailer to the other in kind of a mosh pit maneuver…"

"Exactly my concern," I added.

"They'd have to hit the wall pretty hard to make the thing roll over," Andrew continued, "and even then, the wall would probably punch through before the trailer rolled."

"Comforting," I said.

We turned our attention now to earning a living. Much of Andrew's time had been taken up in the effort of acquiring and moving the trailer, so he needed to focus on his paying projects. I continued my intangibly valuable work in the house and pens, and the chickens, ducks, geese, partridge and pheasant all continued to grow rapidly. The chickens and partridge were now out of the brooder and in the chicken pen, happily comfortable with the natural ground cover of rocks, juniper trees, and pine branches. The pheasant were completing their last two weeks of brooder time, and we had moved the geese and ducks into the dog pen to cope with the overcrowding. The dog was locked in the house anytime we had to leave for town, which put a time limit on our trips and added to the stress level.

Trailer work continued after business hours. Early in the rehab effort, Andrew thought about writing a letter to the trailer manufacturer suggesting that carpet should not be used as a structural element. In places it was the only thing holding the walls together. The whole interior had to be painted, preferably in some kind of paint that also worked as a sealant and barrier to ancient cigarette and cooking smells.

Andrew came up with fixtures and appliances for remarkably low prices from sources like the Salvation Army, or the dump. The dryer had a sticky price tag of forty-five dollars that resisted all efforts to remove it. The refrigerator was divine and cost less than two hundred dollars. It had an icemaker and a water nozzle built into the door. We sent grateful thoughts to the person who had decided that they had to have a brand new Subzero instead of an almost brand new Kitchen-Aide. Juno developed a habit of showering with the water nozzle to cool off, flooding the kitchen floor.

The oven had seemed like a great deal; cheap, miniaturized, and easy to convert to propane from natural gas. I soon discovered it also had a simple cooking method. All settings on the oven dial gave the same result and it could cremate food in a remarkably short amount of time. I began to refer to it as The Incinerator. Using it prompted me to demand that Andrew get the exhaust fan working.

"It is working," he said.

"It doesn't look like it," I said. "I can see all the inside parts. Where is the ON switch?"

"You just twist these two wires together like this," he said, demonstrating and then screaming like a girl as the fan roared to life.

"Scared you?" I asked compassionately.

"Electrocuted me!" he said in surprise. "On second thought, leave the fan alone for now."

Since the trailer was only fourteen feet wide, opening

all the windows in a stiff breeze would effectively clear out cooking smoke. In future months, I discovered that it would also dispose of pesky paperwork and unsecured heirlooms. Finally, the electricians, plumbers, and safety inspectors completed their work and drove away, shaking their heads and wishing us luck. I invited a friend over to celebrate move-in day for our new home.

"Here it is," I gestured grandly. "Our grand plan and new home!"

"Where is it going to go?" she asked dubiously. I stared at the installed trailer, which was plumbed, powered up and in place.

"What do you mean?" I asked blankly. "It's going to go right here."

"Oh!" she exclaimed in surprise. "It just looks a little… temporary?"

I cocked my head and tried to look at it with fresh eyes. It certainly did look more mobile than home, precariously perched on cinderblocks set back only six feet from the dirt road. In fact, it looked like it was parked in the road.

"Convenient access," I said.

"Why don't you rent the trailer and live in the house?" she asked.

"We can get more money for the house," I said.

"Well," she sighed. "Good luck."

Lack of vision, I decided, and we moved in.

I woke up after my first night in the trailer to cool fresh air pouring in through the closed window. It was like luxury camping. The great outdoors felt much closer and more intimate than it had when we had lived in the house. I stared sleepily at a herd of someone else's cattle ranging freely on the other side of the thin trailer wall.

"Look, Honey!" I said, nudging Andrew awake. "Isn't that a bull?"

Andrew bleared out the window groggily.

"It's a huge bull," he agreed, collapsing back on his pillow.

"What's that white pipe he is standing on?" I asked.

"The only white pipe out there is the sewer pipe," he mumbled.

"Don't people usually bury the sewer pipe in the ground?" I asked.

"Yes," Andrew answered, annoyed, "but usually the house isn't three feet up in the air, so people usually don't have to haul in tons of dirt in order to bury their sewer pipes."

"So it would suck completely if the bull broke through that pipe," I observed.

"Completely," Andrew agreed.

There was a loud crack and the bull stumbled forward. I wriggled back into the warm covers and joined Andrew staring at the low ceiling decorated with stiff plastic flowers.

"I vote for never getting up again," I said.

A muscle in Andrew's jaw jumped. Two warm bodies hurtled onto our bed and thrust cold feet down inside our cotton sanctuary.

"What's that smell, Mommy?" Blue said instead of "Good morning."

"It tinks," Juno said, sniffing loudly.

Chapter Three

We began to settle into our new lives in the old trailer. I gave the girls tasks while I began to clean up the house, preparing it for rental. They scooted around the honey-colored wood floors with rags tied to their feet, sliding on floor polish. I cleaned corners I had never become acquainted with when I'd lived there. All of the furniture was out of the downstairs rooms and I found a full-size snakeskin where my desk had been. This indicated that at one time, there had been a full size snake behind my desk. I wondered where it was now.

Our rental ad was in the paper and Andrew was taking the calls. We were ready for it to take some time to find the right tenant. It would also take some time to get the house ready, so that part of our plan was progressing as expected.

In the meantime, I was getting ready to move all of the chicks out of the brooder space for good. The chicken pen and metal-walled workshop both lay at the eastern edge of our two acres. It was a short walk uphill from the trailer to the pen, and both structures were downwind of both the trailer and the house. The chicken pen stood about twenty feet away from the side of the metal building, and I had always thought that if I was going to expand the poultry pen, I could use the side of the metal building to do it. But for now, all I had was the chicken pen.

The chickens and the Chukar Partridge had been living harmoniously together in the chicken pen for the last two weeks despite warnings in the old poultry husbandry books that different species and different ages of birds would not mix well. I was testing this advice because I needed them to mix well. My whole plan was based on mixing the poultry – I couldn't afford separate pens for each type.

These same books had warned that game birds, like the partridge and pheasant, were particularly sensitive to overcrowding and would resort to cannibalism when under such stress. When my square footage calculations came up short for the space the partridge were sharing with the chickens, I went on cannibal watch. I carefully watched as my pheasant and partridge picked each other bare of feathers, pulled each other's tail feathers out until they bled, nailed each other's toes, and hammered each other between the eyes. But I was satisfied that no chick was hunkered down behind the water bucket with chunks of another chick in its claws.

Just as the pheasant were ready for release into the pen, I discovered the best information source I had ever seen; it beat the pants off the old library collection. I found Dr. Leland Hayes on the Internet. He had a website, and an Ezine - an email magazine - all up-to-date and accessible for questions about game birds. I read all of his materials, straight through the night. Many things became clear, like the true definition of poultry cannibalism: feather pulling, tail pulling, toe picking, and eye pecking.

I had taken pride in my cannibal-free pheasant flock while they picked each other bare. Humbled, I joined the anti-cannibal fight and varied the diet, provided more space, added other peck-able items, added vitamin supplements, and provided plenty of shade. None of which stopped the cannibalism, but it kept me busy.

It was July now and the days were hot, the evenings warm. I was feeling optimistic when I dropped the first pheasant chick into the already colorfully populated pen. The chickens stopped and stared. Although the chickens were twice the size of the pheasant, the chickens were soon on the run, chased by the wing shaking, posturing pheasant. But by the time the last pheasant chick was released from the brooder, the chickens had regrouped and were showing the pheasant the true meaning of "pecking order." I got a little worried; the chukar and the chickens hadn't fought when they were first released together.

Andrew's crew was working in the wood shop at our home that day, busy antiquing a custom door for a client while Andrew was in town on a job site. Antiquing the doors involved taking a new unfinished door and making it look ancient by hammering on it, burning it, and scraping it. With the final coat of sealant, it looked spectacular. I waited until one of the men had stepped back from abusing the door and waved to get his attention. I knew that this man had a family farm in Mexico because his immigration paperwork was structured for him to return regularly to his hometown during harvest season. I thought that he must know something about chickens, so I started some elaborate pantomiming to bolster my limping Spanish.

"Son buenos?" I asked, pointing to the pen filled with three species of three varying ages of poultry.

"Si Senora," replied the man politely, "son bueno con limon y arroz."

"No, no," I said, waving my hands in marginal Spanish. "Son buenos juntas? Together?"

The man shrugged his shoulders kindly, and said "No."

"I mean," I said, slipping into marginal English, "are they going to be okay all together mixed in the pen like that?"

"Just got to wait and see," he said, in perfect English.

"Hey!" I said, surprised and embarrassed. He gave a lovely smile and went back to beating the door.

After a while everything in the pen looked stable so the girls and I went back to the house to do more cleaning. When Andrew came home, he took the girls out to the newly populated chicken/chukar/pheasant pen. I came up and stood back in satisfaction to watch my family interact with our new farm environment. The girls were becoming chicken-wrangling experts, and loved to nab the hens and cradle them firmly. They didn't even try to catch the Chukar Partridge, which were smaller, quicker, and much more wild. In fact, none of us could catch a chukar and I had a net on order from a poultry supply company to address that problem.

"Daddy!" Blue called out. "There is a pheasant without a head over here!"

Andrew went over to see and immediately called me in to take his place.

"It's yucky," he said, "and it's over there."

Blue and Juno and I stood gravely over the little corpse.

"Murder most fowl," I said.

One of the dark-feathered pheasant chicks was stiffly propped against a rock in the pen. There was a small splash of blood on the surrounding earth. Everything above the beak was missing. The other birds were strolling around innocently, maybe a little too innocently.

"Where is his head?" I asked.

"I think they ate it," said Blue, and gestured at the chickens that were sidling closer to the crime scene.

I looked at Juno, almost three years old. Her eyes and mind were filled with the image of the dead pheasant. A farming childhood had seemed like a good alternative to the violence and injustice of our media-soaked urban world. Perhaps that was because I had not actually seen a farming childhood first hand. Obviously violence was going to be part of the food-generating process and injustice was in the eye of the beholder. Chickens were turning out to have dark souls, but that was from my point of view, bleeding-heart urban transplant that I was.

"Okay girls, listen up," I announced, crouching down. "This is gross and kind of sad, but it is not scary or wrong. This is normal and natural, say after me."

"This is normal and natural," Blue chanted dutifully.

"Dis gwoss," Juno said.

"So let's figure out how he died, okay?" I continued, and got a hearty nod from both my little students-of-nature.

"Pick him up, Blue," I suggested, "and see if his neck is broken," Without hesitation, she picked up the little corpse and gave the chick's neck a good massage.

"No, it feels all stiff and yucky, but not broken," she said.

"Good job," I said. "Then he probably didn't fly into the wire and break his neck."

Juno stood at eye level with the gruesome little bundle in Blue's hands, her fingers stuffed into her mouth and her eyes perfectly round.

"I think one of the chickens pecked him in the head until he was dead," said Blue, still giving the pheasant's body exploratory little squeezes.

"I bet you're right," I said. "I bet this pheasant tried a little kung fu move on a chicken and it backfired."

"Pecked him in the head," Blue repeated, "until he was dead."

Juno's eyes never left the headless pheasant. I scooped her up and held her while we marched in procession to the poultry graveyard behind the pen.

"Don't be afraid of the birds," I told her, after we placed the rock headstone, "but don't let them near your eyes either."

After laying the pheasant chick to rest, we spent the rest of the day separating the pen. Killer chickens on one side, significantly more expensive game birds on the other. Juno resumed her expert chicken catching, carefully holding the bird away from her head and face. I reflected that my fight against cannibalism had graduated from mild to total failure. They had partaken of the forbidden feast. However, my cycle-of-life education plans for the girls were in full swing, complete with graphic illustrations. Overall, I was feeling like I was in over my head. This was a phase of my life where I had chosen learning by doing and the consequences were manifesting. Some of them were going to leave a mark.

A larger pen space was now urgently needed and so once again, Andrew's crew was diverted for half a day. Four men worked hard and accomplished an incredible amount, while almost a hundred poultry did their best to pluck each other bare. Neither of them achieved their goals that day. We were forced to abandon our elegant plans and go for the most direct way to finish the pen. There were plenty of blueprints for large poultry pens in the resource books but we had once again ignored all advice and designed it elaborately from scratch, based on our own inexperience. Now we were just reaching for whatever was at hand in the yard and nailing it into place.

I had become disenchanted with the aging library books, even though they had warned me about mixing species. Sometime between 1975 and today, poultry had changed a great deal. There were not only more breeds available now than were listed in these yellowing books, but all of their feed information was off. The protein percentage in today's feed was tailored to suit the breed of the bird and the purpose of the farmer. Market birds, including ours, were reaching their market weights in half the time the old books said they would. Somebody had been messing with these birds, and compared to 1975, these were a different animal altogether.

Dr. Hayes' information continued to be helpful for the game birds, but he also wrote about not mixing pheasant species. The chickens were alone in their smaller space, but the chukar and pheasant were combined, and their pen section was too small. I had to weigh the costs of overcrowding versus interacting, and went ahead with efforts for the larger pen addition. I could split off sections later if it really was true that I couldn't combine all these birds happily. Maybe they just needed a really large space. As I hauled manure out of the pen in buckets, because we had built the doorways too narrow to accommodate a wheelbarrow, I ruminated on the lasting impressions of lessons learned the hard way.

A week after the chickens were separated from the chukar and pheasant, all of the birds were doing well. There was no fighting among the game birds, no fatalities, and I had no idea why. (I would later learn that it was because nobody messes with a flock of chukar. They are the piranhas of the poultry pen.) The pheasant were spread throughout the available space, but the chukar moved as a single group, blending in with the rocks and dirt of the natural landscape. I couldn't find very much specific information about raising Chukar Partridge, other than feed ratios, but they luckily seemed to be thriving. Dr. Hayes recommended raising partridge on wire, instead of on the ground because of possible trouble with worms and enteritis, so I didn't find much information about the habits of chukar on the ground. I didn't know if it was normal for the partridge to be stuffing themselves into every cranny they could find. The pen had plenty of pits and potholes in the natural ground cover, but the chukar dug more. Elaborate dust holes where they bathed and deep tunnels that headed straight under the wire. I plugged those holes and piled more rocks in the corners so that I could rake the pen easily, and the chukar loved them. They excavated grand caverns under the rocks and once the space was large enough, every chukar in the pen would try to get in the hole. Between a rock and a hard place was a Chukar Partridge, at least at my house.

One day, I found a chukar trapped between a wooden bench and the stucco wall of the chicken house. I thought it was dead and felt like a negligent partridge farmer for having something in the pen that proved dangerous to the birds, even though I never imagined that a bird would cram itself down in such a small space. I carefully eased it out from the wall and, once free, it suddenly flapped out of my hand, scaring me half to death. It had abrasions on one shoulder so I decided to give it some first aid. I had salvaged materials from the chicken house when we took the last of the brooders down and was able to make a hospital cage out of the lumber, wire, and heat lamps. The injured bird went inside for a holiday of solitary confinement.

The bird healed, and about three days later I fished it out of the hospital brooder. I held it in one hand, with my palm over one of its wings. The other wing was tucked against my side. I'd seen pigeon fanciers hold their birds like this on TV. But this was not a pigeon, and with one great pump of its now-healed wing, it slipped out of my hands and flew away. I had a grand view of its strong wing beats and heavy trailing legs as it rapidly headed west and out of sight.

In order to legally raise pheasant and partridge in my county, I'd needed a game bird permit. It wasn't hard to get but during the application process, I had sworn an oath not to release the birds into the wild. My permit, this first year, was provisional, and specified that New Mexico Fish and Game reserved the right to come inspect my facilities at any time. I thought that it was unlikely for a warden to come visit so long as I kept paying my $10 a year, but now I worried that if he did, he'd find partridge in the wild. Alternately, I worried that my poor partridge wouldn't survive very long in the wild by itself. Mostly, I just wanted my bird back.

Later that day, I took some vegetable kitchen scraps to the pen. Many of the birds were strutting along the fence line and I slowly realized that one of the strutting birds was outside of the fence. It was the runaway! He had returned to his flock and was trying to get in the pen from the outside. I was excited and cast around for something to catch him with. I didn't yet have the professional net that I would later use almost daily. What I did have was my daughter's pink toy butterfly net. The partridge was soon back inside with his covey, and the torn and soiled butterfly net was hidden in the trash.

My success with the injured chukar bolstered my confidence, which had waned as I tried to deal with the partridge whose eye had been pecked out as a chick in the brooder. The one eyed partridge had survived, but never thrived, and lately was looking more and more depressed. When she was a tiny chick, I'd held her in my hand and thought that I should cull her. It would be the farmer thing to do. Just close my massive, callused fist around her tiny neck and snap it. But I didn't do it. I didn't know how to snap a bird's neck, and my urban hand wouldn't follow my farmer mind's advice.

One-eye usually stood isolated from the flock, feathers unhappily fluffed. Her helpful flock mates would peck at her blind side anytime they had the chance, and showed her no mercy. One afternoon I made my usual rounds and found her stunned and stumbling in a back corner of the pen. She must have gotten her head caught in the wire and panicked, because she had a horrible wire cut. She was suffering, and I sadly asked Andrew to give her the Favor of the Wolf.

"What's the Favor of the Wolf?" asked Blue. She and Juno were staring wide-eyed at the vicious wound on the bird's head.

"It's like this," I began, smoothing her feathers with my fingers, "a sick or injured animal gets a promise from nature that when it is in pain, the wolf will come and kill it quickly, setting its spirit free."

"We don't have any wolves here," Blue said.

"Well, then the fox," I said. "The fox kills the injured bird, and eats it," I continued, "and by eating the bird, the fox is able to feed her own babies."

"Is a fox going to come for this bird?" asked Blue.

"Well, not a fox, actually," I said, "but Daddy is going to chop off her head and set her spirit free."

"So it's really the Favor of the Daddy," concluded Blue.

"I'm calling it the Favor of the Wolf to represent how it works in the wild," I countered.

"And we aren't going to eat her either, because she's sick," Blue pointed out. "You said we couldn't eat a sick bird."

"It's symbolic," I said, with emphasis. "We aren't going to eat her, but a fox or wolf would."

The injured bird twitched in my hand.

"Please try to absorb the essence of the lesson," I said,

"and quit playing with the hatchet."

Now I knew that it would have been kinder to close my fumbling farmer fist on the injured chukar when she was a day-old chick. Poultry had no patience for the disabled. Thrive or die were the options, and my bleeding-heart efforts served only to extend her suffering. A small injury like the abraded wing was manageable, but anything more was a hopeless case. I was going to have to toughen up and learn to cull. All of this was supposed to be a learning environment for my children and a small business venture for myself but so far, my learning curve was a vertical line and my bottom line was a seeping, blood red stain.

We had moved the waterfowl to the dog pen to help make room for the chicken/pheasant separation. They were happy there, with a dinosaur-shaped wading pool and weather tight doghouse as a shelter. The goslings were almost ready to feather out, and the ducks already had. We were going to need the dog pen pretty soon to contain the dog, and the waterfowl occupation was supposed to be temporary. The new goose/duck pen was planned as an extension to the other new unfinished pen, sealed off from the chickens and game birds. We had expected to be able to build it quickly because it would use two sides of the existing pen, but we had made no progress at all as we concentrated our efforts on expanding space for the game birds.

Andrew and I stood watching the geese and ducks, as the girls played with rocks outside the pen. We were taking a moment's reprieve from the tremendous work ahead of us. We were enjoying the sunshine and waterfowl pong in the summer heat. We listened to the variety of deafening sounds uttered by our flock of geese as they maneuvered to be as far away from us as possible.

"Which of these geese is going to be Thanksgiving dinner?" asked Andrew, blasting a hole in the moment.

"What do you mean, which goose?" I asked, shocked. "No goose! These will be my layers!"

"No way!" debated Andrew. "I want goose for Thanksgiving and Christmas dinner. These are geese, therefore they are dinner!"

"These are GIRL geese," I said. "Nice, polite, *useful* girl geese."

"Just what are you trying to say?" bristled Andrew.

"I'm saying get your hands off my egg-laying girl geese," I said.

Finding a solution to the housing problem was left behind as we started our day in a huff. Andrew had to go to town to work and I went through the routines of my housework. The next morning, I followed Andrew out to feed the geese, ready for another round of arguments and was startled to see two new goslings in the flock. I blinked and counted again, but there were definitely two more birds than existed the previous day. Andrew stood looking at me, his body language defiant.

"Look!" I said to him. "See how fertile they are? They've increased the flock already!"

"I bought two NEW geese," Andrew said, irritably. "They are boy geese. I'm going to eat these geese for Thanksgiving and Christmas dinner."

I looked at the new goslings, which had already become indistinguishable from the original goslings.

"How do you know that these are boy geese?" I asked.

"Because they were the last goslings at the feed store," Andrew said. "They were the ones nobody wanted. So they are obviously boy geese."

"Obviously," I agreed, staring thoughtfully at him.

Andrew's strange goose-sexing selection method proved effective. The two new geese were indeed boys. I could eventually tell because the ganders grew faster than the geese, had massive legs, and attacked keepers on sight to defend their womenfolk.

I kept forgetting the Spanish word for goose when I was talking to Andrew's crew.

"Estos son las Lindas, very pretty," I said, proudly showing off my goslings.

"Gansos," Andrew's crew said politely.

"Right," I said, and promptly forgot the word again.

I was calling the goslings "Las Lindas" because they were the prettiest of the poultry chicks. It occurred to me that it was a great name for the girl geese, and naming them all the same name would save a lot of effort in trying to tell them apart. So the geese became Linda and the ganders were both Luke. One of the geese was a White Chinese and became China Linda. One other was a Toulouse, and became Toulouse Linda. The rest of the flock were Africans, and were all therefore African Linda, except for the smallest one - the only one I could tell apart. She was Little Linda.

One approach to poultry farming is to plan ahead for adequate square footage per bird and build suitable pens on a reasonable budget. We did not do this. When the need for the new pen became gruesomely obvious, I had asked Andrew to accelerate all of our pen construction projects, but do it in a way to contain the costs. The two requests seemed to be mutually exclusive and I didn't think we were making fast enough progress, so I asked him to get creative to make it happen. Saturday morning dawned and Andrew's crew showed up while I was still nursing my first cup of coffee and began to unload a truck full of supplies. Before I could start complaining about the costs, Andrew bounced up with an explanation.

"The guys are trading me for work on their own houses next weekend," he said breathlessly. "It's a group trade – they all have projects they need a crew for, and the materials are from the recycling yard."

Just four hours later I was looking at a finished pen. I stood in stunned amazement, flies warbling in and out of my open mouth. The crew had started with telephone pole remnants that they chain sawed into even lengths and then sank three feet into the ground. These were cemented into place, each one six feet apart, then laced together with a long cable and six-foot tall horse fence. Game bird netting draped along cables from the roof of the workshop to the fence, and the bottom half was laced with chicken wire. Rocks dug out for the postholes pinned a skirt of more chicken wire several feet out from the perimeter as an anti-dig zone. It was 1200 square feet of predator-proof aviary, and it was beautiful.

Andrew created an elaborate doorway out of netting and planks that connected to the old pen, and propped it open for the game birds to pass. Now that this new space was available, and all the birds were a couple weeks older, I opened the chicken pen as well and allowed all birds except the waterfowl to enjoy the entire space. We watched in satisfaction as the chukar tut-tutted in their new dirt, and the pheasant hid behind new trees. The crew packed up tools and trash, agreeing to meet again the following weekend at one of their houses, Andrew included.

For the first time since the chicks arrived, I felt in control of my project. I looked forward to some peace and quiet; at least until the waterfowl pen construction was underway. The chukar in particular had a beautiful little song that sometimes rolled across the landscape, but more often was too soft to hear. As I basked in this success, enjoying chukar song, the ground began to rumble. I looked around in alarm. An enormous backhoe was lumbering up our private road, headed straight for our new pen. Andrew leapt up and waved it to a standstill, the growling engine churning under any chance I had to overhear. After a short conversation, he waved the driver to the south and came running back to me.

"We have a new neighbor," he exclaimed, out of breath. "That's her contractor, he's starting construction on her new house."

"Next to our chicken pen?" I said in horror.

"Looks that way," he confirmed. And so it was. Construction vehicles of all description began to trundle by our trailer, which we had just finished placing within the barest legal clearance of the road. By my estimate, our new neighbor's house was going to be about fifty yards from our new goose pen. What a rural welcome that would be.

I stood a moment, wondering about this new neighbor. Was she coming to live out here for the same reasons we had, which was an attempt to touch the pioneering lifestyle of olden times? Or was she coming because this was the prettiest land in the area within her price range? Close enough to Santa Fe to work, far enough out to be affordable.

Andrew's family came to California on the Oregon Trail in covered wagons and stayed. He was the first to move out of California in over a hundred years and it caused some comment at family gatherings. My heritage was all over the world. If anything, we were a tribe of expatriots, either engaged in Foreign Service or private companies posting overseas. I was a wanderer and Andrew was rooted. He had wandered this far with me, in search of a homesteading dream, and then he dug in deep.

We hadn't been the first people to live here. There were three neighbors within sight who had initially settled this area, but a new neighbor was a big development. For more than ten years, there had been no new faces. Now there would be several as we rented the house, welcomed the neighbor, and raised our geese.

Chapter Four

There is a saying in New Mexico: If you don't like the weather, wait five minutes, and it will change. Our hot July days were interrupted by thunderstorms, some tremendously powerful, some noisy but accompanied by only gentle rains. Clouds piled up on every horizon, catching my attention for minutes at a time, like artwork in a gallery, compelling, distracting, inspiring. Summer brought shades of green to the landscape as the natural plants and weeds leafed out and grew tall. We pulled up the wild plants by the armful, anything that looked succulent and tasty, and tossed it in the bird pens. The poultry chose their forage from those piles and I couldn't keep track of their likes and dislikes.

We were moving forward with our plans in distinct though arduous steps. We were busily spending too much money fixing up the house for rental. The house got a new stove. The house got a refinished floor. All of the doors at the house were given a tune up. Finally, the house was ready, but the geese and ducks were still sharing the dog pen, which was only about fifty feet west of the house. The

pen full of waterfowl so close to the house was a deterrent
to renters, especially the odor, which had begun to kill every
living thing downwind for a couple of acres after it passed
through the house.

I was constantly inviting friends out to the property to
share the wonders of the bird project. On the rare occasion
that somebody agreed to come, I led them out to the dog
pen and turned the hose on the geese and ducks. I marveled
aloud at their beautiful water play as the geese lined up in the
hose spray and snapped backlit rainbow water drops out of
the air. The ducks did a running duck-dive into the wading
pool that propelled them underwater and out the other side
in the same move.

Most of the time, our friends stared in polite horror at the
ramshackle pens and overload of birds. One day, they were
so quiet that I assumed they were mute with admiration, but
when I turned around to say something, there was no one
behind me. Everyone was in the house, waving to me from
the window. The smell had proved too much for them.

Naturally, I had expected some odor. Odor is a natural
part of poultry. Most people notice the unique relationship
between poultry and sulfur right away. What I did not expect
was to be developing a new kind of biological weapon. Why
did I imagine that summer rains would gracefully wash the
pen clean? Maybe too much time spent curled up in a window
seat reading about poultry and not enough getting out to the
poultry pen in rubber boots and work gloves?

In the lightest rain shower, the pen became a mud pit
from side to side. I tossed clean hay on the mud in an amateur
hope that this would help, and the birds' paddle feet turned

the straw, mud, and manure into an impenetrable adobe floor. The birds were paving the pen in some places, excavating it in others, and sabotaging our efforts at a drainage system. The top layer of mud was the consistency of grease and lay on the packed earth like a practical joke. It was miserable to change the water and feed every day. The birds were unhappy too, unable to keep their feathers clean and waterproof. Overcrowding and lack of drainage were the heart of the problem.

"Are you still having odor problems with your waterfowl?" asked my mom one day over the phone.

"It's getting a little better now that we've dug more rock drains in the dog pen," I said.

"Well, I think you should just slaughter them all," said my mom definitively. "It would fix the odor problem permanently."

"Well, yes," I said. "I suppose that is one solution to the problem."

"You should do it," emphasized my mother.

"But it kind of defeats the whole purpose of having the ducks and geese in the first place," I said.

"They take up too much time," Mom said. "Now, how are your girls?"

"I'm afraid to say," I said. "Lest any problems I'm having fall afoul of your suggested solutions."

"Very funny," she said.

We were forced to complete the new waterfowl pen before we showed the house to prospective tenants. It was finally done and proved easier and cheaper than the previous pens because it shared two walls with the chicken pen, and had no netting over the top. The waterfowl were too large for our aerial predators and according to my books, domestic ducks and geese don't fly. As the day came for moving the waterfowl, I started to worry about how we were going to do it because the geese were hard to catch. That morning, Blue was helping me with the water and feeding chores when I noticed China Linda eyeing her with suspicious interest. As the goose stalked Blue, I stalked the goose, and successfully completed the capture before China Linda could finish her planned ambush. A new goose catching method had presented itself.

"But Mom," objected Blue. "I don't *like* being bait."

"Ah, you're okay!" I said enthusiastically. "I'll catch them quick!"

"Maybe it would be better if I had some knee pads or something," she said.

"It's faster if you just stand there as you are," I said.

"Or something like a catcher's mask," she said, "like they have in hockey games."

"Hold still now," I said. "Here comes another one!"

Andrew didn't like my plan of catching and carrying the nine geese one at a time. He declared it too arduous and had already come up with a plan to herd them, complete with a diagram illustrating each person's position during the operation. He cut some Chamisa branches for us to use as herding sticks. We stripped the narrow leaves and their strong smell filled the air. I held the door and Andrew waved the geese out of the dog pen, keeping back the ducks.

The geese stepped briskly out of the pen and went

straight for some wild greens. They ignored our diagram and our herding sticks. Demoted from goose farmers to urban transplants in an instant, we were at a loss for what to do. I handed Blue a bunch of weeds and told her to be the goose girl. She stepped right up to the task, waved the weeds in front of the flock, and took off walking. The geese followed her and we followed the geese, Juno bravely bringing up the rear. It was just about the most bucolic thing I'd ever seen.

Helpfully, the geese stayed together in a tight flock for the whole hike, never scattering or overtaking their little leader until the goose walk was concluded and they were all safe in their new pen. We waved our Chamisa wands in happy victory, danced our goose farmer dance, and gave each other high fives. Then we realized that we still had to move the ducks.

Undeterred by the failure of his first plan, Andrew had another ready. He had been studying a picture in our old collection of National Geographic magazines. It showed a child in rural China, about Blue's age, herding a huge flock of white ducks with nothing more than a long stick. This formed the base of Andrew's plan, and we stationed ourselves in our proper places. Blue was outside the pen with her Chamisa stick and Andrew was in the dog pen, behind the ducks, ready to encourage them to move toward the open door. I was ready with another long stick, modeled on the one in the magazine picture. Juno was in the baby backpack on Andrew's back.

The ducks were milling in a tight group, moving away from Andrew and all was going well until they stepped outside the pen. As they soon as they were out of the pen, their tight formation crumbled and they stampeded hysterically in every direction. They ran peeping, stumbling, crowding each other, and veering away from us in a panic. Ducks spilled from the doorway and continued, like water, to take the path of least resistance downhill. They poured out of the pen and some went under a tree. The rest headed east very fast, breaking up into smaller duck clots at every bush.

Things deteriorated quickly after that. Blue got a splinter and dissolved into tears. We shouted at her to keep herding ducks and she cried that we didn't care about her. Andrew dove into a duck-infested pine tree and Juno started to cry, whipped by pine needles. I shouted at him to mind the baby on his back and he bellowed directions at me for some incomprehensible maneuver. Ducks streamed through Andrew's legs toward the pen where I was holding the door, so I yelled at him to get behind them and herd them back into the pen. He hollered back about a new plan. Blue continued to cry that her finger was falling off and in the meantime the ducks split up into three groups heading for Texas, Mexico, and Colorado.

I used the basic obedience training invested in our dog to create one sitting barrier the ducks would not approach. I used our sobbing, immobilized little girl as another barrier, and eventually got the ducks back into the dog pen. We were back where we started, and had the scars to prove it. We re-grouped and stood observing the sixteen freaked-out ducks in the pen while I called a family meeting to discuss the merits of handing off leadership when necessary. We counseled Blue on how a duck farmer must keep mustering ducks, even when wounded.

"What about if my finger was all the way cut off?"

asked Blue.

"Then you scoop it up and put it in your pocket and keep the muster," I said.

"What about if I am dead?" asked Blue.

"Then you have to let your corpse fall in the right direction to keep the muster," I said.

"Can I have a band-aid now?" asked Blue

"Why didn't our herding plan work?" wondered Andrew. "We had mostly the same equipment as that Chinese girl in the picture."

"I think these are not Chinese ducks," I said.

In the end, we decided to carry the ducks to the new pen one at a time. I started the move while Andrew fed the girls lunch and applied band-aids. I felt confident doing it alone. How hard could it be? The ducklings were so cute and fragile as hatchlings. They had a lot of spirit and spunk, but not much physically to back up their micro-attitudes. We were gentle with them as babies, catching them by looping thumb and forefinger around their necks then scooping them up with the other hand. We could snuggle them against our cheeks without losing an eye, unlike the other needle-beaked chicks. Ducklings were sweet. Which is why, when it came time to pick up the almost full-grown ducks and move them to the new pen, I didn't give it another thought. The duck was facing me, quacking angrily, and I reached out with both hands on the soft feathers under the wings, and brought it up close. Eye to eye with the duckling I knew so well, I reflected on how heavy this duck had become. They grew fast, these birds.

First to go was my hearing, as the duck slammed her fully

feathered wings against my ears. My ears were ringing and my glasses were dangling. I would have held the duck farther away from my head, but her wingspan was greater than my reach and she kept pounding me. It felt like she had a small baseball bat concealed under her wings. Her beak wasn't idle either. She seized my nose in a very strong and effective grip. Where had the weak little duckling gone? This animal was something else entirely. She had my lower lip in a vice grip and was pulling it off, pushing against my ears with her wings. Her webbed feet had been raking down my front this whole time, shredding my sweatshirt and starting on my skin with a set of talons that would rival an eagle. Both of my forearms were bleeding profusely with deep scratches from her claws. I'd never really noticed claws on those flat-paddling feet before now. They were long, sharp, and exceptionally effective. I made a stumbling run to the new pen and pitched her in, then stood shaking and traumatized as I examined my wounds. I'd certainly done that the wrong way.

Much as I really wanted to stop and go cry somewhere, I was no quitter. I took a canvas apron from the wood shop and moved on the next duck. This time, I caught her by the neck and quickly pinned her wings. I swung her under one arm and used a hand to hold her neck so she couldn't get to my face. Feet firmly held in my other hand, wings pinned, I carried her as if she were loaded, which, actually, she was. By the time Andrew came out to help, the girls safely stashed in front of a children's video, I had mastered the technique.

"I've worked out a system," I said, as I returned from ditching my third duck in the new pen.

"It's okay," he said. "I can figure it out," and reached for a duck head on.

"You'll want to watch out!" I warned. "Let me show you how to do it."

"I've got it!" he said. "It's a duckling. How hard can it be?"

That was the day we ran out of band-aids.

When July turned into August, our newspaper ad for the house rental finally began generating some interest. I took the calls so that Andrew could concentrate on his business, and I learned to mention the forty-five minute one-way commute early in the conversation to save myself a lot of time. The distance put off many callers. Many more were dissuaded by the small square footage of the house. Finally, I got a caller who could not be put off by any of my house and location descriptions. She said that she didn't work in Santa Fe and her maybe-will-move-in boyfriend was familiar with the area, so she knew where it was.

The couple drove up in a black Trans-Am with windows tinted so dark I could see only the overhead clouds reflected in them. We had a nice introduction. The boyfriend was shapely in his clean, white wife-beater tank top. His tattoos looked older than he was. Her tattoo was in color and disappeared inside her seventies-style teddy. I lost touch with propriety as my eyes followed the tattoo. I recovered quickly and hoped she hadn't noticed my stare.

As they walked through the house, the boyfriend and I talked about the local neighborhood. He knew my neighbors better than I did. He said he was drinking buddies with one neighbor and was friends with the wife of another neighbor

who was a waitress at a local bar where he was a regular. I
didn't know there was a local bar. I couldn't get a word in
edgewise, but I was learning a lot about them. Things I think
I couldn't have legally asked them, so I just kept quiet and
began to realize that although I had been a renter many times,
I knew nothing about being a landlord. I felt another vertical
learning curve coming on.

The woman mentioned that she had three young children.
He only had two and they mostly lived with his ex. By my
count, that made five kids, all under age thirteen. This was
a two-bedroom house. The woman asked when the house
would be available, and I asked her when she would want
to move. She said she would have to give thirty days notice
and had only paid the rent yesterday. It was the tenth of the
month and I realized that she was telling me that she had paid
her rent late. She wanted month to month and when I asked
about references, she said she wasn't sure she could provide
any. In the last place she lived, the landlord had moved and
she couldn't contact them. But she'd try to drum some up.

They smelled like cigarette smoke, but it must have been
my imagination, because I had specifically said non-smoker
in the ad. I was afraid they were going to notice me staring
at their hickies. After a while, they began to gaze more at
each other than at my house. We exchanged handshakes, and
promised to call each other in that way people do when they
have no intention of doing so.

After they drove away, I walked slowly back to the trailer
feeling like each step was taking me deeper and deeper into
a dark and unknown place. Renting the house had felt a lot
simpler when it had been a chapter in a "change your financial

life" book than when I was walking around the house asking colorful characters for references. I felt a kind of quiet, depressing panic, knowing that backing out now would cost us as much as moving forward.

We showed the house to a surprising number of people. Most declined because the small bedrooms wouldn't fit their bedroom sets. One older lady almost took it, but was talked out of it by her townie friends who were concerned with her ability to safely maintain a wood stove and drive through two feet of snow on a dirt road in the winter. Another couple almost took it, but the upstairs room wouldn't fit their dining room set. An ex-nun almost rented it, but neither the upstairs nor downstairs would fit her book collection. Finally a young couple, two babies in tow and another on the way, said yes and moved in quickly. They had dogs, rabbits, chickens, and four goats. We neglected to ask how many dogs they had because it didn't occur to us that someone would have eight dogs.

But the house was finally rented and we had the first month's rent in hand. It was the first tangible income we'd received since we had started our plan and it was encouraging. The critics in our peanut gallery were amazed. Many of them had doubted that we would find a renter for such an out-of-the-way place. Others doubted that the trailer could be made livable in such a short time. So we basked in our moment of hard-earned victory. The rental income flowed over our parched desert of personal finance like a long-awaited monsoon. It was just as quickly absorbed, but there would be another check in another month. It was good.

Two weeks later, the well pump crapped out. It was too much of a strain for the faithful, twenty-year-old machinery to supply two households. It sighed and died, leaving the tenants mid-bath with soap in their hair. They were not happy. Our short-lived victory glow faded. Fixing the well cost several thousand dollars and more than a week, even though we worked on it right away. It was frustrating, confrontational, arduous, and stressful in the extreme. New building codes dictated new rules for the new well configuration and Andrew's crew were once again digging at our place. We got it fixed, but it took a toll on our bank account and on my spirits.

Chapter Five

By mid-August, our little rural oasis had been transformed into a social hub with a traffic problem. Our new neighbor had moved in and claimed that she wasn't bothered by the sounds of nature. I thought this was very fortunate, because the geese were naturally loud. Our new tenants were almost talking to us again, now that they had reliable clean running water. Early every morning, three sets of cars drove past our trailer on their way to work, giving me the opportunity to regret putting the trailer so close to the road.

I was losing my cheerful disposition and Andrew tried to help by pointing out that things were actually going pretty well. The girls were flourishing in their simple, rural home. They were mostly polite, agile, intelligent, active, and could play for hours with just a stick and a rock. Because they were growing up in this place, they could run barefoot on the rocks, catch a chicken with one hand, and knew only one fast food menu by heart. Like Andrew, they were exhausting optimists. He argued that as parents we were staying true to our wedding vow to raise our children ourselves, at home, in the bosom of their loving mother. I argued that I was not totally enjoying being that bosom under these financial and physical circumstances.

One solution to our dilemma was for me to go back to full-time work, but Andrew was adamantly opposed. He was happy in his entrepreneurial efforts as a contractor and could see a near future when his income would meet our expenses and more. He had some bids out that were going to come through, on jobs that were going to go well. He was going to get referrals from satisfied customers and, pretty soon, we'd be in the black. I just had to keep the faith.

Andrew was very happy with our arrangement. He was facing the increasing challenge of providing for us with a frisson of excitement. Adversity seemed to answer a need in his soul, and he grew stronger with every setback and rejection. He was educating himself in business with a growing library of how-to books, and conversations about anything other than business didn't hold him for very long anymore. The unpredictable business of contracting exercised his body and soul and he was in his element. He suggested that I approach my role as housewife and mother with a more accepting attitude.

"I'm not June Cleaver!" I retorted angrily. "I'm June *with* a cleaver!"

I thought what I needed was to get a job. We were racking up debt like we were in the Oval Office. But Andrew seemed troubled by my suggested defection.

"The girls need to be with their mother," he said.

"They'd be with somebody's mother in day care," I pointed out. "Most of those women have kids of their own."

"I thought you believed in this parenting style," he said. "I thought we were on the same page, had the same vision."

"The searing hot poker of reality has blinded my vision," I said. "I'm not sure the page I am on is even in the same book as yours."

"One of my business books says that women hate debt," Andrew said. "It's like a chick thing."

"I have a plan for your business books," I muttered, "it's like a Bic lighter thing."

"We can get out of debt with a single good construction job," Andrew insisted.

"Now you sound like a farmer," I said. "One good crop can pay off the farm."

"Well it can!" he said.

"Locusts," I said, "hail, blight, drought."

"What a depressing perspective," Andrew said.

"Well pumps," I said.

The same driving forces that had led us to consider renting the house had inspired me to create the egg business, but it seemed to be coming together very slowly. The need to change our financial situation was urgent yet our solutions were not. I felt the weight of the debt and the insecurity of Andrew's contracting business acutely. I was definitely depressed, probably clinically. At this time in my life, I was having trouble with the sheer number of roles I was expected to play. I woke up each morning as a mother, wife, daughter, friend, farmer, and dragged on the least-stained of my plus-sized shirts. As a sister, granddaughter, cousin, citizen, taxpayer, consumer, I stuffed the wrong-size coffee filter into the basket and dumped in too many grounds. As a parent, democrat, speeder, homeowner, ex-renter, new landlord, I started the hamster-wheel of chores that filled my day.

Most mornings I felt lost, like I'd taken a wrong turn somewhere. I had followed my heart, but it refused to ask for directions. I had listened to all of the sage wisdom out there about pursuing my dreams, following my heart, but I had made the critical mistake of assuming that if I did that, I would gain peace and happiness. I realized that none of the people giving that advice had actually said that the result would be peace and happiness. That had been my interpretation. Now I wondered what the real punch line was to that mantra. Follow your heart and you will live in interesting times? Wasn't that an ancient Chinese curse? Follow your heart because life's a bitch and then you die? And so you might as well? I was feeling pessimistic.

All of our actions made sense on paper, or as an overall plan, but I deeply hated the debt. I had badly underestimated the process, effort, and expense of both of our current projects. I hadn't given up on the dream of a blown egg business or a smoothly functioning rental income, but I was coming up with a bad case of reality.

"Reality," I told my sister on one of my endless sympathy calls, "is a white sand beach and an emerald green sea, but the beach is infested with sand flies and the water is full of reef sharks."

"Oh, that's real all right!" she agreed. "You should write that down."

"Thanks," I said.

"And move into town," she said. "Your life sounds awful."

I'd had my struggles with anxiety attacks before we started down this covered-wagon-style financial road. I'd put in my time on couches with licensed therapists, learning how to breathe through it, how to relax into it, but the discomfort grew beyond what I could handle by breathing.

"I'm thinking of trying an antidepressant," I said to some of the moms from preschool at the summer get-together.

"What about Zoloft?" said one, whipping out her pill bottle.

"I've had luck with Effexor," said another, dipping into her purse.

"Wellbutrin is good," said a third with another bottle in hand.

"I swear by Lexapro," contested another mom.

"Prozac is the mother of them all," a voice from the edge of the group suggested.

"Are there any side-effects?" I asked nervously.

"Not really," said one.

"Not many," said another

"I never experienced that sexual side effect," said a third.

"What sexual side-effect?" I asked. "Like, good side-effect or bad side-effect?"

"Well, if it were a good side-effect," the third mom said, "they'd change the marketing and charge ten times more."

I smiled obligingly along with the laughing women and thought to myself that the drugs certainly seemed to be working for them. I made an appointment with a doctor, still totally baffled about the real meaning of a "sexual side-effect." It was like grade school again with all those mysterious terms and knowledgeable sniggers. The doctor gave me both a prescription and some answers.

"Why don't they just say "inability to climax"? I asked.

"Talk to the FCC," she suggested. "Or would it be the FDA?"

The drug helped, but it wasn't the sunrise-after-a-long-cold-night that I had hoped for. My spinning thoughts of doom and panic slowed. An unlisted side effect was an incredible increase in my sense of smell. This was not a gift. The world is a stinky place and the extra sensitivity was a burden. I didn't want to admit that it had been a mistake for us to get all these birds while making such a big change as moving into the trailer and renting the house, but it was certainly a challenge. We were all feeling the strain, including the girls. One night, in our one shared bedroom in the trailer, Juno was tucked into the deep comfort of toddler sleep, but Blue was still awake and having trouble falling asleep.

"Mommy, I'm scared," she said.

"Scared of what?" I asked, sitting down on the side of her bed.

"Monsters," she said.

"I have eaten all the monsters," I said, starting an old game we used to play when she was smaller.

"Monsters outside," she said.

"I have stomped all the outside monsters until they are flat," I said.

"I'm still scared," she said.

"That used to work for you when you were little," I mourned. "It was an artful and creative use of my extra body fat!"

"That sounds scary, too," she said, undeterred.

"Baby, believe me," I sighed. "I am the scariest thing around here and I love you, and that makes you safe."

"You aren't scary," she said, faithfully.

"I am," I insisted. "I am an angry, unemployed, disenfranchised, medicated stay-home-mom who is not earning any social security credit for her admittedly valuable efforts!"

"Okay," she said, doubtfully.

"What if I just sit here with you until you fall asleep," I said finally.

"That would be great," she said in relief.

And so I sat with her and tried to count my blessings. Tried not to notice the smell of the dishes in the kitchen sink, the laundry on the bathroom floor, and the garbage in the cans outside the trailer.

Summer was winding down as September brought us into the school season. We had long hot days and infrequent rainstorms, and the occasional day that smelled like autumn. It wasn't just the hint of wood smoke in the air; it was the smell of the trees and grasses. This was one of the things I liked best about the place - that I could tell where we were using only my nose. The smell of the changing seasons was a rare delight in our potpourri of earthy organic aromas. The junipers and piñon did not change for the seasons, but there were enough leaf-dropping trees in the landscape that the turn of the season would add yellow and red to our backdrop. For now, every conceivable shade of green contrasted with the reds and browns of the mesas, rocks, and earth.

Two weeks before their fifth month, the chickens began to lay. Blue triumphantly found the very first chicken egg during our morning chores before we left for school. It was small, white, and gleamed in the straw of the chicken house. She was so happy clutching the egg that she did a first-egg dance, then named the egg and kissed it. We all did the first-egg dance and congratulated her on her find. Then she tripped while dancing and landed on the egg, so we cleaned up the egg and mourned the egg.

The next day, there were two eggs, small, white and gleaming in the straw. We did more dancing until I broke those two eggs by trying to carry them in my shirt, so we did more mourning and cleaning. On the third day, we made a proper egg-collecting basket and did our dancing at least thirty feet away from them.

I'd chosen a business involving the care and handling of fragile items and I was starting to feel that reality. My mom is a very meticulous stuff keeper, providing museum-quality care to the heirlooms in her keeping. I'm more of the wrecking ball of the family. My children and I can reduce stuff to its molecular components in a shockingly short period of time. Now that I had eggs in hand, I started to share my dream of a blown-egg business with my extended family and they were more honest than supportive.

"Aren't you the one that goes out and buys a complete set of new dishes every Thanksgiving?" my sister asked. "Out of necessity?"

"But blown eggs are fragile," said my other sister, "and you are, well, how you are."

My mom took a less personal approach to the business issue.

"Who's going to want to buy a blown egg?" she said. "When they can blow an egg themselves?"

I gave the same answer to everyone.

"I'm sorry, you're breaking up, I can't hear you through the static!" and hung up.

Within a week, we had our first dozen eggs. We discovered that chickens like to lay in a communal nest box and if one hen snuck off to lay away from the flock, other hens would find the renegade nest and lay there too. Eventually, the colossal pile of eggs rising out of the straw revealed the secret nest. Two weeks after the first egg, the chickens reached their magical five-month age milestone and were laying an egg a day. I was getting an average of twenty eggs a day out of twenty-four chickens. The hens broke their share of eggs, it wasn't just me.

The ducks started laying too, five eggs a day, which gave me a clue to how many duck hens I had in my fifteen-strong flock. Drakes have distinctive tail feathers that curl, and strange voices that cannot quack but sort of blart instead, but it was still early in their development for me to tell them apart. However my estimate of five females out of fifteen ducks was not good news.

Two dozen eggs a day and the egg inventory waiting for processing was immense. I was collecting, washing, letting dry, and packing more than fourteen dozen eggs a week, even taking into account the breakage. Some of the hens started eating eggs, and I was unable to stop them. Like feather picking, this was a common bad habit in poultry and the farmer was supposed to be able to control it. I tried all of the recommended solutions: varying the diet, adding interesting peckable items like mealworms, collecting the eggs several times a day, feeding boiled crumbled eggs and shells back to the birds. But nothing helped. The chickens had developed their egg eating habit almost as soon as they started laying the eggs. My farmer books sternly instructed me to find and cull the offending hens, but that was beyond me in so many ways.

Andrew and the girls went around the neighborhood selling eggs every weekend and we quickly saturated our local market. The tiny nearby grocery store bought regularly for resale to their customers, but we outstripped their sale capacity, and were also in competition with everyone else in the rural neighborhood that had their own ultra-productive chicken flocks.

I had eggs in the sink, across the counter, and in bowls on the floor. It was exciting, but I was getting overwhelmed. I brought a carton of fresh eggs to my friends whenever I visited them. One day I opened my friend's refrigerator to put the eggs inside and found it filled with stocked egg cartons.

"You have an egg problem like mine," I observed cheerfully.

"You've been bringing me a dozen eggs every time you visit," she said.

"Yes," I acknowledged. "It's a fringe benefit of being friends with a bird farmer."

"You've visited me almost every day this week," she

said.

"Oh," I said, "then I'd better bring you some soufflé recipes too."

It was time to start blowing and selling them. Time to implement my grand original plan. I sat down with a dozen test eggs, poked a small hole in the top and bottom of the egg, mashed my lips on the bottom of the egg and began to blow. Several minutes later, I worried that I had incurred brain damage while the egg remained unblown. I took a skewer and rattled it around inside the egg and tried again. This helped, as the egg and yolk mixed and was forced through the top hole more easily, but it was still a frustratingly arduous process and completely impractical for the number of eggs I was going to have to blow every week. Andrew helpfully cruised the Internet while I gave myself a headache and spattered my face with raw egg.

"Did you know that the standard of the blown egg industry is a single hole in the bottom of the egg?" he called from the computer.

"Blown egg industry?" I exclaimed and choked on egg.

"There's a goose egg hatchery selling them by the case," he said, over his shoulder, "and a duck hatchery offering about three different sizes."

"One hole?" I coughed.

I looked over the mess I'd made of my test eggs, and the bowl of pre-scrambled egg I'd blown out. On the bright side, egg blowing was quite difficult, and that boded well for a market. Surely people would want to buy pre-blown eggs, especially at Easter. And the presence of blown egg sellers on the Internet must also indicate that there was a market, otherwise they wouldn't already be out there offering me marketing competition before I'd even begun. But my process of egg blowing was going to have to improve and the issue of blowing an egg with a single hole was a stopping point. I cleaned up, made an omelet with crumbled cheese and sliced green onion on top, and slid it in front of my Internet surfing contractor of a husband.

"Hey, thanks!" he said, delighted.

"You've got a lot of tools in your workshop," I said to him.

"I love tools," he mumbled with his mouth full.

"You've probably got a drill or two up there as well," I said.

"Lots of drills," he agreed, clicking away unaware.

"So you could probably figure out how to drill a hole in these eggs with a tool you have in your workshop," I suggested, and he stopped chewing.

"In fact, as the wily inventor that you are," I continued, "you could probably figure out how to drill a hole and evacuate the egg contents all through a single hole!"

"Oh man," he sighed.

"My hero!" I said.

Within a week, Andrew did indeed invent an egg blowing system using one hole. It was fast, efficient, and very clever. He took a drill press and fitted it with a diamond drill bit, then experimented with the bit diameter until he had the smallest hole that would still allow the egg blowing to proceed with reasonable speed. He figured out that if the hole was large enough, then air introduced through the hole with a needle would push the egg contents out at the same time.

He got the needle from the feed store on a run for bird food. There were plenty of horse care supplies at the feed store, including gigantic needles attached to enormous syringes. He made an adapter to his compressor and fixed a long flexible hose to the regulator to make it easy to handle. An adjustable trigger would start the rig and air would be injected into the egg through the needle. The yolk and egg white would squirt out the hole and the egg would be empty in no time. Then he took another needle and created a connection to a short section of garden hose, which he adapted to the kitchen sink with a screw on adaptor. Now water would flow through the hose and needle, washing out the egg in the same way the air evacuated the egg contents.

It was a brilliant system and it worked exceptionally well. He set it up and I stood over the sink with the first egg in hand. I was easing the horse needle into the egg hole that we had just drilled with the drill press set up on the kitchen table.

"There are some things to watch out for with the compressed air," he said, as I pressed firmly on the air trigger. The egg shot out of my hand and across the room, hitting the wall with an effect like an egg grenade.

"You have to ease into the air trigger first," Andrew continued, undeterred, as egg and shell slid down the trailer wall. I held the next egg more firmly and again eased down on the valve. The egg exploded in my hand with a muted thunk and yolk splashed over my face, shirt, and cupboards.

"You have to just barely touch it until the egg contents start to come out through the hole," Andrew said, patiently wiping the egg off his face and neck with a kitchen towel. "It just takes some practice to find the edges of the system."

"Anything else I should know right now?" I finally asked, not touching any triggers or valves.

"Well," he paused, thinking, "if you stick yourself with the needle while triggering the compressed air you could get an air embolism in your bloodstream."

"Which would be bad?" I prompted.

"Totally fatal," he said, and set about dulling the needle end to make such an outcome a little more difficult.

Hundreds of eggs later, I was getting into my groove. I learned to let the drill bit do the work of drilling the hole. If I crunched down too hard with the drill press, I would create fracture lines in the shell that would later crack open in the air or water process. I learned the limits of the air pressure and how to balance between fast blowing and rocket launching. There were blown eggs in square cardboard flats on every surface of the house. Single-hole blown eggs.

We had raw scrambled egg in every container we owned. The girls got tired of omelets for breakfast, lunch, and dinner, and I started to worry about infant cholesterol levels. The dog had a sleek glossy coat and was getting almost spherical from her kibbled egg twice a day meal. The eggy smell from all this blowing, cooking, and storing became overwhelming, and I developed a habit of leaving every door and window in the trailer open night and day.

We cooked the egg and fed it back to the birds, as recommended by every chicken book I consulted. The experts also advocated grinding up the shells and feeding those back as well but I was using the shells, so it was scrambled egg with oyster shell for them. Even with these efforts, and freezing as much of it as we could store, we had more than we could handle. The raw egg went bad in a remarkably short period of time, a matter of hours in the still warm September days. I made a note for a future new product of egg contents – maybe as an animal food additive but, in the meantime, the excess had to go down the sink.

"Are you sure we can't find a better solution to this?" Andrew lamented, as he sluiced egg down the drain.

"It's the ultimate growth medium," I said yet again, "it starts growing things as soon as it's exposed to the air."

"What a horrible waste," Andrew sighed.

"Well what about every breakfast restaurant in the country?" I suggested. "Throwing the cracked eggshells into the trash – that's a waste from my point of view."

"I suppose so," he said. "But it will feel much better when we can work out a way to deal with the egg."

Later that year, when we called out the septic service to do our regular septic pump out (necessary because I was a lousy septic system housewife and used all the products that are contra-indicated for septic system health) the pump operator exclaimed that we hadn't needed his services after all. The septic system was working great. The egg, it turned out, was a wonderfully effective septic treatment and promoted all the kinds of bacteria growth that drives a septic system.

"So there!" I said graciously to Andrew.

My first blown-egg sale took place within a month of collecting our first egg from the chickens. I had spent a number of hours figuring out the eBay online selling system and setting up all the various accounts and payment methods.

I joined the blown-egg sellers that serviced an active market for blown eggs. It was a great moment, vindication of my idea and a source of hope regarding the eventual success of my vision. It was only a ten-dollar sale, and didn't make a very big dent in my bleeding bottom line — but it was a start. It made me feel a lot better than the anti-depressant prescription ever had.

Chapter Six

$\mathscr{A}$ s the leaves turned in late September, we enjoyed
occasional glimpses of migrating birds. Twice we thought
we saw an osprey flying up the river canyon. We had a clear
view and I had seen osprey before, on the Florida coast, but
it was hard to believe that a sea eagle would be flying up
our neck of the Pecos River. I asked the County Extension
Office in Santa Fe and discovered that it was true. Osprey
winter over in rivers and lakes, escaping unruly weather in
their usual territory.

We also saw Golden Eagles, Red-Tailed Hawks, and Great
Blue Herons. The Sandhill Crane migration took place mostly
northwest of us, over Los Alamos. The cranes were on their
way to the Bosque Del Apache south of Albuquerque but we
would occasionally see strings of them far overhead flying at
higher altitudes than the other bird species we watched. My
domestic duck and geese were affected by the season and
the bird migrations. They would freeze all movement and
fall silent whenever a bird flew overhead. There was unrest
in the pens.

To save money, I had ordered the "Ducks Deluxe Mix" from the hatchery catalog. It was a straight run collection of hatchery choice ducklings. This meant a mix of male and female chicks in the same proportion as they had hatched, and a chance to try and guess what breeds we had in our pen. I had expected that about half the ducks would be females, and since I wanted the duck eggs more than I wanted ducks for eating, this had seemed a cheaper way to get them. It hadn't occurred to me that "straight run" might not result in such a fair sex distribution.

I was regretting my economizing now. A gang of ten non-egg-producing drakes the size of Tyrannosaurs lurched over the remains of two empty fifty-pound feed bags which they had consumed in half the time I expected. They were developing brilliant head and wing plumage, which gave me feather product ideas, and Andrew was happy to have the boys as a food source. But I didn't see him sharpening the axe as my grocery budget started to drain away into the duck pen. And although I did have two of my coveted Khaki Campbells, the best egg-producing ducks of all, both of them grew the distinctive curly tail feathers of drakes.

Andrew and I had come to an agreement about this aspect of our farming effort. I would worry excessively about every aspect of the birds' lives, do copious research, and build a business from scratch. For his part, he would construct stuff at short notice, do the heavy lifting, and chop off heads at butchering time. It was obviously butchering time in the duck pen but Andrew was suspiciously extra busy at work. He was having a difficult time with the killing part of our farming plan as well.

The duck flock went about their business in safety, and I stayed busy replacing their pond water every day and refilling their feeder way too often. Every time I brought out the hose, several of the smaller ducks would begin flapping their wings in excitement. One day I turned around to shut off the hose and found myself suddenly eye to eye with a hovering duck. The duck was flying.

I didn't know that domestic ducks could fly, and the pen they shared with the geese was not covered. Pretty soon I was spending my days tossing ducks back into the pen they flew out of. They would fly a short distance, land heavily, then waddle back to the pen and quack or belch frantically as they tried to rejoin their flock. Rachel, our dog, was my patient ally. I put her on a sit-stay at one corner post and herded the duck from the other. The door was in the middle and to avoid Rachel, the duck would scramble in the open door. Without Rachel sitting at the corner post the duck would just go round and round the outside of the pen in an exhibition of inscrutable duck logic.

Frustrated, I stood in the pen with an out-dated library book under one arm and a duck hovering overhead. They were now flying quite competently and there wasn't even a chapter on flying ducks in these books. The ducks in the books didn't fly. Was I supposed to clip their wings? I didn't know how to clip wings. Where would they fly? Would they fly home again?

"I think they are Flying Mallards," said Andrew, leafing through the hatchery catalog.

"I didn't order any Flying Mallards," I protested.

"Hatchery choice," Andrew replied, "and they must not

be popular because we sure have a lot of them."

"I can see why nobody wants them, they are teaching the other ducks to fly," I said, watching the enormous White Pekin drake flap hard enough to hurt himself. "They can't do it but they are really trying."

"I saw one of ours flying down the river canyon yesterday," Andrew said. "Then it came back and landed on my windshield."

"I'm not supposed to let them back in with the flock," I revealed. "The books say not to let the free ducks mix with our penned ducks to prevent disease."

"Too late now," Andrew pronounced.

"They are teaching the geese to fly," I observed.

"Domestic geese can't fly, can they?" Andrew asked in alarm.

"I don't know," I said for the hundredth time, and called the hatchery.

"May I take your order?" said the hatchery.

"I'd like to know if the geese I ordered are going to be able to fly," I said.

"Well, not when they are mature, that's for sure," said the hatchery.

"They aren't mature yet," I said. "Are they going to be able to fly before they get mature?"

"Not really," said the hatchery, "not unless someone teaches them."

"What?" I said. "They can be taught?"

"They'd have to be," the hatchery assured me. "They don't know how on their own. Don't let them learn and they won't fly away!"

The Flying Mallards went to the top of my dinner list although by the time the butchering actually happened most of them had flown the coop. The geese weren't successfully flying, but they spent large amounts of time racing with outstretched wings from one end of their pen to the other. They did get a couple of inches off the ground before they slammed into the wire.

It wasn't hard to decide which ducks to slaughter. Most of the flock was male so we could easily keep the females off the list we were compiling for who stays and who permanently goes. The females, however, seemed prone to dying on their own. One White Pekin duck had keeled over of a probable heart attack one day when I was chasing her around the pen trying to catch her for the girls to hold.

"Oops," I said, standing over the duck's outstretched corpse.

"Maybe we shouldn't chase the ducks anymore," said Blue.

"Maybe not," I concurred.

We crept quietly out of the pen with the limp duck in hand. My library books reassured me that White Pekin ducks could have heart problems. Those ducks need to be culled when they show up in the flock. Our culling method was not the most common, but it was effective nonetheless.

The Blue Swedish duck, with beautiful blue chest feathers and a white bib, volunteered by kicking the bucket unexpectedly one afternoon. Just quacked and died. This made our duck mortality rate much higher than any of the other poultry species. At the library I looked up "sudden death" under Poultry Diseases. I found chapters titled

"Botulism" and "Cholera" and quickly put the book back on the shelf.

Another of the White Pekin ducks had spraddled four days after the big duck relocation. Spraddle is an injury to the legs or hips of the duck resulting in paralysis, or at least an inability to walk. Sometimes tying the ducks' legs together as they grow can cure it, but with the tremendous growth rate of White Pekin ducks and their heavy weight at maturity, we resigned ourselves to the fact that this duck was not going to heal. We moved her from food to water and kept her in the shade for three days before we finally sharpened the axe. The bird wasn't ill but without the ability to walk she would have been vulnerable to the ants and sun.

We prepared for our first butchering experience by reading all of the illustrated poultry manuals we could find. This part of our poultry-farming adventure was critically important. It was up to us to teach our girls about where food really comes from and how to be practical yet respectful about it. Unfortunately, I had no idea how to accomplish this because I had not grown up with it. I was completely under the influence of the "Bambi Complex," because food animals throughout my childhood had been anthropomorphized in cartoons and movies. They all were talking in books and were strewn about my bed in stuffed attitudes of affection. I felt awful about transitioning from nurturing the animal, caring for it, and struggling against the forces of nature that were conspiring to kill it, to chopping off its head and cooking it for dinner. I was right up against the fact that taking care of poultry went hand in hand with taking lives. Spraddle duck was a perfect example of how I wasn't going to be able to avoid the killing part even if I was simply raising the birds as pets. There was no cure for this kind of spraddle. But I wasn't raising the birds as pets. I was trying to farm them and strike a balance between giving them a great life and then taking them as a food source. I went for a walk in the chicken pen to think it over and try to come up with a reasonable approach to the coming slaughter.

As I strolled, musing, I thought I heard the sound of a rooster crowing from behind a juniper bush inside the pen. This was surprising because I had paid extra for my chicken chicks to ensure that they were all female. I walked behind the tree and looked closely at the chickens. They all continued to cluck and peck and strut and fertilize the ground, except for one with a bright red comb, huge wattle, and enormous poof of tail feathers who was eyeing the prettiest hen lustfully. He stretched up on his toes, beat his wings, and crowed again.

I sighed. I didn't want a rooster. Roosters were only required if we wanted fertile eggs to hatch up to be new chickens for the flock. The hens would lay eggs without the presence of a rooster, but the eggs would never hatch. Roosters are beautiful, with grand feathers grown to impress the hens, but they can be a noisy handful.

Four years ago, Andrew and I had five Buff Orpington chickens that we got as day-old chicks from the local feed store. They were gorgeous and one of them was a rooster. He was really beautiful and we thought it would be fun to see if the hens would successfully hatch their eggs. Plus, we were not really serious about chicken farming and reluctant to do any head lopping. We were still urban and the young rooster was still harmless.

One morning in that long-ago time, Andrew went out to the pen with his usual steaming mug of tea in hand, dressed only in his terrycloth robe. This was his treasured morning routine. It was very pleasant in the morning, the New Mexico sky truly as represented by Georgia O'Keeffe. There was fresh air, quietude, and the healthful happiness of the eye-pleasing chickens.

Andrew was completely occupied feeding the chickens when the rooster sauntered within striking distance and launched himself, spurs maliciously outstretched, and eyes crazed with bloodlust. Andrew screamed and dragged the heavy galvanized feed can over his own toes and in front of himself for protection. The rooster landed gracefully on top of the can and attacked again. Andrew brought up the metal lid as a shield and the fiendish rooster whomped into it with a feathery crunching sound. Wielding the shield, Andrew escaped from the pen and returned shuddering to the house for some first aid and empathy.

From then on, we had to go into the pen armed with a trash can lid to repel attacks from the rooster. We got pretty good at bouncing him off the inside of the lid, and he got pretty good at devising new angles of attack. We named him Captain America, not because he held the shield, but because we had to. He finally threw his back out after one particularly vigorous attack. It would have been a good time to retire him forever but instead we called the vet. We were young back then.

"No one has actually brought me a chicken before," said the country vet, eyeing the brand new cat carrier I was lugging into his office.

"Really?" I said, genuinely surprised. "Chickens are that durable and healthy?"

"Not really," he replied. "Soup is just that popular."

He eased the rooster out of the carrier and gently turned him over, examining the bird's now useless legs.

"You must really love this rooster," he commented.

"I think I hate this rooster," I said honestly.

"Ah," he said, "I see. New to country living then?"

"No!" I countered defensively. "What do you think is wrong with the rooster?"

"I have no idea," the vet answered. "He appears to be crippled."

"I think he threw his back out while he was attacking us," I said.

"In good conscience, I can't suggest that you eat a bird that is anything less than healthy," he said, holding the rooster up to eye level.

"Well, what would you recommend?" I asked.

"Rosemary," he replied, "and green chile." He caught my frown and shrugged apologetically.

"I could put a shot of steroids in his back," he said. "That's really all I can think of."

Two days later, in that long ago time, the rooster walked. By the end of the week, he was dominating the hens and making us regret our vet bill. I called the vet and told him the dubious good news. He deferred the congratulations, admitting surprise that the steroids had done any good at all.

"It was a laying-on-of-hands, then," I said. "Chickens all over the country will come. You'll become a legend."

That was the beginning of a long relationship with the vet, but we never again brought him a chicken. It took two more years from the day of the miracle cure, but we finally grew up and ate the rooster. So that morning in September, I was not excited to hear that familiar crowing sound. I looked around carefully and noticed a second rooster in the flock. I added them both to the butcher list.

Butchering day arrived and we started with a moment of respectful silence for the birds and a thank-you prayer. Juno helpfully began to name the birds, which I had resisted doing previously, in an effort to avoid identifying too closely with them. The girls approached the whole day with a practical attitude full of equal parts curiosity and disgust. I tried not to cry or wring my hands too obviously.

The library books, which devoted entire chapters to butchering advice, insisted that we needed to use a cone of metal or plastic to restrain the bird during head lopping. We didn't have a cone, but quickly discovered that the cone is indeed necessary because it is true that chickens run around with their heads cut off. They flap madly as well and in the case of one duck, actually gained some altitude and flew into the side of my car, although completely headless.

This is alarming, messy, and upsetting for the butcher. Poultry professionals therefore use the cone, which has an opening at the pointed end just big enough for the head of the bird. The bird slides into the cone, the butcher whacks off the bird's head as it protrudes from the end of the cone, and the interior of the cone restrains the mad flapping.

It was a long day and hard work. I spent several hours

dry plucking the best and most glamorous feathers, especially from the roosters. Fly-tying feather buyers prized their neck and shoulder feathers. I just had to work out a method of cleaning them without using toxic chemicals, which are common in the feather industry. As we worked, I kept track of the hours and equipment we had either bought for the task or were planning to buy for next time. Overall, I was keeping an honest accounting of the bird expenses. I realized that we could raise poultry humanely by giving them lots of room, clean water, drug-free food, and vibrant lives interacting with their own kind, but I could already see that I wasn't going to make a profit unless I did some creative bookkeeping — like not including my time or the cost of the pens.

"You have to count the cost of the pens!" Andrew said.

"That's a couple thousand dollars," I objected, "and it's going to put my bird business permanently in the red."

"You could amortize them," Andrew suggested.

"Gesundheit," I said.

"And you should count your time at the rate you would have to pay someone to do what you are doing," Andrew continued.

I pushed my ledger over to him and gave him the pencil after he had wiped off gruesomely messy hands.

"It looks like you'd have to pay about thirty dollars a bird to buy a roasting chicken like the ones we are raising," he soon concluded.

"I pay about seven dollars for a chicken at the store," I said.

"And contribute to the abusive ways of an unreformed

poultry industry," Andrew countered.

"But I don't want to pay more than seven dollars!" I protested.

"And that is the heart of the problem," Andrew said. "We've become accustomed to cheap meat and are insulated from the crimes of production that make it possible."

"I feel suitably guilty but I don't want to be a vegetarian," I said. "I tried it once and you started to look really juicy to me for unwholesome reasons."

"That's why we are doing this," Andrew said. "This is bigger than just teaching the girls about where food comes from."

"This is big all right," I said, recalculating my bottom line. "I'm going to have to sell a lot of eggs to make this work. And I want to do it in a way that doesn't perpetuate the wrong system."

"I'll clean up and make dinner while you reflect on your sins," Andrew said. "Roast duck okay?"

The girls ate heartily and Andrew made lip-smacking sounds. The dinner was a victory. I had scored an old family recipe book for cooking wild game from my friend. While the duck didn't really meet the criteria of "wild game" it certainly did benefit from the special techniques. My friend had grown up in New Mexico and her family had been hunting for generations. She had the inside scoop on cooking lore that made the roast duck delicious, and a practical attitude that I hoped to someday adopt myself.

I was feeling a lot better though, even with my grieving urban heart. Overall our plans were moving forward in every way. The tenants had water and were quietly leading their frenetic lives which involved a great deal of driving up and down the road we had naively assumed would stay less traveled. The chickens and ducks were laying, the eggs were selling, and our dreams were looking less ridiculous to everyone around us.

As I sorted the feathers from butchering day and started to clean them, I began to envision a feather product and tried to figure out who my market would be. If I could stay as organic as we already were, which was everything but certified, I could probably appeal to buyers who, like myself, wanted the animals to be treated humanely. Additionally, many of the most attractive feathers on the market came from Asia and my birds were all domestic; born and raised in the U.S.A. I was nearly organic, domestic, and humane. "Organic, domestic, humane." I had my business mission statement.

Chapter Seven

The chickens and ducks were laying. The Chukar Partridge, pheasant, and geese were not. The pheasant and partridge, considered game birds, were much less domesticated than the chickens and ducks. They were being raised domestically, but retained enough wild instincts and lifestyle to thrive in self-sustaining populations wherever the climate and habitat suited them. Many chicken, duck and goose breeds, and almost all turkey breeds were not likely to brood up their own chicks or breed successfully. The geese weren't laying because they took longer to reach egg-laying maturity, but they were also expected to live a very long time. The game birds weren't laying because they thought that five months was a ridiculously young age to start trying to reproduce. It was also much too close to winter, an unwise time of year to try and raise babies. I imagined that the game birds looked down on the domestic breeds that cranked out hundreds of eggs a year in an amazing display of productivity. Game birds were naturally haughty.

The ability of the domestic breeds of chickens, ducks,

and geese to build healthy populations on their own was being rapidly bred out of them. There is a growing movement in the animal husbandry world to counter this effect. The Heritage Movement consists of people dedicated to supporting breeds that can procreate themselves and live longer and healthier lives. Heritage breeds are generally smaller, lighter, more agile and less productive of eggs and meat than commercial breeds. However, they are superior in every way from the point of view of an organic, domestic, humane farmer. I had some heritage breeds in my cornucopia of poultry, but I had not specifically chosen them because, at the time, I didn't realize the difference. However, seeing the pheasant and the partridge grow side-by-side with the chickens and the ducks really brought the issue to my attention. The game birds were very different and I was learning my way around them with every passing day.

In the cooling nights of October, the chickens roosted in the upper level of their chicken house. The pheasant had an open-sided shelter that did a great job of keeping out wind and rain, but they stubbornly resisted roosting under cover unless it was actually raining. Each pheasant had a special space, either a tree branch or wooden bar that it would return to every night.

The Chukar Partridge roosted anywhere except for the chicken house. They could have had the lower level all to themselves, accessed through a tiny doorway cut at ground level, but they adamantly refused to roost inside. By day, they were a mob, never out of sight of each other and never going anywhere alone. By night, they fluffed what feathers they had into round dormancy like softballs with legs, and roosted by themselves all over the place. Chukar were particularly susceptible to feather picking, which had been triggered in my flock by overcrowding. Even though they had adequate space now, they had continued to pull out each other's feathers until their backs were completely bare. Our nights were nearing freezing, and I didn't think they had enough feathers to safely stay outside. So I went out every evening and collected them, picking up one at a time, and pitched them underhand into the lower level of the chicken house.

Their favorite roost was the roof of the chicken pen, directly under the wire and vulnerable to owl attack. When twilight turned to deep blue, almost dark, they became docile and I could pick them up single-handed if I could reach them. They exhibited the same behavior during rainstorms. The chickens shook off the first raindrops and filed into shelter. The pheasant would give it a little longer, but once mud formed, they delicately picked their way under the roof that stretched over a good third of the pen. But the chukar just hunkered down and fluffed out; or they would have, if they'd had feathers.

Late on a sunny October afternoon, the girls and I were cleaning the waterfowl pen when I noticed a lone, black cloud drifting in from the west. The cloud wasn't very big, but it was very black and something about it made me nervous. It looked ominous, and although small, it was big enough to cover the entire pen area, which it did as it drifted to a halt and blocked our sun.

Great fat raindrops started to come down so I put the girls in the woodshop while I continued to work just outside the door in the goose pen. They happily settled down to play tea party with the bird food and I kept filling waterfowl ponds until the rain began to drench. I joined the girls under cover and waited for it to pass as these rainstorms usually did. But it didn't pass. It rained harder and harder, until little trickles of rainwater started turning into streams, which were filling low spots and causing flooding that was starting to rise. I could see the mesa on the horizon from the shop with the roll-up door wide open. It was surreal to be watching floodwaters begin to damage areas of the pens when I could still see calm sunny weather farther out on the property. The water kept pouring down and around and was beginning to take rocks and dirt away.

Then it began to hail. Big round hailstones that bounced and rolled close enough for me to catch some for the girls to marvel over. But marveling turned to distress when the hail began to pound the ground with awful ferocity. We had to cover our ears against the demented hammering of hailstones on the metal roof and snow-white drifts of hail began to pile up against every tree. I was getting seriously worried now about the chukar, which I imagined standing out in the rising water and under the driving hail. I'd never seen a hailstorm like this and I feared it could kill them. There was a chance that they had finally taken shelter in the chicken house but if I was wrong, I could lose birds.

I needed to check on the birds, but I'd have to leave the girls alone during this intense cloudburst, and they were scared. The hail was not letting up and the floodwaters were now pushing ice floes across the woodshop floor. Torn between responsibilities, I lifted both girls up onto a worktable and told Blue to keep Juno under the roof and not to go out into the hail, no matter what. They solemnly nodded and stared with great round eyes as I put a box over my head to protect from the pounding hail. "Stay here," I shouted, "no matter what!" but I was drowned out by the hellish thunder of the hail.

I ran awkwardly to the pen door, slipping on the ice underfoot. I went through the main pen, full of sheltering pheasant, to what had been the original chicken pen. The door had swung closed in the storm and a broken tree branch was pinning it. I tore the branch away and flung the door open. A foot of ice water cascaded out over my shins, flooding the ground and depositing two saturated chukar at my feet. I snatched them up and waded into the pen. The force of the flowing water had pinned more chukar against the wire. They were barely keeping their beaks above the rushing floodwater. I grabbed them without ceremony, grasping any part of them that I could touch, and stuffed them inside my tee shirt to free my hands for more. I ran my hands along the wire as I slogged deeper into the pen and grabbed chukar that were underwater or buffeted against my legs at ground level, pushed by the violent currents.

This portion of the pen was a raging stream, completely flooded by water blasting into it from a previously overlooked small arroyo. It was an arroyo I'd never noticed before, but it drained directly into the pen. Access to the chicken house was only about eight inches above the ground and the water was rising fast. I worried that it, too, would flood, but I had no choice. I pitched the partridge into the small doorway, not waiting to see if they landed on their feet. Everywhere I looked, sodden chukar were struggling in the deep icy water.

I snatched them up faster and faster, as they got weaker with the cold. There was no high ground, the whole pen was underwater and several chukar were piled up in corner eddies where the floodwaters had forced them. The ice water numbed my feet and hands. When I finally grabbed the last bird, I searched around frantically, afraid that I'd missed one that could be trapped under the still rising water. Once again, I'd forgotten to count my chukar.

Wading back to the front entrance of the chicken house, I hauled open the door and stepped inside. The upper level was calm, all the chickens roosting dry and safe. The lower level was filled with soaked, miserable chukar. I plugged in one of the heat lamps left over from when the chicken house was the brooder space. A circle of warmth shone on the lower straw for the wet partridge and I pushed them all into it. The water drained as quickly as it had come, flowing through the lowest part of the larger pen area and away.

I went back to my frightened girls, who had faithfully stayed exactly where I had left them, and thanked them for being so steadfast. Cool night was falling and the chukar were still completely saturated. We crouched together for the next hour in the chicken house, taking turns with a blow dryer aimed at the still stunned and bedraggled birds. They all survived, none had been left behind, and I spent the next day with Andrew digging a series of channels on the treacherous invisible arroyo above the chicken pen to divert future blasting floods.

Our tenants had watched the local housing market and lowering interest rates like wolves watch a dying elk and decided it was time for them to buy instead of rent. They moved to a property several miles east that offered more acres and more bedroom space, leaving us facing our second adventure in landlording. Even though every book on being a landlord recommended choosing tenants with good credit ratings, we succumbed to the charismatic charms of another young couple, also expecting a baby, whose credit was not as cheerful as their smiles. Actually, none of the prospective tenants that answered our newspaper ad had shiny credit ratings. People with good credit were busy buying properties, lured by low introductory payments and assurances that with their good credit, they'd be able to easily refinance these purchases when the payments were due to go up. We were reviewing rental applications from the small group of people who were not in a position to buy and, for reasons of their own, wanted to live this far out in the country.

Although the second round of tenants was employed when they moved in, they didn't stay that way. The woman, beautifully graceful and very pregnant, left her job to care for her own health. Left alone day after day as her young husband went into town to work, she became isolated and despondent. She was desperate to keep him home with her. He took a night shift schedule to try and comfort her, but that soon failed, as the nights in our area were darker and deeper than nights in cities the woman had previously lived in.

One day Andrew met the husband on the road as he was coming in and the tenant was leaving for work. Andrew pulled over to make room on the one lane road and the man pulled his truck window to window.

"Hey," Andrew greeted him. "How's it going?"

"Oh man," said the tenant. "I just don't know. I don't know how I'm supposed to make it work."

"It's a hard time," Andrew sympathized, "expecting a baby and trying to bring in a living, I get it, brother!"

"Yeah?" asked the man. "Was it hard when your wife was pregnant?"

"You have no idea," Andrew said, "my wife about lost her mind in that last trimester."

"Did she, really?" the man asked. "Is that normal then? For my wife to be a little irrational?"

"Totally," Andrew comforted, "they get moody with the hormones, but it all works out in the end."

"I'm really glad to hear that," the man said, "because I've been worried, man, I've been real worried. She won't let me go to work and I've got to earn a living or I don't know what we're going to do!"

"Just hang in there," Andrew encouraged.

"No really, man," the man insisted, "she won't let me go, and I just don't know what to do," and he slowly pulled ahead. As his pickup passed, Andrew stared in shock at the woman, sitting upright and determined in the bed of the truck dressed only in her nightgown and slippers. She was silent; staring unfocussed at the sky, with her arms crossed.

For at least an hour, the man drove gently up and down the road to the house, past the trailer, with his pregnant wife perched implacably in the bed of his truck. Finally the truck stayed parked at the house and the lights went out, one by one. We were disappointed, but not surprised, when the first of the month dawned and the rent was not paid. Still hoping in vain for a good outcome, Andrew and I gave them more time, until it became obvious that they simply did not have the means. We sat down for an unpleasant conversation with each other.

"You were the one who wanted to give this young couple a chance," Andrew began magnanimously.

"I get it," I said, "no good deed goes unpunished."

"We are going to have to evict them," Andrew said.

"But I really did like them," I said, "and suppose there is a special kind of hell for landlords who toss out pregnant women?"

"Then I suppose it's going to be a very crowded kind of hell," Andrew said, "and there is something a little strange about that particular pregnant woman."

In the end Andrew paid them to leave. The same landlord books that had warned us about renting to less than optimal tenants in the first place went on to suggest paying them to leave as the easiest way to accomplish an eviction when compared to courts and the sheriff's office. They drove off into the sunset, leaving us with an empty house and a feeling of regret. It would have made a good story if it had worked out, but… it didn't. Our rental ad went back into the newspaper and the house sat empty and immaculately clean, evidence of what the odd pregnant woman had been doing with her time.

Although our projects were not total failures in their small forward progress (one successful rental and several small blown egg sales) we were still trying to find our way through our budget maze and waiting for a good tenant prospect to respond to our ad. I had some new ideas for egg products, but Andrew was insisting that I wait until I had more egg sales before I did any more brainstorming. Andrew doing his bookkeeping and running up yet another bid for yet another project. Summer was over and he needed to secure a project that would take him through the winter. He had reams of paper piled on every surface in his attempt to track expenses, income, personal accounts, debts, and client balances.

"I own my job," Andrew sighed, "not a business."

"I'm not sure I understand the difference," I said, unable to budge the enormous credit card balance off the chair to sit down.

"If I owned a business, I'd be making money even when I wasn't there," he said.

"What is getting in the way of it being a business?" I asked, finally just sitting on the paperwork. "Why are so many bids getting declined?"

"I'm more expensive than a lot of my competition," he said, "people can generally find someone to do it for less."

"Why can other contractors do it for less?" I asked.

"Some of them don't have as much debt," Andrew replied. "Some of them are more efficient, or faster, or more experienced."

"You said some," I prompted,

"And others of them are not licensed, or not insured, or hire illegal workers," he admitted.

"Well if we can't compete with the big boys," I said, with a pirate leer, "then let's compete with the bad boys, and be unlicensed and uninsured."

"I'm really proud of my contractor's license," Andrew said, looking at me out of huge angelic eyes. "I don't want to do things illegally. It isn't right and it isn't me."

I looked at him for a long time, having learned something new about my old man. I remembered a time early in our relationship when Andrew was helping me drive back from a trip I made to North Carolina. It was one of our first long trips as a couple, and Andrew was driving my car when we approached the California state line and an agricultural inspection station. He began to sweat bullets because we had an expensive gift box of Southern oranges destined for his parents on the back seat.

"They are going to ask if I have any fruit!" he said, worrying.

"We have no stinkin' fruit," I said confidently.

"Yes we do!" he said.

"Don't even think of giving up that fruit," I said. "That is for your parents and I'm not buying anything else in its place!"

"But they'll ask," he said, gasping for air, "and I'll have to lie!"

"I'll do the talking," I said. "You just drive."

He sat tensely through the ordeal as I waved at the inspection station officer and denied everything. He popped the clutch as we were waved forward and we almost stalled.

"You're going to get us busted," I said supportively.

"That sucked!" he exclaimed. "We lied!"

"I lied," I said calmly, "and besides, we also have a box of fireworks in the trunk, an open bottle of schnapps in the cooler, and a loaded firearm in a zippered case under the seat."

He stared at me in horror.

"It would take an hour to unload the car," I explained kindly. "Traffic would back up horribly. We did them a favor."

There was plenty of silence in the car for the next couple of hours. Andrew was not entranced with the pirate side of my personality, which he was seeing for the first time, and I was realizing Andrew would not make a good partner for a life of crime. I wasn't really planning to lead a life of crime, but I also didn't want to limit my options so early in the game. Still, he was very cute, and I was just beginning to see that he was, even deep down, a really good man — annoying at agricultural inspection stations though.

Back in our rectangular trailer, I found myself facing the angel in Andrew again, only now there was more at stake than a box of oranges.

"I don't know that I'm up for following all of society's rules while we starve or go bankrupt," I said.

"Hard work has to make a difference," Andrew replied, "and there are still things I know I can do. I haven't run through all my ideas yet. I can get more work."

"I'm not afraid of hard work," I said. "I just want to start seeing things get better because of it."

"Things will get better soon," he said confidently.

"If those other contractors have a way to undersell you, then we need a way to make people want to hire you even though you are more expensive," I mused.

"Well, I do a way better job," Andrew observed.

"I was thinking more along the lines of tighter pants,"

I said.

"Nobody likes plumber's crack!" Andrew cried.

"Depends on the plumber," I said, eyeing his attire.

"Hey!" he protested.

"Well, alternately, I was thinking of looking into pot farming," I said.

"I'll check my closet for tight pants," he muttered, and turned back to his piles of redlined papers.

Chapter Eight

$\mathscr{F}$all was in full swing and the October sunlight lacked the power of summer. There was no way the game birds were going to start laying now. The number of sunlight hours in a day determines a hen's laying cycle, and these wild birds were not only too young, but they were also too wise. However, the chickens and ducks were producing a tremendous number of eggs and I was busy at least two days a week blowing eggs and filling orders for blown egg sales. Every now and then, an egg would slip out of my grasp and I'd call in the dog for Hoover duty. One day Blue inspected the egg on the floor most carefully, before the dog brigade could arrive.

"Which part is the chick?" she asked, indicating the yolk and white and linoleum mix.

"Uhhhhhhhh," I said, "well, ummmmm."

"You don't know?" she asked, amazed.

"No, but I do know where to look it up," I said.

I strapped myself to the Internet to read about eggs and immediately learned that I didn't have to wash the eggs at all if they weren't soiled, which was very welcome news at the rate I was sluicing soapy water into the septic system. I found an extensive diagram of a hen's plumbing through a university extension website.

"Hey, look!" I said to the girls, who were using my desk chair as a carousel ride. "There is a thin protective membrane around the egg which lets in air but keeps out bacteria. Washing removes this membrane and shortens the egg shelf life. So I'm not supposed to wash the eggs."

"Isn't that the hen's bottom?" Blue asked, pointing to the screen.

"It's called a vent," I said.

"Where does the poo come out?" she asked.

"From the vent," I answered confidently, due to the caption helpfully displayed under the diagram.

"And where does the egg come out?"

"Also from the vent," I said, once again checking the text.

"So they come out the same place?" Blue asked.

"Yucky," added Juno.

"And you aren't going to wash the eggs?" Blue said, incredulous.

"Well, now that you put it that way," I said.

"It's a good thing you have us around, Mom," Blue said, helping Juno up to see the screen. "Or we'd all maybe die of poo poisoning."

We continued to learn life-changing facts as we studied the oviduct of the hen. We learned that fresh eggs are difficult to peel when hard-boiled simply because they are fresh. As eggs age, air collects between the inside membrane and the shell. This air provides breathing room for the chick in the last stages of development. The air collecting under the shell also facilitates peeling the egg after it is hard boiled, so an egg has to be at least a week old before it will be easy to peel.

"Look!" I said. "It says that fresh eggs will sink in a bowl of water and older eggs will float or hover."

"Let's try it!" Blue suggested.

We lined up the eggs that had been laid that morning and pulled some much older eggs from the backed up inventory waiting to be blown for sale. I kept reading while Blue filled a clear bowl with cold water.

"It also says that we don't have to refrigerate fresh eggs," I said, "only if we intend to keep them a really long time."

"Was that the same site that said we didn't have to wash them?" Blue asked.

"You are the oldest seven-year old I've ever met," I said.

Juno eased the fresh eggs into the bowl of water and Blue dropped the older eggs in gently. Sure enough, the fresh eggs sank to the bottom and the older eggs hovered and bobbed just under the surface.

"Yay!" yelled Juno, and snatched one of the fresh eggs back out of the water.

"Careful!" I said, uselessly, as the egg slipped out of Juno's hand and cracked open on the kitchen counter.

"Sowwy, mommy," Juno said sheepishly.

"Gross!" Blue yelled loudly. I looked at the shattered egg and was shocked to see an extensive network of veins and blood leaking slowly over the countertop in a viscous muddle of egg white and yolk.

"Oh my gosh!" I exclaimed in astonishment. "That IS gross!"

"What is that?" demanded Blue

"Well, I think that part is the chick," I said. "See, here is the egg white, and here is the egg yolk, and so here…"

"I think I'm unna be sick," said Blue.

"Me, too!" agreed Juno.

"Come on now," I said, cleaning up the graphic illustration of a developing chick's life cycle. "You wanted to know which part is the chick, and now we know that it isn't the white and it isn't the yolk."

The girls clutched their stomachs.

"And we also know why the website recommends cracking fresh eggs into a bowl before adding them to your recipe," I concluded, making a mental note to always do that from this day on. We went back to the computer.

"Here it is," I said. "This little dot, called the germ, is the chick. It grows using the nutrients in the egg white and egg yolk. The egg is like a little machine that provides a place for the chick to develop outside the mother's body." Juno climbed into my lap and tried unsuccessfully to spin the chair again.

"But it says that not every egg will grow a chick," said Blue, reading ahead precociously.

"That's right," I said, distracted, "only if there are roosters living with the hens can the eggs be fertile and hatch a chick."

I wrestled a permanent marker from Juno's hand and replaced it with a highlighter.

"When the roosters mate with the hens, they make the germ appear in the egg – more or less," I added vaguely.

"But we ate our roosters," Blue said.

"Yes we did," I agreed, swapping a piece of scrap paper for the library book Juno had been decorating with the highlighter.

"So how did the chick germ get inside the egg?" Blue asked.

"Um," I said, and pinched the phone cord out of the base so that the numbers Juno had just dialed wouldn't ring through.

"It's called sex," I said, steeling myself for yet another explanation of The Subject Of Life. "The rooster and the hen have to…"

"No," Blue interrupted. "I know that part. I mean how did the chick get in *this* egg when we have no roosters?"

"Oh my!" I blurted, stunned in my tracks. She was absolutely right. We had no roosters. It should have been impossible for the broken egg to be fertile. I'd read of an all-female flock producing hens that feathered out like roosters, but they were still girls. They couldn't impregnate each other. But the egg had undeniably been fertile; that had been graphically and unpleasantly obvious.

"The chickens are all mixed in with the pheasant now," I gasped, as the answer dawned.

"Yes," said Blue. "I've seen the pheasant fighting with the chickens too!"

"That's it!" I exclaimed. "They must have been doing

more than fighting!"

"Those naughty pheasant boys!" Blue said, scandalized.

"Boys, boys, boys," Juno echoed into the phone, shaking her head like her big sister.

As the autumn cold began to creep in, all of the birds had molted their ragged summer feathers and put on their winter coats, including the partridge. The pheasant were beginning to grow distinctive feathers that helped me identify some of their breeds, and I had plenty of males. This was great news because the male pheasant, known in the industry as cock pheasant, but referred to in our family vernacular as rooster pheasant, had truly spectacular feathers. I knew that I had one Reeves pheasant rooster, with his robin-hood style dark feathers banding his eyes. I had several Melanistic Mutants, which is a crow black version of the Ringneck pheasant that flashes iridescent purple, blue and green in bright sunlight. I had a single Ringneck pheasant rooster, who was much more beautiful than I expected, and three Golden pheasant roosters, already wooing the girls with a weaving hissing dance that was a delight to watch. There were two white-colored pheasant roosters that I was having trouble identifying. They had turned a completely uniform peach-white color and developed rich-red face armor, with enormous spurs. Completely out of resources, I tried posting to an Internet chat group dedicated to game birds.

"What kind of pheasant is this white pheasant?" I posted, along with a nicely pixilated picture of the bird.

"It's a White Pheasant," somebody posted back

quickly.

"Yes, I know," I typed, "but what kind of pheasant is it?"

Internet chat groups are not known for their patience. I'd like to point out that White Pheasant hadn't been listed in the hatchery catalog, so there was no way I could be expected to know that there was such a thing as a White Pheasant.

The most numerous pheasant were the ones I had the hardest time identifying. They were energetic, cheeky brown birds with bright red legs. They were brown through all their numerous molts, with only the occasional black and white kinky tail feather emerging. They were always at my feet. I often had to move them out of the way with a gentle soccer punt. I called them Red-Leggers, but I was totally unable to identify them through any of the books or Internet sites that I found. In frustration, I resorted to a fine art book of stylized pheasant photographs. It was the only book in the library to feature images of juvenile pheasant and there I learned that my Red-Leggers were actually Silver Pheasants; a bird very much in demand in the feather market. At maturity, they would have valuable black, white, and zebra striped feathers. The book warned the keeper not to push Silver Pheasant around, for instance, with one's foot when coming into the pen. Apparently they had a great reputation for attacking the keeper and were easily offended by such handling. I was pleased to have identified my birds, but it would have been handy to have found this book several weeks earlier.

We did not see a male Lady Amherst pheasant in our pens, which was a disappointment since that bird was the whole reason I got the pheasant in the first place. However, there was one mystery pheasant hen that did not look like any of the other birds, or like any of the pictures we kept bringing up from all sources to try and identify them.

"Have you seen the spurs on that one pheasant female?" Andrew asked one day.

"Yes," I said. "Pretty amazing."

"I thought you said that only the male pheasants had spurs," Andrew observed.

"Well, the girls can grow spur bumps," I said quickly. "The Chukar Partridge females have little spur bumps."

"Yeah," Andrew agreed, "but are spur bumps supposed to get really sharp and pointy?"

"No," I mused.

"And what about that one crimson feather?" Andrew said.

"What?" I exclaimed. "What crimson feather?"

"The one on her back, underneath her wings when she has them folded up," Andrew answered to empty air. I was rocketing up to the pen in great excitement. Pursued at high speed around the pen, the pheasant female finally took flight and revealed her crimson feather. She was also sporting one medallion-shaped greenish feather on her neck. I held my breath and crept closer, willing her not to fly away again. Sure enough, she had a mint-colored patch under her mint-colored eye and I whooped in delight. These were the hallmarks of a Lady Amherst Pheasant rooster – there could be no doubt. He had been slow to develop his distinctive feathers and we had mistaken him for a hen this whole time, but he was what he was. Amidst the racket of startled, flapping birds, I danced the Lady Amherst victory dance. We had a Lady Amherst

Pheasant all to ourselves, our very own. We were complete.

"Are you very pleased?" I asked Andrew.

"I am," he said, "very pleased."

"Why is it called a Lady Amherst Pheasant?" Blue asked.

"A long time ago, there was a British Countess called Lady Amherst stationed, with her husband, in India," I said. "She got a pair as a gift and took them back to England where they promptly croaked."

"How do you know this stuff?" Andrew asked, staring at me.

"But she got some more?" Blue asked, anxiously.

"She did," I confirmed, "and they became a popular zoo and aviary bird."

"You should wear a tee-shirt with footnotes," Andrew said, "citing your sources."

"I'm weawing footnotes," said Juno, proudly showing her new sandals.

I was filling a steady stream of blown egg orders and the range of egg sizes I was getting from the ducks had my entrepreneurial mind racing. I could already imagine a line-up of eggs featuring goose, duck, chicken, partridge, and pheasant sitting in beautiful, natural glory. They could be sold as a collection on little stands in order of largest to smallest. The geese, pheasant, and partridge would lay eggs eventually, although I didn't know exactly when, and based on the production I was already managing, I might have a steady supply of such collections.

I kept coming back to one more kind of bird that would

add a crowning glory to the egg collection. It was the Button Quail, also known as the Chinese Painted Quail. It was the smallest bird in the quail family and laid a little brown speckled egg. Button Quail eggs sold continuously on eBay for prices I couldn't begin to afford, but would love to receive.

Andrew remained adamant on not expanding the bird business until we were in a better financial position. So far, the egg sales were almost covering the feed bill but he kept waving the pen construction bill like a flag of surrender. He was utterly right, I knew that, but the little birds came to mind every time I closed my eyes. A valid objection was the fact that their care was completely different from the poultry setup I already had. Button Quail had to be kept out of the weather and in a heated space in the winter. The only common point they had with my existing endeavor was that they ate the same game bird food. I was plotting how to use Andrew's workshop as a quail house, and Andrew was counter-plotting how to keep me out.

Unexpectedly, we got a call from a couple who had been living nearby for some time but whose current lease was ending. They wanted to move into our rental house for a year before they moved to the big city. They had a project in the area they wanted to complete and felt our little house on the river would be perfect for their needs. Their arrival was like an electric bolt of good luck and we were delightedly amazed. They had perfect credit, knew exactly where the house was in relation to town, and had the means to pay the rent. We danced the Unbelievably Good Tenant dance and slept well for the first time in weeks.

It seemed too good to be true, but they moved in

promptly and proved to be everything we hoped they were. It was our third year-long lease signed in less than twelve months and we had finally caught a break. It felt very good to have the house rented and I started every discreet luck-building ritual I could think of to ensure our fortune would hold. I also read more and more about Button Quail.

Button Quail had a massive following on the Internet, so I was able to collect detailed information on how to raise them. They were on the fringe of the pet industry; too small for the commercial quail meat markets but still not a common find at pet stores. One day I made a visit to the pet store in town seeking a jar of mealworms to supplement the feed store grain. I was surprised to see what I thought were two Button Quail nervously skittering around in the bottom of a large parrot cage.

"Are those Button Quail?" I asked the bored-looking clerk.

"I dunno," said the clerk. She went to find the manager after I stared at her for a while.

"These are Button Quail," confirmed the manager.

"Are they male or female?" I asked.

"They are both female," said the manager firmly.

"And are they laying yet?" I asked, thinking that my research indicated that they'd be laying every day by the time they were as fully feathered as these were.

"No," said the manager uncertainly. "I would have noticed if they were laying."

"But you're sure they are female?" I asked again.

"Definitely," he said.

It was possible that they were too nervous in their

new environment to lay. I decided to buy them since a bird in the hand was worth a pile of little fresh eggs. I figured that Andrew couldn't object now that we had great tenants firmly established in the rental house. The clerk prepared a cardboard transport box and netted the quail. She was unnervingly casual taking the birds out of the net.

"It's okay," she said. "They don't fly."

But thanks to the Internet I knew that they did jump and was ready as she dropped the first bird into the box.

"Good catch!" she exclaimed, as I stuffed the first bird back into the box.

"Look at him go!" she cried as I caught the second bird mid-flight and put it in the box as well.

I went on my way to the muffled beat of little quail heads impacting the soft cardboard of the transport box. At home, I put them into the hospital brooder with wood shavings, natural logs, and juniper branches. They looked very picturesque with their reddish breast feathers and intricate back feathers. They both had a darling little white chinstrap that I fell in love with. They were pecking the game bird food happily when I went inside and pulled up one of the Button Quail websites. I quickly found great pictures of birds that matched my new quail. They were both unquestionably male.

The girls marched up to the workshop from the trailer to see the new quail cage.

"Aren't they pretty?" I said.

"What are they doing?" Blue asked.

"They seem to be fighting," I said.

"Are they going to hurt each other?" Blue asked.

"According to the website, they may kill each other," I said, thinking uncharitable thoughts about male quail and their lack of egg laying abilities.

Blue and Juno looked at me in shock.

"Which is why we are going to prepare another cage!" I continued quickly. "Can't let that happen!"

We made up a second cage, complete with water, food, branches, and wood chips. It was a very pretty, natural looking habitat. Two quail, two cages, two waterers to change, two feeders to fill. This already wasn't going well. With the second cage ready, it was time to move one of the quail so I reached inside the occupied cage and tried to gently pick one up.

"Wow, Mom!" said Blue. "Did you see that one pop up in the air?"

"You almost had him that time, Mom!" Blue cheered, while Juno clapped.

"Get him, Mom, he was on your arm," Blue admonished.

"Are you supposed to be squashing him like that?" Blue said, finally.

I had the tiny bird pinned in my fist. He was even smaller than he looked, his fluffed up feathers doubled his body size. I walked carefully to the other cage with the girls following every move.

"Oh, Mommy!" Blue cried. "You're holding him too tight!"

I felt somewhat unsympathetic to the bird, after the run-around he had given me in the beginning, but on Blue's warning I stopped to look him over. Maybe his eyes were bugging out a bit, and I heard a little squeaking chirping sound.

"Well," I said reluctantly. "I can ease up a bit, I think."

I relaxed the pressure of my hand and he was instantly airborne. His tiny wings were a blur as he flew expertly into the blue New Mexico sky. We watched silently until he was a tiny dot against the clouds, and then saw him drop in a graceful dive and run quickly under a distant bush. Although we immediately searched that bush and every bush for a mile, we never found that expensive little bird.

Within an hour, the other quail rooster began to call piteously into the vast emptiness of the woodshop, devoid of quail mates or even quail foe. His lonely song pierced my heart. I argued with Andrew that I was still no closer to my goal of having lucrative little piles of Button Quail eggs, but I was already taking care of a quail, so I should find a good source on the Internet and order up some girls for my lonely boy.

"What is the most efficient number of Button Quail to order in regard to the shipping cost?" I emailed the most reputable breeder of them all.

"Sixteen," came the reply. Sixteen, I thought. Andrew would be so pleased.

"Okay," I sent, optimistically. "I'll take one male and fifteen females… because I already have a male here, but it would be good to have one back-up boy in case I decide to breed the quail."

"Um," wrote the breeder, politely, "do you know very much about Button Quail? Because they do best in pairs or small harems of one cock and two hens."

"Oh," I wrote back, my disillusionment showing. "Then

I'd appreciate it if you would send the right combination of cocks and hens based on your experience."

"Also," she wrote. "The birds are all molting. They look terrible although they are healthy."

"That's okay," I wrote back. "I've only seen one up close and one flying away, so I don't have much to compare them to."

"Great," she wrote dubiously.

Soon I got a phone call from the breeder. The birds had boarded a plane in Sacramento and were headed my way. Within twenty-four hours, I had the massive chick-shipping box in my hands and was standing in the bathroom with the door closed. I had individual cages ready; eight cages for eight happy pairs or small harems. Eight waterers, eight feeders, and eight litter pans to clean. Eight optimistic little nesting boxes. I pried up the edge of the enormous cardboard box. It was divided inside into four compartments of four quail each, and the breeder had placed small pieces of sponge in the waterers to provide moisture for the birds during shipment. Many of the sponges were still wet and there were apple slices as well. The birds were in great condition. I was relieved since shipping adult birds is tricky. They don't have the couple of days of absorbed yolk to live on like the day-old chicks do, and are vulnerable to heat or cold if the postal service and the airlines don't handle them properly.

I mastered a method of sliding my hand inside, trapping a quail in a cage made of my fingers, then gently sliding my bird-filled fist out and dropping the creature into the new cage. By the time all sixteen quail were in their new homes, I had also mastered a method of catching loose quail by stalking them and throwing a towel over them. I felt like a village matchmaker as I divided the flock into pairs and harems and placed them in their luxury apartments. Once I had them all safely caged, I brought the girls in to celebrate the exciting moment. Sixteen healthy adult Button Quail were in my house, soon to be laying valuable Button Quail eggs.

"What are those?" Blue asked.

"Well they are Button Quail, of course," I said, "like I've been talking about."

"Where are their feathers?" she said.

"It's still hot in California," I answered. "So they took them off."

The birds were sparsely feathered on their wings and on their heads, but they were naked everywhere else just as the breeder had warned me. They were obviously healthy, but they looked like winged mice. They moved around the box incessantly, nervously, maniacally. Some birds, possibly the males, were posturing at each other through the bars. Other pairs were already fighting. Each was no longer than my finger.

The enthusiastic websites I'd researched so heavily talked about how tame the quail could be. I began spending time every day trying to coax them onto my hand, using tidbits and mealworms, but I never had the success described on the Internet. For me, handling them was a race between restraining their slippery clever selves and popping them into the next available cage.

The quail fan sites were also overly optimistic about the amount of care that Button Quail required. They declared that maintenance was minimal and the birds didn't smell. I didn't know what kind of Button Quail those freaky authors had, but my Button Quail seemed to import poop from another dimension, cast off feathers as soon as they grew them, wreck the cage from one end to the other, fight with each other, injure themselves, eat like elephants and stink like skunks. I struggled for a sense of daily equilibrium in the Button Housing Project. Each couple lived in a decent-size cage, complete with natural log (which they pooped on), a more or less fresh sprig of juniper (which they pooped on), natural dirt (which they bathed in, then pooped in), wood shavings, food, grit, oyster shell, mealworms, and water (all for them to poop in).

Couples counseling began within weeks of the Buttons' arrival. One female took such exception to her husband that she beat him incessantly and I feared for his life. He became thin and nervous and ended up in a cage of his own to recover. Another hen later vehemently rejected the same male, so I juggled more quail. I was mystified by the constant complaints about the rejected male. To me, he looked like he was doing everything Buttonly possible to please. He held tidbits and clucked cajolingly. He offered the hen most of the mealworms before eating his own. He fluffed his feathers coyly, and he regularly chased her round the cage trying to mount her with verve and gusto. But to a Button Quail hen, he was an irredeemable jerk.

Only one of the pairings was a joy to see. As the nights began to get cool, I saw "The Prince," (the pet store male), and his wife "Canny Hen" (cannily attempting escape at every water change), snuggled up rear-to-rear with his feathers fanned out to almost completely over hers. It was a sweet scene and I was touched. I almost forgot for a moment how frustrating my Button Quail were and waxed as romantic as the websites. Then I went back to fiddling with the temperature to make sure they didn't freeze to death or die of heat prostration, changing their water daily to make sure they didn't die of enteritis, adding calcium supplements to make sure they didn't lay themselves to death (not that they were laying at the time), cleaning their cages every other day to cope with the incredible amount of poop they produced, and adding padding to the tops of their cages so they wouldn't bonk themselves into a coma and death.

"You sure are spending a lot of time in that workshop," Andrew observed one night over a dinner of peanut butter and jelly sandwiches.

"I don't want to talk about it," I said.

"Mommy doesn't call them Button Quail," Blue offered. "She calls them f*$#%ng quail."

Soon after that, I started my morning quail chores to a happy surprise. In the front of one quail apartment was a little brown egg and the quail were strutting circles around it. I was so happy that I did a quiet little first-egg jig and thanked the couple profusely. My doubts disappeared, faith in my business plan reappeared, and I became suddenly fond of Button Quail. I crowded up to the cage to give the birds a koochee-koo of congratulations. So I had a bird's eye view as they quickly ate that first egg.

Chapter Nine

*E*arly November can capture the wonderful weather of October, or it can rage. We were thankfully enjoying mild sunny days, low winds, and few thunderstorms. Early morning smelled like ice and the afternoon smelled like browning grasses in the warm sun. Andrew had a remodel job in hand and the new tenants were happy. The laying birds were producing nicely and Blue was enjoying school. Juno spent many of her days pretending to go to school, complete with packed lunch.

The angle of the sunlight in November was fair warning that winter was coming, but the mild weather gave us time enough to prepare. We started to split wood and cut construction scrap to the right lengths for the woodstove. Propane was our basic heat source but it was much more economical to keep a fire going in the woodstove.

Early mornings and late nights got chilly enough to warrant our winter jackets, so I went into the workshop to find them. The shop was stuffed with everything we could possibly need but would never find due to the disorganization.

I chose a box at random, looking for the jackets, and found a sweatshirt that a mouse had made into a nest. The hole in the sweatshirt was packed with shredding from what could only be my summer clothes storage box. A shower of mouse poop rained down on me like a bride's send-off when I took another box down from the upper shelf.

I got a little upset. I do like mice, I think they are fascinating, but the damage was unpleasant. Plus, I suspected I was losing a significant amount of poultry feed to their raids. The shop was a mouse palace; there was no downside for them in living here, especially with a plentiful food source nearby. Poisoning them was totally out. Poison a mouse and the poison spreads to the entire surrounding area, all the way up the food chain until a beautiful soaring eagle falls in a crumpled heap from the sky. Trapping them was slow and gruesome and no deterrent. To fix the problem I'd have to make the shop a whole lot less desirable than the great outdoors. I would have to get a cat.

I'd never had a cat because Andrew is horribly allergic to them and I'm more of a dog person. The cat would have to live in the shop with the door wide-open most of the time. I wouldn't be able to protect it from the neighborhood dogs, coyotes, foxes, eagles, owls, and bobcats. Basically, I could provide support, a warm place to sleep, and a whole bunch of mice. It sounded like a decent deal for the right cat, except for the lurking predator part. But I didn't want to pay money for a cat that might take off forever the first night or turn into a snack after the second night. I needed a free cat and wasn't the world swimming in excess cats? It was beginning to feel like a matter of principle as well as a budget issue.

I went to a pet store and prepared for my free cat with the requisite food, litter box, feeder, waterer, cat litter, and litter scooper. I spent too much money and still didn't have the cat itself. The animal shelter was full of cats, but at $65 each, they didn't really qualify as free. Not that the $65 wasn't a great deal, since the cats were neutered and vaccinated. I also didn't think that some of these pampered, cosseted, urban cats would be very happy with my barn.

"Do you have a financial-aid package for your cat adoption fees?" I asked the animal shelter. "Or a multi-cat adoption discount?"

"No," said the volunteer, "we think that if you can't afford $65 to adopt a cat then you can't afford to have a cat."

"It's just that I need the cat for my workshop," I pressed, "and it might disappear after the first night, and then I'd need another one and that would start to get expensive."

"These aren't bags of potato chips!" said the volunteer angrily. "Your home doesn't sound like a good place for a cat at all!" And then she cat-blacklisted me. I began to put out the word for a free cat.

"I'd like to get a free cat to live in the shop and eat mice," I told my friends.

"If you know anyone who is giving away kittens, let me know," I told every waitress and checkout clerk and receptionist I met.

"I've got a good home for a free cat," I told Blue's teachers, Juno's babysitter, and the tire guy.

"I'm calling about the free kitten ad in the paper," I said to answering machines, wrong numbers, and people who never called me back.

One day I was picking up my mail and chatting with the postmistress.

"I'm starting to despair of ever getting my hands on a free cat," I said.

"You want a free cat?" she asked.

"Yes," I said, "my shop is crawling with mice and I can give it a good-ish home, but I don't want to pay for the cat itself. Kind of a philosophical thing," I said.

"I might know somebody who is giving away kittens," she said.

The next day, I was dialing Rosie, a local-who-had-kittens.

"Mi'ja!" said Rosie in a thick New Mexico mountain accent. "I have to go outside and catch them. I'll take them to the post office and you meet me, no?"

"Today? You can give them to me today?" I said, caught off guard with the possibility of an imminent cat.

"Sure, just I have to catch them, dear," said Rosie.

"How many kittens do you have?" I asked.

"Oh, I can give you them all," said Rosie, putting down the phone. "I'll call you soon, you can meet me."

I waited all day and the next. I called Rosie and left messages. Three days passed and I tried to accept defeat. My cat litter stayed pristine and trackless. My cat food sat forlorn and full on the shelf. Blue compiled a longer and longer list of possible kitten names. Then the phone finally rang.

"Mi'ja!" said Rosie. "I'm at the post office, where are you?"

"Rosie?" I said. "I'm on my way. I have an animal carrier

we can put them in to bring them home."

"Uh, noooo," said Rosie, "maybe you don't want to try and pick up the momma cat."

"Oh, okay," I said.

"You take my box and give it back to me tomorrow," she suggested, and it was settled.

We loaded up and headed for the post office. It sounded like the momma cat was feral, but that was no problem. It was actually better as she would be more likely to clear the mice out of the shop. And if she'd been living outside, my shop might be better accommodation than she was used to. That's what I needed. Some cat that would think my shop was nice. Blue, however, had been looking forward to a kitten to snuggle and play with. I told the girls what I was thinking, trying to prepare them for a bunch of cats that we would be able to report occasional sightings of, but nothing more.

"Mom," said Blue, after a silence. "Maybe the cats don't let the Rosie-lady pet them, but they'll let us pet them because we will *love* them."

"I'mna chase dem," Juno said.

"No you won't!" cried Blue. Juno smiled wickedly at her.

"Mom!" Blue yelled.

We arrived at the post office and drove to the only car in sight with a lady standing patiently next to it. She waved and lifted the hatchback of her car as we pulled up. I stared at an industrial-strength badger trap filling the back of Rosie's car. I got an impression of angry lambent eyes and welded heavy-gauge steel.

"This going to fit in your car, Mi'ja?" Rosie asked, looking dubiously at my kid-filled compact car.

I suddenly realized that Rosie's delay in calling me had been because she had to actually trap her cats. When she had said she needed to catch the cats, she had been speaking literally.

As I wrestled the trap into the front seat of the car, I got a better look at the occupants. There was a gray tortoiseshell adult cat, with a clean white bib and dainty white paws. Her pretext of domesticity was marred by the vicious expression on her face. I could see all of her sharp, white teeth. There were two very young black kittens, and a tousled, wobbly mouse-sized thing that I belatedly recognized as an infant kitten. Its eyes were still closed.

"That baby stays with the momma cat," Rosie said, pointing to the tiny thing. "It still needs her milk."

"Okay," I said. "Thanks!"

I squeezed the passenger door closed on the cage of free cats, shook hands with a relieved-looking Rosie, and started off home. Blue was ecstatic. She was delightfully exploring the world of cat names and enjoying the tingle of power that bestowing names brings. Juno was echoing each name that Blue considered and adding extra vowels to each one. I was becoming concerned about my car engine. There was a very low grinding sound coming from the front of the car.

"What is that sound?" I said.

"What is that *smell?*" I added, a moment later.

I looked over at the cats, perched on claws in the cage. Three and a half pairs of distrustful eyes glared back at me. Little wavy stink lines threaded up through the steel, diffusing into the air. I leaned closer to the cage and realized the grinding sound was coming steadily from the direction of the momma cat. I'd never heard that kind of sound from a cat before: a deep, threatening, promising growl, a Stephen King kind of sound.

"Girls!" I announced, straightening up. "New Family Rule! Never Touch Momma Cat!"

"Okay," promised Blue,

"Otay," promised Juno.

"This momma cat will rip off your arm if you try and touch her," I said, eyeing the girls for effect. Juno mimed ripping off an arm and waving it at her sister.

"Mom!" Blue protested.

By the time we got home, our cats had become Momma Cat Charlotte, Little Cat, and "The Dodos," The two black kittens were identical, so I insisted that Blue name them both the same name. In the shop, with the door closed, we opened the trap and stepped aside as Charlotte streaked out. The Dodos slunk around the edges and hovered as I reached in and extracted Little Cat. Blue and Juno settled in to snuggle this tiny piece of kitten, almost sharing admirably. Charlotte melted away into the shop's corners and crevices, and each time I reached for a Dodo, it stepped just out of reach and hissed tiredly. As we made a cat nest under a heat lamp and put the kitten in the middle, Charlotte came to the food bowl to devour the canned food. She cast an evaluating glance at the girls, then climbed into the bed and wound around her kitten. We left her for the night.

The next day our dog Rachel came in and stared in amazement at the new cats. Charlotte the Cat walked directly up to Rachel the Dog and swatted her in the face. Rachel backed up and Charlotte came on again until a bewildered Rachel was expelled from the shop and their relationship was established. As I cleaned the shop and the girls snuggled the kitten, Charlotte stayed close. All the cats, it seemed, were using the cat box. Several times over in fact. I had acquired another daily chore to spend my copious spare time on.

Later that afternoon, I went to refill the cat food bowl and to my amazement and delight, found a huge gray and white carcass, larger than the kitten. Charlotte had presented us with a wood rat. Less than twenty-four hours of cattage in the shop and they were already reducing the rattage. Andrew did an attitudinal about-face about cats in general and our own cat specifically. He went from distrust and disgust to pride and celebration. He now made sure that Charlotte got her canned food in the evening and began to talk to her as he worked in the shop. We were all very pleased with our box of cats, except Rachel, who was offended by the whole thing.

Three days after the cats had arrived, I was getting faster at my morning cat chores. We were late for appointments in town that morning so the girls were in the car, strapped in their car seats, while I quickly finished the chores. I approached the cat bed to check on Little Cat. Charlotte was in the bed, curled up around her not-so-good-looking kitten. There was something about the position of the tiny kitten, something not so flexible. Stiff. I'd asked Blue and Juno to postpone their kitten snuggle time till the evening. Now they would have to postpone it permanently.

"Damn," I said to Charlotte. "I'm sorry, Mama Cat."

Charlotte responded with a quiet series of growling threats and profanities. I wasn't sure of dead kitten protocol.

Charlotte was still snuggling the kitten, but it was rigid and rather flat. I didn't want to lose my arm to retrieve it and I was late. So I left it with her, feeling bad about the whole thing. I resolved to tell the girls after school, putting it off, and got back in the car.

"Mom," said Blue immediately, "did Little Cat make it through the night?"

There was a pause, a lengthening pause. There was a really long pause.

"No, honey," I said finally, "I'm sorry, Little Cat died."

We both cried as Juno looked at us curiously.

Despite my speed habits, the ride to pre-school was twice as long that morning. I told Blue what I believed about soul migration.

"So what you are saying," said Blue, "is that some other kitty's soul could come into Little Cat's body and make him alive again when we get home?"

"No," I said hurriedly, "once an animal or person is dead, they stay dead. Their body breaks down into the earth, and the soul goes somewhere else."

"So is Little Cat being born right now into another kitten?" she asked.

"Maybe!" I agreed with relief. "Somewhere maybe a cat is having kittens and Little Cat is starting over."

"So what happens to *that* baby kitten's soul if Little Cat's soul is in there instead?"

I am not qualified for this, I thought.

"Maybe it's like standing in line at the store," I suggested, "and Little Cat has taken his place in line and his time will come."

"I hope we meet Little Cat again," she said softly, looking at the window, "when we get another kitten."

"Me, too," I said, and drove even faster to school in apprehension of the gears turning in her head.

That evening, we came home to the unwelcome task of burying Little Cat. This many hours post-mortem, I was worried about how earthy and biologically graphic this task might be. I went into the shop and discovered that my decision to leave Charlotte with her board-like baby had been a good one. Charlotte was curled up in the bed and the kitten had been discarded some distance away. I picked up Little Cat cautiously between thumb and forefinger and was relieved. He was just a little whiffy, not bad. Charlotte went to rub heads with the Dodos.

Blue, Juno, and I took the kitten out to our pet graveyard and I dug a grave in the rocky ground. I scraped and stabbed at the earth, jumping up and down on the shovel. A tiny pile of earth and roots began to grow by the shallow hole. Our pet graveyard was a garden of rock cairns due to the effort of digging anything more than six inches deep. Fortunately the scavengers seemed to find the earth just as difficult. A knee-high memorial of river stones piled on the graves had so far guaranteed a restful interment for our departed animals. I finally stood back to let Blue put the kitten in. She had collected stones for the cairn, including a special cairn topper rock with a fossil in it and gave a beautiful eulogy.

"Little Cat, I'm sorry you couldn't stay with us because we really wanted you. I know you had to go, and I hope that your soul will go to another kitten that we can have and take care of someday," she said.

I was so proud of her. She held the icky kitten and looked at it closely and stroked it. Little Cat was no longer stiff and lolled in her arms. I got a little uncomfortable as the tender affections went on.

"You should put him in the grave now, love," I said.

Juno was watching it all with great interest. The kitten in Blue's arms was just above her eye level, and she studied it closely. Blue reverently placed the kitten in the earth and sprinkled a handful of dirt on him.

"Hey guys!" Juno announced, "dat's GWOSS!"

It was like having my Dad around.

Overall, we were happy with our free cats. I was learning a great deal about how to manage a shop of feral cats, and the mouse population began to fall. A couple of weeks after little cat expired I discovered that feral cats often come with complications. The girls developed ringworm. We spent almost $50 in anti-fungal ointments and a trip to the doctor. But the cats had been free.

We had the month of November to give the poultry a dietary boost that would prepare them for the coming cold weather. We usually got our first snow in October but it was a light dusting. The heavy storms often held off until December, so we had one month to get ready. The chicken house would have a heat lamp on cold winter nights, but the chickens' best defense against the weather was access to foods that would supply all their vitamin and energy needs.

We were feeding them high protein pellets and crumble from the feed store, as well as tossing in handfuls of oyster shell for calcium, but we knew that they needed fresh greens to have a truly balanced diet. In late summer, the land produced all kinds of greens without any effort on my part. I ripped up armfuls of succulent green weeds and tossed them in huge piles in the pens, but now the weeds and natural grasses were drying out and developing spikes.

I had big plans for an organic circular system of refuse with the birds. We would take our kitchen vegetable waste and toss it into the bird pens. The birds would eat it all up, then we'd gather their waste and toss it into the compost heap. The compost heap would fertilize the garden and grow vegetables for us to eat. The vegetable waste from our garden meals could go back to the birds where the cycle could start again.

This did work in theory. Those times that the vegetable waste managed to make it up to the bird pens rather than turning into compost on the kitchen counter, the birds deeply enjoyed it. But I knew I needed a greater nutritional range. Supermarkets regularly threw away tons of fresh-enough greens so I sent Andrew to one market after another, asking for access to their trash.

"We can't," said a huge chain-store produce manager.

"Why not?" asked Andrew.

"Because you could sue us," the manager said.

"I promise I wouldn't sue you," Andrew said.

"We did that once," said the manager, "and somebody ate it and got sick and sued us."

Andrew persevered until he found a manager of an environmentally motivated store. She had a degree in recycling and compost and was trying to start a program of reusing their "fall down," greens and fruits that were no longer saleable. This manager had to wade upstream against a torrent of liability-conscious superiors, but she didn't quit until she had found a way to divert the vegetable waste away from the dumpster. Andrew signed several liability wavers, promised not to eat the stuff, and got bags and bags of off-the-shelf greens.

The waste produce was divine. There was every imaginable item in the bag and they all looked so good and fresh that the promise not to consume it ourselves suddenly made sense. The geese dined on organic spring greens, radicchio, kale, red-leaf lettuce, butter lettuce, and bok choy. The other birds feasted on a buffet of apples, mango, pineapple, pears, grapes (red and green), strawberries, raspberries, carrots with the tops, broccoli, cabbage, and beets. We had almost every vegetable and fruit known to man spread in front of our lucky birds. One day a shipment of baby spring greens came in with too high a moisture content to be sold in the store. The geese stood breast-high in a buffet of greens that stretched from fence line to gate. The ducks didn't have to bend their necks to waffle up the crisp tasty leaves.

Andrew went twice a week to the store, timing his visits to the rhythm of the produce department. English cucumbers tumbled over cauliflower heads. Endive and escarole intertwined leaves with watercress. The only effort I had to expend was to remove the rubber bands and identification tags that someone else had laboriously put on. Green leaf lettuce and spinach were as popular with the geese as the tops of red radishes and rutabagas were with the chickens. At the bottom of one rich bag that Andrew tossed in the pen was a collection of expensive, top of the line, organic, ripe Hass Avocado.

Andrew was working in the shop that day, preparing door jams for installation in an ongoing job. The avocado went into the pen at about noon. I came home with the girls at six in the evening, saw the avocado, and took it out. There was a ghost of a wisp of a cousin of a thought in my mind that avocado may not be good - some really obscure reference that I had skimmed in my copious research. I took the avocado out of the pens as an afterthought.

During the night, the first Chukar Partridge died. We found him in the morning under one of the pine trees. All of the other chukar were looking unhappy. They stood apart from each other, heads tucked in between shoulders, moving as little as possible and puffed up to twice their usual size with fluffed out feathers. I took the dead chukar out of the pen and placed him on the shop worktable. Then I remembered the cats and placed him head-down in a bucket. Then I remembered the dog and moved the bucket to a hook attached to a high shop shelf.

For the next forty-eight hours, chukar continued to die until there was a bouquet of chukar feet blooming from the bucket hanging in the shop. Six partridge died from that mistake, and we felt awful. I started researching avocado poisoning and found all kinds of vehement websites under pet bird searches. My research had been in game birds, a very different fan base. Every parrot website I visited had the avocado warning in clear view, at the top of the page. The experts writing on behalf of parrots, doves, budgies, and finches said that there was no cure for avocado poisoning. There was nothing I could do. Sometimes avocado is deadly poisonous to birds — not all kinds of avocado, and not all kinds of birds — but, sometimes, it kills.

To combat my feelings of helplessness, I read every word on every site I found, looking for more warnings. Parsley and onion were also on the no-give list, but more because of the flavor they could impart to the eggs than for their poisonous properties. I discovered that the fumes from an overheated Teflon pan coating could be deadly to birds, which are extremely sensitive to it. At first, I dismissed this as a threat since I didn't have an indoor bird. But then I started to reflect on how often I overheated my Teflon pans, which was every time I used one. If I did have an indoor bird, it wouldn't have lasted very long. I figured that my cooking style was probably not very good for my little girls either and resolved to stop flaming my pots and pans.

It was a hard week. Some bird days were better than others. I lived and learned. I killed and learned. It occurred to me that I didn't have that much more education as a parent than I had as a game bird farmer, and mistakes were so easy to make. That thought earned me a few more sleepless nights. Would there come a day when I felt like I knew what I was doing? It wasn't this day, that was for sure.

The cascade of riches from the supermarket refuse bins stopped with a change in ownership of the parent company. The new managers of the produce department closed their doors, afraid of lawsuits, and we once again had to rely only on our kitchen. But the time of plenty had been enough to prepare the birds well for the deep cold and waning daylight.

Chapter Ten

$\mathcal{W}$e lost the cornucopia of fresh greens just as late November settled in with a vengeance. Mild sunny days were gone and it was cold. Enough of the deciduous trees had lost their leaves to take the glow out of the landscape, leaving it feeling bare even though there were still plenty of juniper and piñon. Those trees did not change with the seasons, but the winter look was on the land. It was time to hunker down. The birds fluffed out and they suddenly all looked very good. To maintain their good health, we had to find another source of nutritional supplement that was affordable and attractive to the wide range of preferences in our poultry species. The bird books had waxed poetic about mealworms as an essential live food that was packed with protein and easy to raise. The books said that it was more economical to raise mealworms than to buy them so to get started, the girls and I went down to the pet store and bought 500 mealworms in a small plastic tub with tiny holes in the top.

"Oh Momma!" breathed Blue, enraptured by the baby rabbits, "can I have a baby rabbit?"

"Sorry, no," I said.

"I wanna bird!" shouted Juno. "I wan DAT bird!" She was pointing to an enormous $900 parrot winking wickedly from a thick branch by the register.

"Sorry, no, we already have too many birds," I said.

"How about a little mouse?" asked Blue. "I would take really good care of it!"

"No," I said, distracted by the scorpions in their tanks, "we have too many of those as well."

"Don' wan dat," Juno said, following my gaze and shuddering.

"Hamster?" Blue offered.

"Sorry girls," I said, "but look what we *can* have!" and I took the plastic tub from the cashier with my receipt.

"Worms?" Blue said incredulously. "You really honestly bought us worms?"

"Hard to believe," I agreed. "Am I the best mom in the world or what?"

"Wha?" said Juno.

Following Internet directions from a grade school teacher, we also got a large box, a feed-store size bag of bran, some yeast powder, some apple halves, and some pieces of raw potato. My box was a Styrofoam cooler which I had on hand and seemed durable yet still lightweight. As an art project, the girls glued window screen to a hole we cut in the top. In the end, we had a tight fitting lid with screened ventilation. It gave us a nice view of the burlap bag that would sit on top of the wheat-germ-and-yeast medium. The worm box would stay in the second bathroom of the trailer where it could take advantage of our heated household. Apparently a cold environment would slow down the worm life cycle and dampen our plans for hundreds of tasty worms for the birds.

When we were finally ready to release the worms into the Styrofoam box, I opened the pet store container and gazed indulgently at the seething herd of worms at the surface of the tub. They were a nice honey color, with neat and tidy segments that slid gracefully over each other as they moved. Their heads were tiny and their little jaws even smaller.

"Want to hold one?" I asked the girls, offering up the tub.

"NO!" they answered in unison.

"Come on," I urged, "they really are harmless. They don't eat hand meat."

They stared at me with undisguised distrust.

"Look," I said. "I'll go first, see? I've got them in my hand and they are…"

"What?" Blue asked, instantly alert to stress in an adult voice.

"They're fine," I said between gritted teeth. Blue and Juno came closer, studying the bead of sweat rolling down my temple.

"Try it!" I grunted, holding my wrist with my other hand as the worms writhed into the creases of my palm and gave me a serious case of the heebies.

"No. Way," enunciated Juno, as clearly as a teenager.

"Fine!" I exclaimed, dumping the wormy handful back into the tub. "But look! No bite marks!" The girls examined my palm as closely as I did myself, incredulous that there were

no signs of worm attack. Blue ceremoniously poured the rest
of the mealworms into the bran mix and we watched as they
all slithered out of sight. We closed the lid.

"Now what?" Blue asked.

"Now we wait," I said. "Let's have lunch."

"I'm not hungry," said Blue.

"Me eider," said Juno.

"Nor me," I said, and closed the door on the bathroom
and worm box.

We waited for weeks. The apples withered and went
soft. The potato halves dried out and went hard. A sharp
fruity odor of mold wafted up each time I opened the box
lid. My instructions had said to remove any moldy stuff, but
when I stared to dig out the moldy bits I found no end to
them. The apples had dissolved into the medium and I was
only succeeding in mixing it around, fluffing the mold into
the air.

More time passed and the worms got bigger and gnarlier
looking. They grew too big to feed to the Button Quail and
I began to wonder if I'd have to build a pen for them too.
I was getting frustrated with my mealworm project. I was
expecting to have an endless supply of protein-packed live
food for my birds but instead I was just feeding more and
more produce to a box of large worms.

"What's up with the stinky box in the bathroom?"
Andrew eventually said.

"I've got it under control," I said. "No need to worry."

"It's a bit much," Andrew pressed. "I don't think it should
be in the bathroom."

"I'm dealing with it," I said.

"And I also don't think you should be keeping a bunch of gigantic worms in the house," he continued. "What if they escape?"

I shivered at the mental image of escaping worms.

"I'm going to have to insist," Andrew said firmly.

"What*ever!*" I said maturely, but I moved the box up to the Button Quail section of the woodshop, now heated with hanging lamps to protect the quail from the pressing November cold.

Soon after that, I opened the box to add another apple and saw a strange new thing on the surface of the wheat germ. A worm had suddenly changed shape. It was motionless until I poked at it, then it gave a crazed wiggle and leapt away like a popcorn kernel. I dragged the girls from their playroom to the cold shop and showed them my new discovery.

"This is even more revolting than the worms," Blue announced.

Juno poked at the thing until it pinged across the box and squealed in delighted disgust.

"This is the second stage," I marveled. "Do you see? The life cycle change has begun!"

"So is this thing going to hatch into a hundred worms?" Blue asked.

"Well no," I said. "I don't think so, there is a beetle somewhere in the life cycle, and then an egg, and then another worm!"

"So you are doing all of this just to get to another worm?" Blue said.

"Yes!" I crowed. "Brilliant, isn't it?"

"But you had a worm to begin with," she persisted.

"But now I'm going to have lots and lots *more* worms," I insisted.

"Wha'eva," said Juno, poking the popcorn worm again.

"Hey, man," I protested. "where'd you learn to talk like that?"

The next day, many of the worms were that strange new shape. Their great sleep had begun. They ate nothing and moved around very little. Soon I found no worms, only these chrysalises. After a comparatively short time, a light brown beetle appeared and I was very excited. I photographed the beetle and carried it around and showed the girls. I turned it upside down, then right side up. They thought I was a little over-fond of my brown beetle.

"My victories are small!" I sang to them. "I have to celebrate them all!"

The next day yielded another brown beetle. Then there were hundreds of beetles, and they began to turn black. Now I was waiting again, feeding a colony of voracious beetles that would devour a whole cabbage head in a matter of days. Thankfully, my Styrofoam box proved beetle-proof, but I was doubly glad I had moved the box to the quail shed. If there was going to be a breakout, I preferred not to have the already dubiously-livable trailer overrun by glossy-black hungry beetles.

More time passed and my mealworm enthusiasm was drowned out by the scratching sound of thousands of black chitinous feet on the underside of the Styrofoam box lid. The beetles were *Tenebrio*, the darkling beetle, and mealworms were their baby phase. I wondered if my research was faulty as I waited and waited. I'd succeeded in raising thousands of beetles, but what I really wanted was more mealworms. I contemplated tossing the whole box into the chicken pen and letting them have a great beetle buffet, but instead began to ignore the creepy mess and just toss in a vegetable or two each week.

One cold morning, I lifted the lid higher than usual to put in another cabbage head, and staggered back in astonishment at a surprising waft of heat that billowed out from inside the box. Lifting the burlap bag, I saw a strange new surface on top of the wheat germ. The mass undulated and I gingerly pinched a sample. It was a sea of worm castings. Underneath it, permeating the wheat germ, were so many mealworms that the friction of their bodies rubbing against each other was making the box almost hot to the touch. I scooped up a hot slick handful and found it brimming with tiny mealworms. I whooped out loud, setting off a bonk session among the Button Quail. I was a successful worm farmer! I was the Worm Queen.

Andrew and the girls were politely enthusiastic and congratulatory on my worm success. Juno finally agreed to hold a small handful of baby worms before scattering them in the bird pens. Blue gently sifted through the worm box and eventually agreed that I now had many more worms than I had started with. I was worm rich.

I had tiny worms to large worms and everything in between. Beetles ran amok through the worms and new chrysalis. Whenever I was in a wormy mood, I sifted cupfuls of the medium and tossed the dozens of resultant worms in with the birds. Devoted male Button Quail would nab a mealworm, give it a few blows to the head to quell (or increase) the wiggling, then chirp-chirp-chirp to his wife to come and eat the mealworm treat.

In the big pens, the chickens became experts at pecking up the mealworms as fast as I could scatter them around, so if the other birds wanted a worm, they had to come close and stand still as they waited for the largesse. In this way, I began to score some truly spectacular close up photos of the shy pheasant.

The Styrofoam box had worked well to insulate the worms from the cold, but the new generation dug a great labyrinth of tunnels in the foam and out underneath the lid, illustrating the flaws of Styrofoam as a worm barrier. Many worm-messiahs led their followers into the promised land of the Button Quail shed through these tunnels. I lost those, but I had plenty more.

Inevitably, after a while, I began to run out of worms. The wheat germ was no longer permeated with them and I learned to look for the "worm party," the happening site where all the worms would be. Often it was the burlap sack, and I could shake down a good jarful of worms there, but then the sack went out of vogue and I had to find them in the apples, or dig under the potato halves. I stopped tossing the dried-out potatoes when I discovered that they were the main worm egg repositories. The potatoes hosted so many hatched wormlings that they would have made a great horror movie close-up shot.

Eventually I stalked a mostly deserted worm-yard and

knew that I had to set them up to reproduce in stages. Maybe a rotating series of boxes accommodating the different life phases would work. I was a worm farmer now and I'd learned the patience of the worm. It was a segmented way of thinking, with a view of the changing state of life. The shape of my inner mind no longer chained me. I knew that I could metamorphose and change my entire being to accomplish a new purpose. I could wait and I could worm. Worm Queen, I set up my boxes and waited for my new subjects.

The now steady supply of mealworms satisfied my compulsion to supplement the basic feed store diet. Along with the kitchen vegetable scraps and oyster shell, I thought we were doing pretty well. The Button Quail hens were laying stockpiles of eggs. This was great for my egg-selling plans, but bad for the hens. They could lay themselves to an early grave, even with all the supplemental foods. I tried dimming the light in the shop to decrease their laying, but it was only effective for a day or two. Once the lights came back on, they were laying an egg a day again.

One of the Button hens was laying her eggs in a distinct nest, while others left eggs all over their cages. If I left the nested eggs alone, instead of taking them away, the hen would stop after laying seven or eight eggs and begin to set them. This would provide a natural break from laying eggs, so I decided to let her fuss over the nest.

Her setting behavior was very different from her usual manic scuttling around. She made a new sound, a melodic chirruping sound, and spent most of her time fluffed out over the eggs. She could fluff out an amazing amount and cover all the eggs at once. The male was also attentive to the eggs. He would run over and check on them when the hen was eating, and bring her food when she was on the nest. Mostly live mealworms, well bashed against the cage, but also large seeds and grains. I didn't really expect the eggs to hatch, which naturally went a long way toward guaranteeing that they would. There is a fine line between not counting chickens before they hatch and keeping an eye out for setting eggs in case they do hatch.

One morning I came in the Button shop, which used to be the workshop, for daily chores and heard a new sound. It was a tiny, almost ultrasonic, peep peep peep. I hurried over to the setting hen's cage and there was a tiny, fragile, yellow chick.

The mother hen was running around the cage, frantic. She was stomping on the little chick as it tried to close in on her. Another little chick lay motionless in front of the water bowl, dead, but not drowned. I had stuffed the water bowl with small rocks to prevent chick drowning, even though I truly didn't expect hatching. The live chick was stumbling around, trying to wiggle its way under the hen's breast feathers, but she was still streaking around in a panic, falling into the water and upsetting the food bowl. The male quail was also running around in a panic and managed to punt the chick across the cage. I waited for several minutes, but it looked like the surviving chick was weakening. It was cold in the shed. The temperature was above freezing and adequate for adult quail, but not comfortable without a jacket. Without the mother's protection, he wasn't going to survive.

I scooped up the chick and dropped it down the front of

my sports bra. There, the chick would be contained and warm, but my hands would be free. I wasn't thinking clearly, just reacting to the immediate situation. The chick was the size of the last joint on my thumb, literally the size of a bumblebee. It quieted right away and seemed to doze off in the sudden heat inside my shirt. There were two unhatched but cracked eggs still in the nest. I picked them up and inspected them. By peeling a tiny part of shell aside, I could see the fully developed chicks. They were also dead. It seemed as if the mother hen hadn't expected the eggs to hatch either, and when they did, she freaked out and abandoned the nest. With the November temperatures, they ran out of time for her to calm down and figure things out.

At first I was frustrated with the distressed little quail hen, but then I began to remember how it had been when I'd had my first baby. I had no actual motherhood responsibilities during those nine months of incubating pregnancy except to keep myself alive and in moderately good condition. After the intense and somewhat appalling experience of birth, the baby was laid in my arms and everyone who had been standing by to help moved on to other tasks. I was suddenly a mother and responsibility settled on me like a foot-thick coating of lead. I wanted to hand that baby back and go on a good long vacation somewhere, but everyone was expecting me to care for her immediately and independently, as if I could tap on some deep root of biological mammalian instinct that would tell me what to do. But I felt no differently than before I had the baby, other than being sure I never wanted to go through *that* again, and I had no idea what I was doing. I held my baby like anyone else would, like a slippery bomb that someone should do something about, and soon. I gradually grew better at the role of mother nurturer, but I remembered those early hours.

The hen must have been so surprised when her inanimate pile of eggs started to crack and pop out live chicks. They would have come at her insistently, clawing at her feathers for warmth and invading her personal space. She ran as if pursued by scarab beetles. Maybe I could give her a helping hand, but not in this cold adult-quail suited environment. She needed a quiet, warm crèche. I caught the poor startled hen, popped her in the kid's bug catcher that I used as a temporary cage when cleaning the Button apartments, and marched down to the trailer. When I stepped inside the trailer door, I called the girls over.

"Look down my shirt," I told them.

"Why?" Blue asked, suspiciously.

"Just look!" I urged Blue. I leaned down and pulled at my collar. Blue cautiously peered into my cleavage and the little yellow chick peeped up at her.

"Oh, My!" Blue exclaimed. "Mommy has a chick in her boobs!" Blue was pulling my collar into a permanent stretch.

"Really, Daddy!" Blue shouted. "Mommy's got a tiny chick!" Juno began to cry in bitter frustration because she was too short to see and Andrew lifted her up for a turn to pull at my collar.

"A tick!" she hiccuped in wonder.

"Look, Daddy, Look!" Blue insisted. "Do you see?"

"Wonderful!" Andrew said.

"Isn't it tiny?" Blue said in excitement.

"The chick is amazing, too," Andrew agreed.

"All right, enough!" I said, fending off the hands that were diving down my shirt. "Let's get this chick back to its mother."

I made a cage out of a big plastic bowl, a towel, a desk lamp, and a network of soft window screen wrapped around the base of the lamp. My real brooder was much too big for this fragment of life; the chick would be able to walk right through the air holes. I put the hen in the makeshift space and gave her a moment to settle in. She pecked the food and drank some water from the shallow, pebble-filled saucer. Then I gently plucked the chick from my bra and boosted him in through a gap in the screen. He made a beeline for the hen and burrowed right into her breast feathers. She gave a startled, whooping cluck, but settled down again. Without her quail husband around and in the smaller space, she seemed more able to accept the chick's insistent presence. The warmth from the light bulb was enough to keep the chick comfortable when it was shaken out of the hen's feathers, and it gradually adventured into the food bowl to peck the smallest grains of feed.

The little cage wasn't really quail proof, but I hoped that the hen wouldn't leave her chick, and it did actually work. The chick was so tiny and frail that I expected it to be dead every anxious morning. However, it thrived and by the time it was a week old, had some tiny primary wing feathers with others on the way. Mother and baby settled happily, and the chick grew. I was able to return them to the quail projects in the workshop before the first real snow of that winter.

We had come full circle in one part of our poultry plan,

and the girls had been able to see the whole cycle. I had been able to see it like never before as well. The heat lamps in the shop made a cheery warm circle as the storm clouds of winter rolled in, and the cold closed like a fist over the pens. Ready or not, our first winter of living in the trailer and managing the flock was here. We fired up the woodstove and taught the tenants how to use theirs. We stocked up on propane and all mutually gasped at the huge bill. The winter coats were ready on the hooks, and boots pulled out of storage and ready by the door. There was very little between us and the cold dark nights now that the thin walls of the trailer sheltered us, but we piled on the blankets and tried to tell ourselves that we were ready.

Chapter Eleven

There was always a certain tension involved in entering the goose pen. I had conquered most of my fear, but being nailed by a sneaky, vindictive goose was no fun. I was learning their ways and was able to side-step most attacks. Yet as the geese matured, their aggression escalated, and I finally learned that the only way to make a goose stop attacking was to attack back. Usually it was a gander that would sally forward and come at me with his head held high and wings outstretched. I had to come back at him like a berserker, grabbing for his neck and ignoring the consequences. This was usually enough to discourage bloodshed, but occasionally a goose would launch a low and silent raid, head and neck parallel to the ground, and those would always catch me unawares. Bitten, scratched or hammered on the ankle, I limped back to the first-aid kit, but one day I was mad enough to chase the offending gander down and scoop him up under my arm. I got the rare chance to snuggle my goose and he had to put up with it, which seemed a fair punishment.

Thanksgiving was only days away and we should have

already butchered one of the ganders to give the meat time to "rest" before roasting. Once again, Andrew was busy and I just couldn't face the effort of butchering such a large bird, so it hadn't happened yet. Plus, the ganders protected the geese admirably (although I was their only foe), so I hadn't pushed the schedule. As I was giving the gander a poke, trying to estimate how big a roasting pan I would need, a new cacophony from the rest of the flock caught my attention. I watched the birds in deafened amazement as they mobbed me. The geese had never attacked as a group before.

It took me a moment to realize it, but I held a gander that was bonded to several of my strongest female geese. The flock was ready to fight to prevent me taking him out. If I took this mate away, the remaining geese might pine away and die. My research had confirmed that geese do mate for life, and if I put that to the test, I might lose my egg-laying investment before they even started. It was too great a risk and I realized that Andrew had just lost Thanksgiving Dinner and I had gained a lifelong non-egg-producing feed consumer.

As a test, I let the gander go and caught the one goose hen that had not been part of the mob, Toulouse Linda. The ear-splitting racket died down and the flock moved away behind a nearby screen of trees in another part of the pen. She emitted some forlorn little honks, but no goose even turned a head. Toulouse Linda was not bonded with anyone. I caught the other gander, to test his bond with any of my future layers, and acquired some new bruises for my collection. Once again, the rest of the flock pitched an alarming fit until I put him down. Both ganders were solidly bonded to the geese. I sighed. It would be ham for Christmas and Thanksgiving yet again, and Andrew was going to be unhappy. But I was secretly glad. The geese were my babies, despite their continued attempts to rid the earth of my presence. The Lukes were here to stay.

Thanksgiving came and went. The chickens and ducks continued to lay regularly despite the shorter, darker days. The poultry books had advocated putting artificial lights in the chicken house to boost the egg-laying cycle, but I didn't do that. For one thing, they were laying plenty, but I also felt the hens would benefit from any natural reduction. They wouldn't lose as many vital minerals and would conserve some of their energy for keeping warm in the nights below ten degrees Fahrenheit. Although I worked hard to supplement their diet and provide supportive warmth in the chicken house overnight, my efforts were not enough to prevent the first death.

One of the Buff Orpington chicken hens had been walking around with her tail down for a day, and the next morning she was dead. I found her in a sitting position, with her beak to the ground, kind of turned to the side. The girls were sad and curious. We held her and poked at her, marveling at how hard she was, as if she had turned into a statue overnight. She did feel like a feathered sculpture. I tried to explain how she would get soft and loose again in about a day, but when the girls begged to keep her around so that they could see that for themselves, I chickened out. I wasn't sure why the hen had died and figured it was unwise to play with her corpse for too long.

All of my reference books had a section on poultry diseases and helpfully listed the symptoms along with a very short list of cures. Unfortunately, the "sudden death" symptom showed up for every truly horrible bird disease. Coccidosis - sudden death, pseudotuberculosis – sudden death, botulism, fowl cholera, tetanus, typhoid, hepatitis, pyrovirus, and of course, avian flu, were all culprits in cases of sudden death. I tried not to get obsessively worried after this deluge of unhelpful information. I was suffering acute ignorancealosis.

I watched my flock carefully. Soon, a Button Quail hen died in exactly the same position as the Buff Orpington chicken hen. Both of the birds had become slow and unhappy, tails down, and the tips of their wings pointed down. They moved around less but didn't look sick until they were dead. I put all the birds on antibiotic and we stopped eating their eggs for seven days.

A second Button Quail hen began to look unhappy. She was ruffled and holding her tail down. I whisked her out of her cage and popped her in the hospital brooder under a forty-Watt heat lamp. I was afraid I'd cook her with any more wattage. She had antibiotics in one cup and electrolytes (dissolved in water) in the other. She had a lump of ground oyster shell, vionate vitamin powder in her mash, and soy protein mixed with scrambled egg. She had a pillowy nest of tissue paper and a quiet room. Every morning, I opened the door to the brooder in unpleasant anticipation; every morning, she was alive.

She was eating well and had a perfectly normal fit of hysteria when I changed her water so I put her back after three days. She snuggled up with her husband and made a mess of her cage. She was fine, but the next morning a different

Button Quail hen was dead. It was beyond frustrating. The newly dead hen was a good layer and nicely bonded with her male. She had no symptoms at all and was eating mealworms and fussing over oyster shell. She'd eaten the vitamin mix with gusto and had a good energy level. This time, there was nothing I could point to that would have predicted her death, not even a sad tail. I dosed all the hens with vitamins again and added fresh fruit and vegetables every day.

I perched in the pens every day for hours, pen in hand, noting down every behavior and symptom I could see. What was the definition of an epidemic, anyway? I had over one hundred birds. Did losing three in one week constitute an epidemic? I worried that I was going to lose my whole flock to inexperience or worse. I imagined the whole state of New Mexico going the way of Hong Kong and having to exterminate every chicken on every farm. I'd be the Chicken Typhoid Mary and would be greatly disliked. I was terrified of being disliked.

The only causes I had been able to identify in my poultry mortality were accidental poisoning by avocado and periodic neck collisions with hatchet blades. The lists of possible diseases that I worried about read like a State Department report on a third world country. But during one research session, at the end of a book featuring necrotic enteritis, infectious bronchitis, streptococcus septicemia, and gizzard worms, I found a description of egg binding.

Egg binding was listed as a notorious hen killer with very few symptoms. The most obvious symptoms were holding the tail very low, rear end tucked, or just looking ruffled, then dying. The book said that laying hens had to have enough calcium in their diets not only to form the eggshell, but also to allow muscles that move the egg to contract properly. Although I had been giving them oyster shell as a calcium supplement, this book swore that oyster shell alone was not enough. Especially when birds were under environmental stresses, such as overcrowding or winter. It seemed that all my supplementing efforts were failing on some hens because of their high production rate and the stresses of winter.

I was alternately elated and mortified. The continental United States and Canada were perhaps saved, but the hens had probably died because of their helpless compulsion to produce more and more eggs to satisfy our human demand. I mourned my hens and showered them with new calcium-specific vitamins. I returned the books of doom to the library. Thankfully, with the addition of an expensive water-soluble calcium, the dying stopped and we were able to go back to our normal routine of killing them for dinner.

The winter cold had encouraged the birds to clean up their feathers and they were looking pristine. The dead Buff-Orpington hen in particular had beautiful orange-cream feathers. We couldn't eat a bird that had died on its own instead of being butchered, but her feathers were too beautiful to waste. This seemed like a good time to get serious about my feather product ideas.

It was cold and windy outside at the pens, and although the girls were bravely trying to play, they were turning blue. I tried to find a place where I could settle in to pluck the dead hen, but there was nowhere warm or out of the wind. The Button Quail cages each had their own heat lamp, which was sufficient for their comfort, but didn't throw off enough heat for us. Cold and frustrated, I cradled the hen under one arm and we all marched down to the trailer.

I stashed the girls in front of the television and sat down on the couch with the dead hen on a towel on my knees. I started to pluck her carefully and respectfully. This was the first hen I had plucked for feathers. Previously, when I took feathers from the roosters, I had only taken a handful before scalding the carcass in a deep pot of almost boiling water, which would loosen the feathers and make the process much easier. But scalding ruined the feathers. Dry plucking, one feather at a time, was very different and much slower.

I divided the different feathers into bags, and it was an education. There were feathers of perfect size and shape for armoring the head and neck. Little feathers gradually melded into larger feathers that gave way to insulating fuzzy feathers close to the skin. Breast feathers were softer than back feathers, which overlapped in a way that made the chicken almost waterproof. The wing feathers were rigid and difficult to pluck. The tops of her wings had little shoulder feathers packed densely, for warmth and good aerodynamics. Feathers around the vent could have been fur, except for the quill that declared them feathers. Andrew came home from work right about then, and greeted the TV-sedated girls.

"I'm just about done with the belly feathers," I said distractedly, as a greeting.

"Is that a dead chicken?" he asked in a strange voice.

"Yeah," I said sadly, turning her over in my hands, "one of the Buff Orpington hens. Sad, I know."

"You're plucking a chicken on the couch?" he asked.

"Oh yes," I said. "Her feathers are just beautiful and I can't let them go to waste."

"You are plucking a chicken on the couch in the house?" he asked again, his voice incredulous. I looked at him suddenly.

"Oh, my God!" I gasped.

"Oh, yeah!" Andrew echoed in kind.

"I'm having a single-wide moment!" I said, horrified.

"You are," Andrew agreed.

"I'm plucking a chicken on the couch in my living room!" I cried, horrified, wrapping the chicken and bolting for the door.

"Should I check the bathroom for goats?" Andrew called after me as I ran, feathers flying, to the workshop.

Back at the workshop, dead hen safely returned to our appropriate agricultural zone, I reflected on how easy it was to stray from the standards of civilization. I had to fight to keep my lifestyle up out of the compost heap because I kept losing battles to the seductions of practicality. Pluck the chicken in the house because it was cold outside. Wear the same stained and stinky clothes from the day before because I would once again be doing dirty work. While I was at it, dress the girls in the same clothes they had worn previously because it saved on the washing, folding, and putting away.

Where was the end to this erosion of proper living? I had to stop it now before I got any closer to barbarity. Like the legendary English colonists who took their fine china, rugs, and window drapes to wild foreign lands, I had to fight to keep a semblance of dignity in these pioneering times.

Trailer was a state of mind as much as a place to live.

Letting things lie in the yard where they landed, or skimping on the cleaning during a week when I was tired were all choices I could make because I was inviting fewer people to come visit and the neighbors out here were the hands-off kind. I did feel demoralized by the imperfect condition of the walls and fixtures, but it was in my own power to make the place tidy and clean regardless of the quality of the windows and roof.

Five years before, I would have sworn that I didn't have prejudices or class consciousness, but I was getting to know myself so much better as my personalities multiplied and my complacency disintegrated. I understood the cultural imperative to climb ever upwards in housing and social standing, collecting meritorious trophies along the way like club memberships, large new cars, and complicated time-share investments. Going so far backwards on the housing ladder to a fourth-hand singlewide was something strange and new in my social world. It also wasn't popular, but I didn't have to let my standards slide along with the quality of my housing.

My own behavior and attitude had to be independent of my living situation. *Trailer trash* was a state of mind, but it was so seductively easy when everything else seemed so hard. I resolved to start taking care of the little things, like having clean shoes to wear and not plucking chickens on the couch. Maybe it was my imagination, but it seemed like clean white shoes were a status symbol in our society. My shoes, while often white, were never clean. My shoes spent most of their time on the raw ground. They often had suspicious organic splashes decorating their designer sides.

Chastened, I went back down to the trailer to microwave something for dinner. I took the harvested feathers with me, resolving to make an effort to figure out how to wash them efficiently, but separately from the family's underwear.

Christmas came, but there was no snow. It was our first Christmas in the trailer and we had decided that it was time for us to create special family traditions of our own that reflected our individual beliefs. The tree was an easy center point and we decided that it represented a celebration of nature and the spring season that would come. Andrew's choice of tree was larger than mine would have been. Some of the furniture had to be moved up to the shop to make room for our celebration. We didn't have any visitors for this Christmas because the previous year had been a big family bash at my parents' house in Reno.

We held hands and gave thanks for everything we had and everyone we loved. We named all of our bird species and gave special recognition to Rachel, our dog. We went over all the departed creatures, which brought us to the cats. In honor of the effort the cats were making, we set aside some special bits from our Christmas ham to take up to the shop after presents. Rachel got her share as well. It was a cozy Christmas, even without our roast goose.

The cats were doing well in the shop in the Christmas cold. They had a heat lamp of their own, high on a shelf above the quail cages, and I often saw all three piled under it together. The so-named "Dodo" twins had arrived as scrawny, dirty, little kittens and they were now gleaming, sleek panthers with enormous yellow eyes. They reigned supreme from the top shelves in the shop and contemptuously blinked at us and looked away whenever we tried to lure them down. They were huge to my uneducated eye and my suspicions that they were both Toms was confirmed one day when they paraded past me, at a safe distance, tails held high. The Dodos were boys.

Charlotte had transformed from the stressed, grungy, spitting cat we had picked up from Rosie at the post office. She was affectionate, clean, and starting to lose her edge-of-the-wild look. She allowed us to pet her and continued to gift us with mouse parts and wood rats almost daily. Her coat was shining, and she was even getting plump. In fact, she was starting to look a little fat around her belly, but nowhere else, curiously. It took me a while, but I finally realized that she was pregnant, and I was dismayed. I never imagined that the male kittens might be old enough to impregnate their mother and I wasn't ready for a pregnant cat.

I felt that it reflected poorly on me to have a cat on the property that had become pregnant by her own sons. I was still urban in my outlook, still far from having a farmer's point of view. In time I would come to understand that a pregnant cat in my barn was a necessity if I wanted to continue to have cats in the barn. Allowing the cats to reproduce naturally, even if they were drawing a straight line instead of a family tree, was the only insurance against the hordes of mice busily reproducing while buoyed by the inexhaustible food supply of the bird project. But at the time that education lay in my future, so I had her spayed as soon as the Christmas holiday was over and felt like a law-abiding kitten murderer.

She disappeared soon after that, leaving me with only

the boys. I mourned Charlotte cat. I struggled not to end the year with a litany of farmer mistakes I had made and instead went through the pens to reaffirm all the things I'd done well enough to get by. It always lifted my spirits to walk the pens and watch the birds. In my preoccupation with the birds, I sometimes overlooked all the accomplishments I was racking up in other areas of my life.

The girls were invariably cheerful and enthusiastic. They were also very good car passengers, having spent so much of their baby days securely strapped in car seats while being driven up and down the considerable distance from town. I played my choices of music for them, regardless of whether it was appropriate for tender ears. Once when we were on the open road on a dim December afternoon, I could see Juno in the rearview mirror. She had her little fist raised in the air.

"Mommy?" she shouted.

"Yes, Juno?" I said.

"Are you weady to wock?" she yelled.

"Yeah!" I said, joining in.

"I said," she continued happily, "are you WEADY to WOCK?"

"YES!" Blue and I said together, looking at each other in the mirror. Juno took a deep breath and raised both arms in the air, fists pumping.

"Den here we go!" she screamed, "ABCD EFG HIJK…"

And we all cracked up laughing.

Chapter Twelve

January was the bleakest month in my opinion. It was cold and dreary, and the ground stayed frozen day and night. Any eggs the ducks laid that I didn't find before nightfall would freeze and crack so Andrew got to work building them a house. They would share it with the geese, who were not yet laying and did not seem to miss having a shelter, but who would benefit anyway. He did a beautiful job framing it, complete with covered porch for the feed bowls to sit out of the elements. It was a work of art, and when it was time to cover the framed structure, we had a healthy discussion about using the stuff lying around in the yard instead of buying expensive brand new stuff.

"We have so much stuff lying around in the yard," I fumed, "that we can't even see the yard!"

"I want the goose house to look nice," he argued. "It's going to look like crap with that stuff on it."

"Then take all this stuff to the dump!" I yelled reasonably. "We can go do it right now!"

"No!" Andrew objected, "That's great stuff, we can't take it to the dump."

"You just said it was crap," I pointed out, "so is it good stuff or not?"

"It's good for something," Andrew said, falling through a rotten spot in the lumber pile, "just not for my beautiful goose house."

Inevitably, the crap in the yard was laboriously screwed to the goose house, giving it a dubious complexion. Andrew resigned himself to knowing that it had a beautiful bone-structure underneath. The finished house looked vaguely dangerous. I thought it looked appropriate to the creatures it would house.

We built beautiful and roomy nesting boxes for the geese in their open-sided shelter, but they had scraped a rocky hollow in the middle of their pen before the deep freeze and insisted on sitting in it no matter the weather. They weren't laying at the time, but they all took turns incubating a light-colored rock. I tried to add some straw and clear some of the other rocks out of their lair, in case they did start laying, but I couldn't budge anything due to the freeze. Early on a Sunday morning, Andrew woke me up by rubbing a huge, snow-white egg on my nose.

"Did the duck that laid that egg survive the experience?" I mumbled.

"That," said Andrew proudly, "is a goose egg!"

"Goose goose goose!" sang Juno, from the backpack, celebrating for all of us who had not yet had our coffee.

It was the first goose egg, and although it was small compared to their future eggs, it was still the biggest egg we had ever handled from our birds. We did our goose egg victory dance and immediately drilled it for blowing.

It was tough, but not brittle, and we scrambled the blown contents.

"You can eat goose egg, right?" Andrew asked, voicing my unspoken question. We stared at it, light and fluffy on the plate with a sprig of celebratory garnish.

"Of course you can!" I claimed, although I had never actually heard of anyone eating goose eggs.

"Wouldn't we have heard about it if you can't eat goose egg?" he asked.

"Like avocado and birds?" I said.

"Well, some people knew about that," he said, "and you can eat turtle eggs."

"We can give some to Rachel and see if she is okay," I mused.

"Rachel eats cow poo and she is okay," Andrew pointed out. Rachel roundly wagged her tail, willing to try anything we wanted to feed her.

We compromised by eating it together, so that neither of us would be burdened by outliving the other. It was divine: fresh and sweet. It was better than chicken egg and better than duck egg. The yolk was smaller than I expected it to be. It was smaller than the duck egg yolk even though the egg itself was half again as large. This meant that the scrambled goose egg was more egg white than egg yolk and it was delicious. We never tried it fried, since we didn't want to crack them and lose the blown eggshell, but it was our breakfast egg of choice for the whole laying season.

"Do you know which goose laid the egg?" I asked, still marveling over my first blown goose egg.

"I think it was Little Linda," Andrew said, "at least, it was

Little Linda who tried to kill me as I picked it up."

"I thought she was a pygmy goose," I said. "I was thinking that she would be on the reduction list if we decided not to keep this many geese."

"Can't judge a goose by her size," said Andrew.

The second goose egg arrived a week after the first, and I was frustrated to find the egg sitting next to the frozen rock in the ridiculous hollow outside the goose house. It was frozen to the ground and I broke it as I tried to pry it up. Fueled by warming anger, I dragged enough planks and branches over to the rock nest to make it difficult for anyone to climb inside. Gradually the other geese began to lay and, to my relief, they chose the goose house.

February in New Mexico was still a deep freeze, but the birds could feel that spring was coming. The first goose egg had been an early indicator that although it still looked like deep winter to me, the birds saw things differently. My cherished peace in the big pen was fracturing. The coming mating season was sending ripples of tension throughout the mixed species. It began slowly with tiny indicators that I might have missed if I wasn't already constantly looking for disaster. One of the mutant pheasant boys had a toe wound that I suspected he incurred while running fast through the pen. Whether running away or chasing after, I didn't know.

The Chukar Partridge hens were missing feathers from the backs of their heads, newly bald when they had finally feathered out from their naked childhood. I watched as a partridge rooster tried to mount an unenthusiastic partridge hen by holding her at the back of her head, which explained the missing feathers. Every evening, we would watch an activity we called "The Sunset Scramble," when the birds would suddenly sprint around the pen. Some ran after others and some ran alone. This was a new behavior heralding spring.

The Silver Pheasant were the most dramatic. The Silver Pheasant roosters now had a full complement of striking black and white feathers and bright red face shields. They postured for each other and for me, standing upright and whirring their wings in a speedy blur. They were a pack and moved everywhere together; practicing stylized dances, brandishing their spurs, and circling each other, but they never fought amongst themselves.

Two of the three Flying Mallards we had left when we put the ducks into the covered pen turned out to be drakes. They both developed the spectacular coloring of the dominant male duck and then squared off with each other in front of the hen. In the off season, the male mallard looks much like the female, feathered with the brown and black pattern that would make them less visible in a lakeshore environment. But our season was turning and beetle-green iridescent feathers were coming out on their heads, while grizzled feathers were decorating their breasts.

This was called the "Nuptial Molt" and it was supposed to drive the female into a romantic swoon. She went about her daily duck business as the males decided to fight for dominance. They grasped each other by the breast feathers and flopped without letting go. Each drake took a turn whapping the other upside the head with his wings. Each drake had a bill full of enemy and it went on for days. I did the chores, went through my day, and when I came back for the evening chores, they were still locked in combat. I worried about them, but didn't interfere.

Finally they separated. At first, I wasn't sure who was the winner. One duck was missing so many feathers on his chest that I worried for his health in the snow flurries, but the missing feathers came back remarkably quickly as the whole duck changed suit. The winner bloomed into full Mallard glory, complete with purple-tipped wing feathers. The loser returned to "eclipse molt," the black and brown drab so similar to the duck.

March arrived; spring, according to the calendar, and I could finally begin to feel the seasonal change. What the birds sensed a month ago was finally revealed to my sense of smell, accompanied by an indescribable feel in the air. The approach of Easter was driving blown egg sales into a frenzy and I was *finally* beginning to make some money with this whole idea.

As the days passed, more pheasant and partridge started to limp. When I looked closely, I saw that they were all suffering toe wounds; in some cases they had broken toes. Although I looked up remedies for broken toes in all my poultry resources, I found no suggestions other than serving the bird up for dinner with a sprig of rosemary. Their toes weren't getting caught in the wire, I was sure. The pen had vast amounts of natural ground cover and the only wire was on the vertical walls. The male pheasant were all gloriously clad in their full mature plumage now and were posturing, thrumming, and dancing for the females. I suspected the broken toes were from fighting, but I hadn't seen it firsthand until one gruesome morning when I came to do the chores and faced a scene of carnage.

A Melanistic Mutant rooster pheasant lay dead under a juniper tree in the pen. Feathers and blood were everywhere, but most significantly concentrated on the beaks and spurs of the Silver Pheasant roosters. All five of them were splashed with incriminating gore and enough of their feathers lay in the crime scene to indicate that the Mutant rooster didn't go quietly. There were other feathers there too, matching the Reeves Pheasant rooster. He was in his usual space, as far from the entrance to the pen as he could get, pacing in his usual way. He wore the longest and sharpest spurs of any pheasant in the pen, and the research I had been trying to ignore had claimed all along that the Reeves Pheasant males were the most intolerant and aggressive of the pheasant species.

I removed the dead pheasant and tried to salvage as many of his sadly beautiful feathers as I could. The mixed pen had once again failed; this time permanently. I could get away with the integration so long as the birds were immature, but it was mating season now, and the males were doing what they did best: fight for the female's attention.

I was going to have to take quick action. In the short time it took me to do my chores, the Silver Pheasant pack began to hunt another pheasant. They had targeted another Melanistic Mutant rooster and had him on the run. They were so intent on slaughter that they didn't even swerve from my feet when I joined the chase to catch the victim and tuck him safely under my arm. I clipped his wings and tossed him in with the geese. It was a makeshift solution. There were too many other potential victims, even if the Silvers only targeted their male competition. I collected all the Mutant Roosters and stashed them, wings clipped, into the goose pen.

Andrew and I got to work immediately on an effort to separate the large pen. While we stretched and anchored netting, the rescued Melanistic Mutant roosters began to fight among themselves. Their fight triggered fights in the rest of the pen, an all-out war between every male bird that could see the conflict. I was in tears as we worked even faster on the pen separation.

"There's no way we can separate them all," Andrew said finally, voicing the unpleasantly obvious fact.

"I know," I muttered.

"You're going to have to choose who stays," he said. I didn't reply.

"Their feathers are gorgeous," he tried again. "It won't be a waste."

The Reeves rooster imprudently chose that moment to stage an attack on Andrew's unprotected back. He landed with a whumping slide that left parallel rips in Andrew's down jacket.

"Aha!" Andrew cried, "a volunteer!"

The Silver Pheasant, which were the most unusual and valuable breed, watched the sun set on their new territory and faced off with the Reeves rooster. These main killers were sequestered in a space we now called "The Shark Pen." The Golden and Lady Amherst Pheasant roosters were proving to be pacifists. They did not join in the rumbles and they did not seem to trigger a killing rage in the more aggressive, more mature males. The Golden Pheasant did not yet have their mature plumage and they stayed with the chickens and partridge.

I told myself that I shouldn't be so sad and horrified at the fact that pheasant roosters will fight to the death. It was a fact of life. It was even a traditional New Mexican sport, although it was more usually confined to chickens and had been recently outlawed. Maybe the cock-fighting cartels hadn't yet discovered pheasant. Maybe there was another income opportunity there. As my imaginary hand rooted around in my imaginary wife-beater pocket for smokes I had never bought I came back to myself with an ugly gasp. Desperation was working an evil juju on me and I shook it off with a middle-class shudder. Cock-fighting was sick and wrong, wife beater t-shirts didn't have pockets, and I didn't even smoke. I needed to get back to the problem of separating the fighting pheasant.

The partridge were only fighting amongst themselves and not to the death, so in the urgency of the moment, I was able to ignore them. The only solutions open to me were to divide or build more pens that could keep the pheasant in a one rooster to three hen ratio, as the books had always recommended, or butcher some pheasant roosters for feathers and food. I couldn't build more pens. I was out of time and money.

The idea of butchering this many roosters using the hatchet and cone was exhausting. I also wasn't totally convinced that it was the most humane method. The whole action of catching the bird and carrying it to the butchering site was stressful and I thought there might be a better way.

We needed to do something that would take the bird from being alive to being dead in a matter of moments, and which would also preserve the valuable neck feathers.

Inevitably, it came to me that we needed a gun. Before I had babies, I had owned a large caliber revolver and was a pretty good shot on the gun range. But a gun like that would leave a pheasant-sized hole in the ground and a lone floating feather if fired at a bird. And I had sold it years ago to a gun store to prevent it from making a smoking crater in one of the girls. We needed a rifle, so Andrew and I went to the local gun store. We took the girls with us because this whole experience was supposed to be educational, and we had no babysitter.

The store was decorated inside with dozens of mounted wild animal heads and the girls were speechless. Standing in front of a stuffed black bear mounted on a pedestal was a woman, stringing a bow.

"Help you?" she said, concentrating on the bow.

"I'd like to know if an air rifle would kill a pheasant," I said.

"Can't shoot a pheasant with an air rifle," she said. "S'illegal."

"Oh, no, no!" I said. "They are my pheasant and they are in a pen. I'd shoot them in the pen."

She looked at me with a disgusted expression.

"I mean," I amended nervously. "I'm looking for a more humane way to kill the birds. I've been using a hatchet to butcher them, and I want to find a way to kill them that doesn't also terrorize them."

"Isn't going to work if you miss," she said.

"I'm a pretty good shot, actually," I said, in a huff.

She concentrated on stringing the bow.

"But if I don't miss," I persisted. "Will the air rifle kill the pheasant with one shot?"

"Might," she allowed.

"Because I was thinking an air rifle might do the job but be less of a hazard to my family," I said.

"Depends on where you point it when you pull the trigger," she said, shrugging.

"Well, yes," I said.

She walked over to the air rifles as I peeled one daughter off the back of a stuffed bobcat and dragged the other, by the collar, away from the trophy photo bulletin board.

"Are all those animals in the photos dead, Mommy?" asked Blue.

"Yes, they are dead," I said, trying to follow the woman who had disappeared behind a wall of armaments.

"Don't touch anything," I said, pinning Juno's arms to her sides. "Anything at all!"

The air rifles were displayed next to the pump-action shotguns and real rifles, one of which Andrew was holding with great enthusiasm.

"Check this out!" he said. "This is the one I learned to shoot on!"

"Honey," I said, not be distracted from our core mission, "put down the gun and hold the baby."

The woman demonstrated how to crack open the air rifle and prime the pump by pulling the barrel toward the stock. She showed me how to avoid loading it backwards, and carefully put the pellet away after the demonstration. She watched impassively as I failed to either crack or pump the air rifle.

"Use both hands," she suggested as she watched Juno put mouth prints on the handgun display glass.

Blue was consoling a stuffed gazelle. Andrew had graduated to heavy loads, the kind of rifle that would take out the bird, the pen, and half an acre as well. I handed the woman my credit card.

"I'll take an extra box of pellets and a packet of targets, please," I said.

The next morning, I called my mom.

"Hello, Mom!" I said.

"How nice to hear from you!" said my mom. "Is it pheasant killing day today?"

"We are trying a new thing," I said. "We are going to shoot them with our new air rifle."

"What?" she exclaimed. "What? Shoot them? What makes you think that's going to work? Neither of you have particularly excelled at target practice!"

"Well, actually," I huffed. "I happen to be a pretty good shot."

My mom snorted so hard I think she hurt herself and I sighed with futility. I called my sister for consolation.

"I'm going to shoot my pheasant," I said.

"Gross," she agreed.

"I'm actually a pretty good shot with a rifle," I said.

"What makes you think that?" she said with genuine amazement.

The lack of marksmanship respect from my family bothered me more than I wanted to admit. I really was a pretty good shot. It was one of the few things I could do in the realm of manly outdoorsy enthusiasms. I also used to be able to ride a horse, long ago and far away. Skills I had developed or discovered after leaving home as a teenager were going unrecognized. It bugged me. It really rankled. I was nettled and vexed. Why couldn't I be happy to have a secret life my family knew nothing about? Why did I need recognition and approval on everything I was doing?

It was natural that they weren't familiar with all the things I had accomplished since I left their nest, and like many normal, natural things, it stank. It was time to shoot the gun and begin to solve my rooster pheasant problem. The phone rang as I was heading for the door.

"It's Mom," said Mom. "Your father is very worried about flying bullets and little children."

"Tell him it's a single-shot deal and the kids are safely stashed in the car with the heater on," I said.

"But it's a flying single shot which could hit the car," she said.

"Not if I place it right," I said.

"Well," she said, "your father is very worried, so maybe you could call us when you're done?"

"Sure Mom," I said. "I'll call. So long as we're not busy applying pressure."

"What do you mean, applying pressure?" asked Mom.

"Artery, eye socket, belly, whatever needs it," I said, and almost didn't feel bad when she gasped.

The girls were securely locked in the warm safe car with

a candy bribe. We practiced in the wood shop with a fancy target that made fluorescent orange blossoms when we hit it. The scope needed severe adjustment for shooting so close, as if that was a setting the manufacturer never expected to actually be used. We used a tripod to rest the rifle on and tested the force of the pellet by shooting a honeydew melon. The pellet passed cleanly through the melon, then zinged off the backboard with enough force to scratch the metal shop wall. Finally, we could justify no more practicing.

Inside the pen, one of the Melanistic Mutant roosters was calmly sitting on a branch, surveying his empire. I could aim the rifle so that the fence post was behind his head in case I missed. He was all alone and content, drowsing in the sun. When I was planning this butchering session, I had wished that I could just transport the bird from that contentment to being dead without the terror and pain of the catching and hatchet process. This was the idea behind the air rifle, and now was the moment of proof. I exhaled and gently squeezed the trigger. There was a loud crack and the rooster erupted in flapping and squirming. Andrew dove forward to grab him and restrain his wings.

"Is he dead?" I squealed.

"He is dead," Andrew confirmed, but I cracked the gun for another pellet just to be sure.

"What's with all the flapping if he is truly dead?" I said, aiming point blank at the back of his skull.

"The birds do that when they die," Andrew said. "Remember, that's why we used the cone."

"Did my first shot kill him?" I asked again.

"Yes," Andrew said again, "for sure, but I do think that

if we shot them close up at the very back of the neck, where it attaches to the spine, it would be even better."

"This is really distressing," I said, "are you sure he was dead with the first shot?"

"I'll show you the bullet hole," Andrew sighed. "Let's go on with the butchering part, okay?"

We released the girls from the car and started the plucking and cleaning process. Once I had the best feathers tucked safely in a bag, we were able to accelerate the process by using the hot water scald. The scalding rinsed him clean, but I still couldn't find the pellet hole.

"How can he be so dead if I missed?" I asked in frustration.

"You didn't miss," Andrew reassured me. "I found the pellet."

"Where?" I peered.

"Right here," he said and brought the rooster's head into the strong light. It was right in the eye. It was embedded so exactly in the eye that I had thought it was the eye, under all the tissue and feathers. I had placed my shot exactly right. It really was a pretty good shot.

It was now Andrew's turn, and the girls went back into the car. The second Mutant rooster was nervous and paced up and down incessantly. We finally netted him, which involved some chasing and wrestling, just what I was trying to avoid. But the idea of wounding a bird and then having to do the chasing and wrestling was worse. Despite my single-shot victory, I didn't feel at all capable of shooting a bird while it was racing up and down the pen in terror of being killed, and Andrew wasn't confident on such a moving target, either. The air rifle worked exactly as we hoped it would and the rooster was dinner with a minimum of pain and shock. Even though we had to catch him, it was quick, tidy, and a better solution. I let the girls out of the car again and called my worried parents.

"Hello?" said my mom, answering on the first ring.

"Ma, it's me!" I said.

"Is everyone alright?" she asked breathlessly.

"Everyone is fine," I said. "Can I talk to Dad? I know he was pretty worried about all this."

"Well," Mom said, "you can tell me, he's kind of engrossed in a football game right now."

"No, no," I said mercilessly. "I really should tell him myself, I feel bad he was so worried."

"Hallo," said my Dad.

"Good game?" I asked.

"You have about five seconds before the next down," he said.

"Hey," I said. "I placed my shot in the bird's eye!"

"Really?" said Dad in surprise, "what were you aiming for?"

"Well his eye, of course!" I exclaimed.

"Lucky shot," Dad said, "here's your mother."

Later, Andrew and the girls were gnawing a somewhat tough but incredibly tasty roast pheasant dinner. I was too exhausted to continue to fight my city-girl roots anymore, so I had a grilled cheese sandwich. After dinner and a fight to put the over-sugared girls to bed, I sat down on the couch next to Andrew. It occurred to me that one of the many exhaustions I was suffering from was the effort to convince my family that I was capable in some ways that they thought I wasn't.

I was spending too much energy trying to convince everybody around me that I was actually a pretty good shot, but it was important to me for them to know. I decided that I would have to choose one person to be my witness in all things important. One person who would recognize my accomplishments. Once recognized by that person, I would then have to be happy with it, as if it were the recognition of the world. I looked over at Andrew, who was dozing off in front of a TV documentary about hot manatee love.

"Andrew!" I said, giving him a loving shoulder shake.

"What? What?" he said, reaching after the dislodged sofa pillow.

"You are going to be my witness in all things important," I said. "Out of all the people in the world, I need you to recognize my accomplishments and cheer me on."

"Okay," Andrew said, distracted by the graphic TV images.

"I'm placing my peace of mind in your hands," I announced.

"Sounds good," he said.

"So long as you recognize my accomplishments, I'm going to be satisfied," I said.

"Okay," Andrew confirmed.

"I am a pretty good shot with a rifle," I said, turning him to face me directly.

"You really are," Andrew said, looking me straight in eyes with warm admiration.

I felt as much peace as I possibly could, given that I'd begun to kill my rooster pheasant in cold blood after witnessing them kill each other in hot rage. It just wasn't destined to be a peaceful time, this coming of spring.

Chapter Thirteen

*M*arch in our county is still a snow-prone month. Wildly unpredictable weather is normal. While I watched eagerly for pheasant or partridge eggs, I also thought that they were probably waiting out the threat of snow by instinct. I made a bet with Andrew that there would be one more snowstorm before spring set in. I was betting on the pheasant's wild wisdom.

One day in the second week of March ended quietly. The sunset was unremarkable and the cold air was still. In the darkness of full night, snow clouds gathered and big flakes began to come down silently, without our knowledge. It must have been an idyllic scene out in the bird pen for a while with the gently falling snow and quiet air. It was a wet snow, which was unusual for our area. We were more used to dry snow or even kernels of snow that sounded like a rain of rice grains coming down. This serene benediction collected peacefully on the overhead pen netting and created an insulating roof above the birds before the ground was even covered.

More snow accumulated, and it kept coming down. We

couldn't be sure exactly when the cables gave way, but there was perhaps a foot of snow on top of the netting when the cable hook pulled out of the support post and whanged across the pen where it slammed into the metal building hard enough to leave a dent. Each of the cables gave way after that and the frosted aviary roof crashed down on the sleeping occupants.

I crunched and scuffed my way through the deep snow to the bird pens the next morning without a clue. I had been surprised to see the snow at all. I'd stepped out of the trailer to do the morning chores wearing my sneakers. The snow came halfway up my calf and all the way into my shoe. I had changed into my knee-high insulated boots and walked up to the bird pen gate where I stood in shock and tried to make sense of the scene in front of me. The entire bird pen, except for the gate, was now only waist high and totally obscured by heaping snow. It took heartbeats to understand and then I gasped in horror, imagining trapped and injured birds inside. I wrenched open the gate and started to tunnel into the pen, under the snow and cables and downed netting.

I quickly discovered whole and healthy birds in every free space that had been preserved by objects inside the pen. Several trees had broken tops but they tented the netting in a wide clearing around their trunks. The shelters also supported the netting, as well as the feeders and various plastic chairs that were there for bird observation times. The pheasant and chukar were clustered in every safe open space, wet and tired. The chickens were all in their chicken house, roosting or rooting in the straw, clucking in surprise when they stepped out in the morning to such disarray.

Every bird was safe. Even the separation of the Shark Pen was preserved. In some places, there was about four feet of open space where the loaded netting slung low but didn't reach all the way to the ground. The birds had marched back and forth over the lightly dusted ground as they observed the damage.

Andrew and the girls arrived to see what was taking me so long up at the pens, and we all marveled over the near-disaster. We had to re-set the cables to repair the snow damage, but before we could do that, we had to shake the snow through the netting and onto the ground. We each took an opposite end of the netting, warned the girls to put up their jacket hoods, and started to rock and roll. The snow bounced up, sideways, and through, coating the girls, the birds, and every surface inside the pen. It piled up once again, this time on the ground, and the birds scattered for shelter. It took most of the morning to repair the cables.

In the end, the only real damage was to the three small trees that had taken the weight of the loaded netting and saved the birds. Their broken tops proved to be fatal wounds and they became rooted roosting places with dried, brittle branches.

The water buckets and dispensers were all frozen solid in the deep cold that followed this big snow. Previously, evening temperature drops had created an icy lid on the water, but the birds could easily peck through that. This time, the birds couldn't peck a hole through the ice because ice constituted the entire bucket. I made a trip to the feed store for a solution. The feed store sold expensive systems for heating buckets, so

I took the opportunity to ask the clerk what the locals do for poultry water during winter (in case it was cheaper).

"I fill up the buckets in the morning," the woman at the counter said, "and they've got to drink their fill quick, before it freezes."

"What do they do during the day while you are at work?" I asked.

"They wait till I get home and fill up the buckets again," she said.

"So they don't get any water during the day?" I probed.

"Not in the winter," she said.

"And this works?" I said.

"For the last twenty years it has," she said.

Well, I decided, that might work for real farmers, but I was a rank amateur urban transplant and wasn't comfortable with the birds going waterless throughout the day. We bought a host of bucket heaters and strung two of them in the chicken pen. We bought a metal water dispenser along with the metal heating stand commercially designed for it, and eventually stopped shocking ourselves when we figured out how much rubber matting to put underneath it.

Now that we knew a big snow could bring down the overhead pen netting, we were much less relaxed about winter storms. With the next snow, which came before the first snow had melted, Andrew and I took turns stomping out to the pen every two hours to shake the snow off the netting. For some obscure reason having to do with my being a stay-home mom and Andrew having to work with power tools the next day, I drew the 3 a.m. shift. I smothered the alarm with my pillow and hauled myself out of my cozy flannel nest and into my yellow down jacket and wet boots. I pulled on my double-lined wool gloves; tugged sweat pants over my pajamas, and stepped outside. My glasses fogged up immediately with the cold. The road was already obscured by the heavy snowfall and I navigated my way to the bird pens by memory and luck through knee-deep snow.

It was a beautiful night, totally socked in with clouds and fog. All of the trees were snow smothered. Any house shining a light was wreathed in halo and a little bit of light went a long way to illuminating the landscape. The quiet was ethereal, that which only a heavy snowstorm can create.

Once inside the aviary, my method for clearing the snow was to lift a push broom into the air and ram it against the underside of the netting. A shower of snow cascaded down, and I waited until it slowed before I looked up for the next place to put the broom. Usually, a last clump of snow would then plop down on my face and my glasses would fog up again. I got wise to the system early on and kept my head down, so the last cascade would then fill up the inside of my glasses against my face. It was very refreshing in a sub-zero super-frustrating kind of way.

When we bought the nylon netting, we'd had a choice of a two-inch or one-inch weave. We chose the smaller weave because the Chukar Partridge were small, and because we wanted to someday be able to raise quail in the large pen. But the one-inch weave stubbornly collected the snow and I had all the time in the world to regret my netting decision as I shook down the snow in the middle of the night.

The birds were awake, shaking themselves off regularly. The ground-loving chukar moved before me, dark shadows against the snow. Despite our recent effort of building lovely wooden perches under sheet metal for additional shelter, most of the pheasant were roosting in the open with an inch of snow on their backs. I got very close as I shook down the snow and they didn't even shift their feet. It was a magical night of truce and hushed silence. I could take my time, defrost my glasses, lean on my broom, and take a rest until the geese started honking, which made me jump. I had expected the geese to be inside their deluxe straw-filled house, but they were out and I had mistaken them for mounds of snow. The goose pen had no cover, so the snow had collected normally on the ground. The geese always slept outside. They had simply tucked their heads under one wing and slept on. I moved to the other end of the aviary and they settled down again, their fresh tracks clearly stamped in the otherwise blank snow.

It occurred to me that anything moving in or around the pens for the next several hours would leave clear tracks. I would be able to see what was visiting the pens in the pre-dawn if I was willing to come up here again in a couple of hours. I had always wondered if we actually did get visits from all the creatures we had proofed the pens against. It was a hard choice: cozy warm sleep or cold hard research, but I really wanted to know.

I went back out to the pen with the first pink edges of dawn coloring the snow. The raking light from clearing skies would help make any animal tracks stand out. My own boot marks were mostly filled in, which gave me an idea of the time any crisper tracks were made. I knew that I had made the last boot prints at 4 a.m. I had an animal track identification book with me, complete with color photographs of exciting footprints.

The first thing I noticed were the mouse prints that led from under every tree and bush straight to my car. There were no tracks leading back. Rabbit tracks criss-crossed the road, followed by canine paw prints. One set led to a low-slung bush with a dog-sized imprint in the snowy branches. Cheeky rabbit tracks left the bush at a right angle, while the dog tracks continued on straight.

I stood at the perimeter of the pen and saw tracks as far as I could see and in every direction. They came from far away on the horizon in a straight line to my pens. Tracks looped around trees and bushes, or came out from under them. Tracks intersected lines of other tracks and made patterns in the snow circling the base of the wire fences. I had suspected that some of the neighborhood dogs and native predators had my bird pens on their regular rounds, but this was far more than I'd dreamed. This was incredible.

I cracked my book and went down on my heels. The book had dog tracks listed for comparison on most of the pages, for freshman trackers whose own faithful companions were standing right behind them with snow covered paws. Many of the largest tracks were dog and had obviously come from the direction of houses and the road. The medium-sized tracks were coyote. The book suggested that the tiniest canine tracks were fox, and there were a lot more of those than I expected. These came in from wilderness directions and tended to be laid down in straight lines, without the larger canine detours to every tree and bush.

There was a feline print that was either one big house cat or a bobcat. Bobcats were native in the area and I had seen one in my headlights late at night in the summer. The tracks came in from the wilderness, went parallel to the fence, then went straight back out. A tree close to the pen had a patch of disturbed snow on a branch and one clear grasp print, perhaps an owl. Claw prints were also splayed on three of the upper post tops that held the netting, definitely owl.

There were whole swatches of disturbed snow where ground dwelling visitors had sat down, watching the birds from within inches of the wire. It was a wonder that the birds weren't nervous wrecks by now from all the hungry eyes and jaws coming so close to them.

For all this evidence of intense pre-dawn activity, I seemed to be alone at the pens, with only the birds and juniper-berry-laced scat piles for company. I began to feel much more content with the expense and effort we had put into construction. Over the ten years we had lived on these two acres, we had seen coyotes, bobcat, a mummified pine marten, owls, hawks, eagles, and an osprey. We'd heard fox mating calls, found bear poop, and heard annual rumors of mountain lions.

In our first year living here, I was awake one night and enjoying the full moon through the glass door when several coyotes came up to the house. They came surprisingly early, slipping through the trees at about 10 p.m. They were totally silent, no crunching footsteps, no loud snuffling. One sauntered in front of the porch door, right on the gravel walkway we used every day. It was smaller than I had expected, with a bushy tail and light, graceful step. It seemed calm and confident, not furtive or watchful. It walked without that goofy rib-cage swing that many dogs have. Its movements were tight and coordinated, but not stealthy. It was just as at home here as I was.

One night soon after that, Rachel woke me up with animated tail wagging. She was very agitated and kept pressing her cold nose on my face then running to the doorway. Having grown up watching Lassie on TV, I knew she meant a small boy had fallen down a well, but I wasn't sure what I should do about it. So I got up and staggered to the door, but as I was about to open it to my now leaping, whining, grimacing dog, I hesitated. I'd never seen her this animated. She really wanted to get outside. What was outside that had triggered this behavior? What if it was a whole pack of slavering coyotes, primed to lure her to a bloody cruel death?

I hesitated some more and Rachel became silently frantic in her desire to go *out*. Now I imagined a bear. A bear with wickedly curved claws that was going through our unprotected garbage. Rachel was a fighter, a tough alpha-queen, and she wouldn't hesitate to take on an intruder. She was sensing something, perhaps even a cougar. I smoothed her coat with my hands and firmly explained why she couldn't go outside. Whatever it was would have to wait until morning, when it would be long gone. It was hard to walk away from her imploring eyes, so I closed my bedroom door.

Morning came and I emerged from my bedroom, ready to let Rachel out for a good sniff around. A mound of dog poop was neatly piled on the carpet by the door. Rachel blinked apologetically at me from her bed. There were no tracks outside other than my own and I felt like I'd been handed my Idiot Diploma.

Chapter Fourteen

$\mathcal{I}$n 2005, Easter came at the end of March. The ground was puddled with ice-rimmed mud that made chores slippery and arduous. Spring winds cut through my clothes and I was very glad for my down jacket. There was no sign of budding green in the trees yet. Everything still seemed to be sleeping and waiting for the earth to tilt just a little more in spring's favor.

The big snows had melted away but we were still making adjustments and repairs to the pen. The new cable attachments that ran from the building roof to the telephone pole posts were twice as strong as before the big snow, and we improved the separation between the main pen and the smaller enclosure for the Silver Pheasant. A new netting sheet was tied to the overhead cable and draped straight down to be secured by railway ties bisecting the pen.

This didn't take care of the sight barrier that professional game bird farmers recommended for pheasant, but it was quick and easy and we had the materials. However, access to the new pen remained a problem. The netted maze we set up when we first separated the Silver Gang was a bitch to get the buckets through every morning.

"That netted maze in the Silver pen is a bitch to get the buckets through," I said to Andrew one morning.

"It's not bad," Andrew claimed, "you just have to pull down one fold before clipping up the other fold, and duck real low at the end."

"Perhaps I wasn't clear," I said, "the Access, otherwise known as the Entry, also referred to as the Doorway, is not working for me!"

"What are you saying?" Andrew asked.

"Look Mr. Custom Door Licensed Contractor Man," I said, "we need a permanent solution for that problem."

"Custom Door Installer," Andrew corrected, "it says "installer" on my card."

"My card says I quit doing pen chores until you fix it," I said.

"What do you mean?" Andrew exclaimed. "I can't do the chores every day by myself!"

"It's not so bad," I sympathized, "you just have to pull down a fold and clip up the other fold, you know how."

"Okay," Andrew sighed. "I will fix the doorway."

The next week, a man who was not Andrew showed up at the bird pen, laden with tools. He installed a beautiful door cast off from a recent renovation job. I assumed he was one of Andrew's guys, but I didn't ask. He was, after all, fixing the door. By the end of the day, the aviary had a nice second-hand door and door jam, complete with doorknob. It functioned perfectly. It functioned much better than the doors in the trailer. I opened and closed it just for fun. It closed with a satisfying thud; a whumping sound that went straight to my heart. There had always been a gate to access the whole pen area, but it was a salvaged, oversized compromise that fastened with a stone age contraption requiring two hands to open or close. Now the shark pen was separated from the main pen by this beautiful new door. Maybe I still had to open the main gate with two hands, but once inside, I could move through the rest of the pen single-handed.

Ten days after the huge snow, the day before Easter, I went up to the pens just to play with the new door and stopped short as I was reaching to open it. Right in front of the doorjamb, near a low bush was an egg. It was the first pheasant egg! A pheasant hen was finally laying, having indeed waited until the last snow had passed. So many months of anticipation had gone into this first egg moment and now it had finally arrived. Since I was standing in the shark pen, I realized that this had to be a Silver Pheasant egg. These pheasant were so unusual in every other way that I held great expectations for the unique qualities their eggs might have. It looked… pretty much like a chicken egg.

"What did you expect it to look like?" said Andrew, when he came home that night and we celebrated the egg. "Did you think it would be spangled and sequined?"

I did, actually, but I didn't want to admit that to him.

The egg was a pretty shape, pointy at one end with a rounded bottom. Egg-shaped, really. It was smaller than a regular chicken egg and a light pinkish brownish color. It had some subtle speckling near the pointed end, but I wasn't sure if that was some crud from the pen or a trendy pattern.

This first egg was out in the middle of the pen, as if the hen was overcome by the laying and then ran away. Later, the Silver hens all used the same small nest box I had built for them. They would lay their eggs and then compete with each other to eat them before I came with my collection basket. Only by touring the pens every hour and a half was I able to stockpile a number of Silver Pheasant eggs. There seemed to be no limit to the lengths the Silvers were willing to go to inconvenience their keeper.

The next day, Easter morning, the girls and I arrived at the pens with a proper Dorothy-and-Toto style basket, complete with cloth. To our combined delight, the girls found a small olive-green egg under a juniper bush in the pen that housed the other pheasant hens. Juno jubilantly found a speckled beige egg under an unusually patient Chukar Partridge hen, and our Easter was complete. I held the perfect new eggs in my hand and breathed a huge sigh of relief and satisfaction. My egg project was a success. I now had goose, duck, chicken, Silver Pheasant, regular pheasant, Chukar Partridge, and Button Quail eggs. Blown and put on little stands, this egg lineup would be the heart of my egg and feather business. Who wouldn't want seven beautiful blown eggs for their mantel? It felt really good, and as soon as I listed the collections, they sold.

The arrival of the first game bird egg was not only the culmination of a year of planning, hope, and dreaming; it was also a herald of the true end of cold weather. It had been a hard winter. The egg, always a pregnant symbol of fertile life, held a different meaning to me that spring. It was a promise of change, a token of progress. We celebrated that triumphant Easter with a roast pheasant dinner. I found it ironic, with my continued self-consciousness about the trailer, to be having such a gourmet dinner in this rough setting. But pheasant farmers eat roast pheasant, just as cattle ranchers eat prime rib, and so we sat down to an aromatic, mouth-watering meal that I had burned only a little bit.

Most pheasant recipes called for skinning the pheasant instead of plucking it. I didn't know the reason for that, whether it was because the pheasant skin was traditionally a trophy from the hunt, or because the cooked skin wasn't as tasty as that of a chicken. As I served it, I decided it was the latter reason. Pheasant was not as fatty as chicken or duck, and the roasted skin had an ebony gloss to it. I carved the roasted pheasant with surgical creativity, and we sat down to eat. It was rewardingly delicious and very flavorful, although not as tender as commercial poultry. But those few times I served store-bought chicken it tasted mushy. I was getting used to my tough old birds.

Andrew and the girls were eating well and enjoying the meal. The girls loved an Easter surrounded by real eggs. Once again, I wasn't filling my plate with slices of roast bird. I ate only a little of the meat, then turned to the side dishes.

"Why aren't you eating the meat, Mommy?" Blue asked.

"I'm not really hungry for pheasant right now," I said.

"Are you *still* having an emotional problem with our home-raised food?" Andrew asked in exasperation, putting down his fork.

"Well, my stomach is a little upset," I tried again.

"Have soma mine?" Juno offered sympathetically.

"No, thank you," I said. Andrew planted his elbows on the table.

"What's up with this?" he demanded.

"Well, if you must know," I said. "I don't really want to eat the bird because I raised it up from a chick and I can't stop thinking about that."

"Oh, Mommy," Blue wailed, "you're making me sad!"

"Which is why I didn't want to tell you!" I said.

"But it taste good," Juno argued, with her little mouth full.

"It does taste good," I agreed, "and we are doing all this specifically so you girls don't get all wrapped up with the silly emotions that I'm having now."

"Because you grew up in the city," Blue said, repeating what I had told her over and over.

"Exactly," I said, proud of her.

"You've got to find a way to grow out of this," Andrew announced, wiping his chin. "This is really divine food!"

"You're saying I should grow the hell up?" I bristled.

"Well, no…" Andrew attempted.

"You're saying I should get real?" I flared.

"No, not at all…" Andrew said.

"Look," I continued. "I'm having a conflict with the whole thing, all right? It's hard for me. Wolves don't rear up baby rabbits! Owls don't set up heat lamps for baby mice! They don't get all committed to the survival of their developing dinners, then turn around and chow down!"

Andrew chewed at me, and the girls just watched.

"I'm admitting to you that my emotions are at war with

my reality," I said. "I really don't want you girls to have this same struggle."

There was a strained silence, chewing sounds lapping on the shores of my frustration. The girls smiled at me encouragingly and took another forkful, except for Juno who was eating with her hands.

"Dessert is chocolate eggs," Blue offered. "You shouldn't have any trouble with those."

"Thank you, honey," I said.

"I do respect you telling us all that," Andrew finally said, through a mouthful of pheasant.

"Well, thanks," I said.

"But you should probably grow up and get real sometime soon," he said.

"Dad!" the girls said loyally.

"I feel bad, too," he continued, ripping a wing off the roast.

"Oh, really?" I said, skeptically.

"But not as bad as you," he finished with gusto.

"This is really very tasty," he said. "You did a nice job spicing it. It's got a kind of smoky flavor to it. What secret farm-wife touch did you give it?"

"Last rites," I said.

Easter really was the end of the snow and cold weather. Spring became obvious even to those of us without the special sensory powers of poultry. Green shoots emerged and the bare branches leafed out in vivid life. Eggs rolled through the pens morning and afternoon, and we went out regularly to collect them while they were still clean and whole. One of the chicken hens, a big Australorp with glossy jet black feathers, became broody and started collecting all the eggs in a huge pile under her warm motherly self. One morning, I noticed fewer eggs coming down from the pen into the kitchen and figured that Andrew hadn't had the time to collect them, so the girls and I went up with the egg basket we had used on Easter day. It had been sitting on the wood stove as an ornament, and I thought it was time to put it into service.

I helped Blue climb up to the laying boxes and she reached in under the big hen, which she had named Big Bertha, of course. Big Bertha moved fast and nipped hard at Blue's hand

"OW!" Blue shouted in pain and outrage, "she *bit* me!"

I comforted Blue and examined the hole in her hand.

"Sorry about that, baby," I said. "Sometimes the hens get broody. That means they protect the eggs so they can set them. Setting them means sitting on them until they hatch into chicks, but that won't happen with these eggs."

Blue frowned with tear-filled eyes at the hen and held the basket out for me. I took it and confidently reached into the laying box. Lightning fast, Big Bertha tried to take off my hand at the wrist.

"OW!" I yelled and jumped back. "Bloody Hell!"

"She did that to Daddy, too," Blue said.

"Oh she did, did she?" I said.

I had touched the pile of eggs under the hen before the attack and discovered that it was huge. Now I understood why no eggs were coming down to the kitchen. It was the Broody Hen Handoff. Andrew was leaving the collecting to me.

I looked at the egg basket and took the cloth out from

inside. I had an idea.

"Maybe if we cover her eyes," I said to Blue. "She'll calm down and let us take the eggs."

"Or maybe," Blue said, warming to the concept, "she'll peck the cloth instead of our hands."

"Exactly," I said, and gently laid the cloth over the broody hen.

"Hey," Blue exclaimed, "it works! She isn't even pecking anymore!"

"I guess that's what the cloth is for in the egg basket," I said.

"Did you know that already?" Blue demanded.

"Not really," I admitted. "I just made the whole egg basket to look like something out of the Wizard of Oz."

"Pitty cool," Juno said, putting a finger on the growing pile of eggs in the basket.

The chukar hens proved to be clever egg hiders. While the pheasant hens generally laid an egg wherever they happened to be sitting at the time, the chukar hens worked together to build a nest, and then used it together. We had placed three straw bales in a U shape and topped it with a discarded door to increase the laying space in the pen. The chukar hens accepted the straw bales with enthusiasm. They tunneled into the bales and made a nest, or they scraped down a big pile of loose straw and made a nest, or they shimmied under a pile of loose straw and made a nest. Then the fiercest chukar hen would snug down to set the eggs and posed a real hazard when collection time came. She resisted the cloth and it was like reaching into a miniature crocodile mound to get the eggs. I resorted to a heavy gardening glove and I won.

The chukar were incredibly productive egg layers and they probably would have brooded up dozens of chukar chicks if I had let them, but their delightful little eggs were big sellers and I was finally making a profit with everything: eggs and feathers. I took the step of setting up a website which I called www.TheFeatheredEgg.com. I put up pictures of my birds and a page describing our operation. What I didn't know about raising poultry was nothing compared to what I didn't know about online business. I learned as I went and the eggs continued to sell.

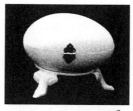

Chapter Fifteen

In my dilapidated singlewide, in my firebox of an oven, a gourmet dinner was cooking. Roast pheasant with rosemary and balsamic vinaigrette glaze. The pheasant was fresh and the ingredients were local. It was stuffed with onion and fresh thyme. Somewhere else in the world, there was an exclusive penthouse apartment with a million dollar view, where a frozen potpie was thawing in a microwave.

Everything was easier as the cold weather lifted. Blue went to school without the additional suitcase of snow clothing. The chores were simple and done in the pleasant morning light. The smell of the greening property was uplifting and joyful. I reflected on one year ago, when all the chicks had been in their brooders and the volatile temperature changes had been such a problem. Now it was easy. The landscape was beautiful again and we were almost ready to turn off the nighttime heat lamps.

Blue was dealing with the childhood ordeal of losing teeth. So far, she had gone through every version of how to deal with a loose tooth except purposefully pulling it out. She lost one in a sticky mouthful of taffy. I couldn't resist teasing her about that being proof that candy makes your teeth fall out. She was not amused and the taffy was nasty afterwards, but I was pleased with my own wit. She lost another by running accidentally into Andrew's leg as they collided in the tiny trailer hallway. Her first loose tooth disappeared in the night because she was too scared to try and pull it out. We never confirmed if it went down into the sheets or was swallowed, even though we looked *everywhere.*

This time she was determined to have it taken out on her terms, so one evening she showed up at my chair armrest with a tissue and a resolute expression.

"Please will you pull out my tooth?" she asked.

"Are you serious?" I cringed. Pulling loose teeth was not my one of my favorite subjects.

"I'm ready right now," she said bravely.

"I'm not!" I said maturely. "Yipers!"

But she was determined, so I washed my hands and took the tissue and had her sit down in a comfortable chair. I tugged experimentally.

"Does that hurt?" I asked.

"Mmrff umggffh," she said, waving her hands, and I tugged some more. The tooth wasn't coming out.

"Hold on now," I told her, pulling even harder and moving sideways for better leverage

"Umrfff gtthh!" she said, pointing to her mouth.

"I'm sorry, honey," I said. "I don't think your tooth is at all ready."

"I said," she said, wiping her mouth, "that you were pulling on the wrong tooth!"

"Oh, sorry!" I said, reaching back in there again. This time the tooth came off into the tissue with barely a touch. "You really are brave," I said to her, leaning back again. "I'm not so brave," she said. "You have to pull it out right now or I'll faint."

"It's already out!" I said proudly.

"Are you serious?" she said, eyes wide. She was pleased and proud and ready for the tooth fairy. I felt like I had accidentally stumbled into a moment of competent parenting.

The warmer weather of April came as an obvious relief to all the birds, despite how capable they were in the cold. Eggs rolled in every direction. We had so many Chukar Partridge eggs that I felt generous enough to let the chukar hens brood up a huge pile of eggs they had carefully collected and valiantly defended. They had chosen a protected corner of the chicken house instead of their usual outside straw bale, and so I marked my calendar and gave them some room.

In the meantime, I struggled to wash and blow the huge numbers of eggs I was now collecting from all the birds. The geese were laying about an egg every other day, and the pheasant didn't lay every day, but together the total was almost 300 eggs a week. The Button Quail were out-producing the chickens, laying an egg a day without fail. I finally had the opportunity to learn first hand about rotten eggs, since I could not keep up with the backlog and blow them all in time.

Rotten eggs were unpredictable and humidity made a big difference. I placed one flat of washed eggs in a plastic bag to see if it kept them from drying out, since that was a problem I was encountering more and more often (eggs that had lost so much moisture inside that the egg and yolk didn't blow easily). The plastic bag eggs rotted much faster than the exposed eggs.

My rotten egg introduction was an egg from the plastic bag. I took one out that had a strange black ring on the outside of the shell. With my usual level of egg-handling proficiency, I dropped it accidentally on the bathroom floor and it went off like a bomb. The effect was absolutely awful; a palpable, volcanic, sulphurous cloud of nastiness. Some component of the rotten egg fumes worked on the human nervous system the same way skunk musk does. I suffered a helplessly compulsive need to sniff the fetid air again and again, as if my brain was repeatedly incredulous that anything could smell so utterly bad.

I quickly learned how to tell if an egg was rotten without drilling into it. The evil black ring was a good indicator, but it wasn't always there. I could hold the eggs in front of a bright light and if there was blackness inside, I carefully set it down. I could sniff the unbroken shell and tell if the insides were rotten, but despite these clues, I still occasionally blew a bad egg and the whole house suffered for hours. The only real remedy was to keep up with the egg blowing. The refrigerator simply wasn't big enough to hold them all.

Before the due date for the chukar hatch, I came within range of the pens and knew the clutch had been a failure. Rotten egg fog clung over the entire bird pen and was not dispersed by the mild breeze of the day. I could smell the pong everywhere on the property and it was a huge effort to go into the chicken house and remove the failed pile of eggs.

The chukar hens had kicked apart the nest, scattering the nasty results throughout the chicken house. The smell was so strong in the confined space that my eyes streamed. I guessed that in the wild, Chukar Partridge could simply relocate their entire flock to another portion of the state when a clutch failed. Here it took weeks for the smell to abate. The chickens seemed unaffected and continued to lay in their usual spaces, but we humans couldn't get past it. For the next month, egg collecting became the punishment chore for anyone hitting a sister or losing a bet.

I named the business "The Feathered Egg" because I was producing feathers and eggs. I was delighted to find that the domain name "www.TheFeatheredEgg.com" was still available by the time I bought it. Many of the cleverest egg business names were already taken. My competition was canny.

The amount of manual labor involved in my grand egg business was appalling to the people watching from afar and applauding my success.

"It's just so much *effort!*" exclaimed my mother, on the phone, as she vacuumed, scrubbed, cooked, cleaned, and made cakes from scratch.

"It sounds like a *huge* amount of work," said my friend, taking her first break in days from her sixty hour a week corporate salaried job.

"I don't know how you find the time," said my sister, on the way to her third marathon run of the year.

But I was making money at it. Nowhere near enough to compare to the wages I'd be making if I were working a more normal job, but enough to give me hope that it could become a contributor to the family income and pay for itself. It was supporting the birds already, and I was counting on it to repay the cost of the pens within another year. The reward from my project was far more than the simple math of income and expense. Somewhere in the first year of scrambling after the birds and creating systems to blow and sell the eggs, I had stopped taking my antidepressant. I was still worried and sometimes distracted by a sense of coming doom, but I no longer swallowed a pill a day to combat it. The business was my cure.

My housekeeping suffered, but frankly, it had suffered before I had the excuse of a hundred birds and daily egg chores to justify the dust bunnies and pale grey cast to all of our laundry. Before I started the bird business, I had railed at the feeling of futility I would have by the end of the day when all the tasks I had accomplished since the morning were waiting to be done again. The food I'd cooked was consumed. The possessions I'd put away were scattered out again. The clothes I'd washed were dirty once more. Knowing that I was making a foundation of good health and happiness for my family wasn't enough to keep me from feeling depressed and set back at the end of the day. Adding the effort of poultry farming and an online business hadn't made me any more efficient or effective at those critical life-sustaining tasks. But even when the money I brought in did not equal the amount that went out, I felt much happier at the end of the day. I wanted to feel more fulfilled by my mothering job, but the truth was that I didn't. I'd been trained since early childhood and throughout college to do complex tasks destined for grateful employers. I could type, knew lots of formulas, and had studied advanced literature, but none of that formal education had prepared me to do the one job I was most likely to have as an adult woman in my society: the job of housewife and mother.

The poultry business truly was a lot of work, but it was my work and I enjoyed it. Having the products sell was like having my hamster wheel of daily chores break off mid-spin and hit the open road. I felt that I was finally getting somewhere, and while I wished I could get the same satisfaction from keeping house for my family, the satisfaction came from using my skills in a business setting. Andrew never saw it my way. He appreciated my creativity with the business, but for him it remained a life cycle experiment gone out of control. He patiently folded his own laundry and packed his own lunch and tried to remain supportive of my mental and emotional struggle.

"The only creatures on earth who don't have to do daily, repetitive, mind-numbing, annoying, or even down-right hazardous tasks to keep themselves alive," he said, "are creatures that are being fattened for another purpose."

I appreciated his point of view, but I quietly resolved to make my egg business so successful that one day he'd come home and take care of the family while I got up every morning to go to work. And then we'd really see if he was content with the daily routine of supporting other people's lives or if we ended up with yet another weird kind of farm.

I joined a local art tour at the kind invitation of a neighboring artist and showed my eggs and feathers to the public for the first time. It was an encouraging success, and with Andrew's help, I developed a new product: a cut, hinged egg. The first hinged egg experiments resulted in a huge pile of broken eggs, but I got better at the process and at using the tools. Soon I was able to produce the most elaborate confections of real blown eggshells, cut and hinged with doors, or sliced across the middle for people to make into jewelry boxes. I once again amazed my family with sales of these products. I was proud of myself for adapting the technology at hand in Andrew's workshop to making this new product.

That summer the Dodo cats lured a pretty female cat into the shop to shack up with them. I called her Not My Cat, and think she may have been someone's escaped housecat. She acted feral until she had a litter of kittens, then she couldn't resist purring around my legs for congratulations on her success. We were back in cats and very relieved. The new kittens were long-haired, wild-child, mouse-catching machines.

My website began to attract traffic worldwide. By the fall and into the Christmas season of 2005, I was truly in business selling blown eggs, hinged eggs, and feathers. Sales were high enough that my flock was securely supporting themselves and the minor business expenses of website and supplies, as long as I didn't count my time as a business expense. I hoped one day that would change but in the meantime, I was very pleased that this experiment had proven successful. It looked like I'd be able to keep my birds for as long as they agreed to lay. I celebrated by buying the family a special present for Christmas, one that was an example of a technological leap even more useful than my hinged egg work.

"What is it?" Blue asked after opening it on behalf of the family.

"It looks like a clock," Andrew observed.

"It is a clock," I said, "but it's a special new kind of clock."

"What's a clock?" asked Juno.

"It's a machine that tells you the time," Blue said.

"Aha!" I said, "That's not quite true. It doesn't really tell you the time. A clock is a machine that *asks* you the time."

"What?" they all said.

"You may think a clock tells you the time," I said again, "but in reality, it only tells you the time after first asking you what time it is."

"I'm confused," Blue said.

"You have to set a regular clock first," I said, "and then it tells you the time. But it's only correct if you told it the right time to begin with."

"So what's different about this clock?" Andrew asked, turning it over in his hands.

"This is an atomic clock," I announced happily. "It sets itself based on a radio signal from the atomic clock in Boulder, Colorado."

"So it really does tell me the time?" Andrew asked.

"It really does," I said with satisfaction.

"That's cool!" Blue said.

We passed around the new fangled clock with great delight and in the process, unintentionally set the clock's alarm for two in the morning. But even as I swam up out of a groggy deep sleep to find and turn off the awful beeping, I was still pleased with my purchase. The time glowing on the LED screen was truly the actual time, down to a fraction of a second.

May of 2006 marked the one-year anniversary of my flock. The first chicks, the ducklings, had arrived on May fifth. They were all, more or less, a year old now and I took a moment to reflect. It would have been much less entertaining with better planning, but I only now knew what to plan for. The idea I'd had about the eggs was a definite success and I could see many ways to expand on it, all taking time and experience that I had to carve out for myself somehow. The second summer of managing the flock was completely different from the first.

The months began to fly by as the flock's second year proved much less adventuresome. The adult birds were stable in their life cycle and in their spaces. Anything that could go wrong had done so in the first twelve months. The laying seasons became established and were different for each bird. The only commonality was that they all laid significantly fewer eggs as they got older. The geese were the exception; they laid larger and thicker-shelled eggs each year.

As we went into the winter of 2006, our second winter in the trailer, I began to wonder how long I should keep my flock. Productivity was lower but so was the drama. With automatic waterers, water heaters, and heat lamps, the adult birds had become very low maintenance.

I was spending more of my time now on the website

and making products from the eggs and feathers. The time I wasn't spending on the birds was all going into the business, and I needed the birds to continue to take care of themselves. Relying on the inventory from their first ultra-productive year was all right for now, but if I were to expand the business, I would need to raise birds again. Just not now.

My poultry literature failed me on advice for flock maintenance. Most poultry farmers didn't keep their flock for more than a year, and most backyard amateurs kept theirs for way longer than that, but didn't write about it. I was running on rumor for how long the flock would continue to lay, and what their production rate would be. Much of the information that was available was from the perspective of incubation and hatching. My needs were entirely different, as I was interested in the quantity and eggshell quality of the eggs produced, so my own notes were going to have to be my guide. In the end, I kept the original flock for an un-farmerish three years, only occasionally butchering an unproductive bird for dinner. Each of the species matured differently in those passing years.

The chickens had begun to lay at about eighteen weeks of age – two weeks earlier than predicted in the hatchery catalog. They laid an average of an egg a day until they were one year old, at which point they went through a spectacular molt and came back to laying at the rate of an egg every other day. Every year from that point on, they were less productive, until the age of four years, when they almost stopped egg laying completely and began to stagger around on arthritic joints.

The ducks were amazingly productive in their first

year. They began laying at almost exactly five months of age and laid an egg a day until the deep cold of December set in. Their eggshells were strong, and the contents richly perfect for baking, but their second laying season showed the strain of that production rate. Second season eggs had much thinner shells and the commercialized duck breeds, like the White Pekin, seemed to age at an accelerated rate. The genetic tweaking that made them get big so fast also resulted in a much shorter lifespan. By the third year, only the Flying Mallards were still comfortably ambling around the pen.

The pheasant hens laid their first eggs at almost ten months old; twice the amount of time it took for the heavily bred chickens to produce their first egg. They laid conservatively, an egg every three to four days, and they stopped at the first hint of cold weather. Their pattern was much more in tune with a real life cycle. They laid only when the newly hatched chicks could have a hope of survival, and they did not seem to exhaust their bodies like the commercial birds did. I never lost a pheasant to egg binding. The male pheasant were also slow to mature, but they had much shorter life spans as well. The pheasant hens began to show their age in the third year, but there were no males by that time. The ones I had not butchered to keep the pens safe died of natural causes within the first two years. The Golden and Lady Amherst Pheasant roosters were the exception. They lived vigorously for four years, and their full plumage was complete in the third year. They probably would have lived longer, but by that time, we were experiencing changes in our own life cycle.

The Chukar Partridge confirmed their wild heritage by

laying only in the warm weather, and only after they were about ten months old. The males burned out earlier than the females. By the third year, I had only one slow moving grandfather chukar who watched his wives die one by one of old age before they turned four. Some partridge farmers argued that it was possible to keep the chukar alive longer than that, but I had them on the ground and in natural surroundings, which they loved, and that was against partridge farming lore. Chukar are susceptible to parasitic worms and intestinal flora, and although I didn't feel my partridge died of infestation, they may have lived longer without their beloved dirt baths.

The Button Quail do not have a long expected lifespan. They laid many eggs and died young: none lived to the fourth year. I figured they were trading long lives for high reproduction rates. Their plan was to flood the world with hysterical, maniacal quail but not stick around to live with the results. Their separate and high maintenance needs wore me out, and I didn't brood up a new generation of quail to replace my original flock. By that time, buying their eggs already blown seemed more profitable, even though I missed their beauty and their funny ways.

Geese apparently are able to live for decades; some have lived almost ninety years. Every year, they lay a larger egg and there are goose eggs for sale that rival the height of a Rhea or Emu egg. Even though they are thoroughly domesticated, they stick to their laying season and do not lay all year round. Our geese had a laying season of only three to four months each year, leaving eight months of the year for me to wonder if it was worth keeping them. It helped that twice a year they molted their long, dramatic wing feathers, which were in great demand in online sales. They were spectacular watchdogs, and, as a flock, quite capable of defending themselves against most single predators.

So even though it was not very logical from a farming perspective, I kept my flock for several years. The second year proved to be a transition from focusing on the birds to developing the business. My website was a tiny thing in the beginning, just a couple of pages, but within six months of setting it up, I was getting significant traffic.

Chapter Sixteen

When we first started the poultry project, everything was fledgling: our flock, children, businesses, housing situation, and experience level. By the middle of 2006, all of those things had matured, although at different rates. Our businesses brought a steadier income and our finances stabilized. Andrew's contracting business grew wings and began to soar. It became a big deal, with a permanent crew and year-round projects, and consumed his attention utterly. The house rental was now stable. There really were people interested in living this far out of town, mainly because the location was so beautiful. These were people who could handle the bad roads and had the ability and intention to pay the rent regularly. New tenants came in. One couple brought an alto flute and ethereally beautiful music floated out over the juniper and piñon trees.

Our family life was changing. Blue was firmly established in public school in Santa Fe and Juno was in a great preschool. I had been looking forward to the day both girls would be in school as a kind of graduation of my own. Just as things got easier with the flock after their first year of life,

I expected things to be easier for me once the girls were in school. I was pleased to see them learning so much every day and making friends, but I had underestimated the amount of schoolwork I would be responsible for personally. As soon as I thought I had lunches, water bottles, backpacks, and permission slips under control, I tripped over the girl's vaccination records.

Andrew and I had gone along with all of the well-established vaccinations like measles and polio. I took those very seriously. I'd had a Brazilian friend in college who suffered the aftereffects of polio and I did not consider it a dead disease. But the host of new vaccines gave me pause, especially as they kept getting recalled. The school district required us to either give the girls the chicken pox vaccine or file a conscientious objection form. I had been filing the form every year and hoping that the girls would catch the chicken pox in the meantime. But they hadn't.

Just before school went back in session after the summer break of 2006, my friend reported that her daughter had a confirmed case of the chicken pox. The poor kid was miserable, but her mom was delighted. She invited all of us over for a Pox Party, complete with balloons and cake. I wasn't the only mom who wanted my children to go through chicken pox early in their lives and therefore gain immunity against a more severe infection as an adult. I wasn't alone in my distrust of the vaccine. We all bravely passed the single lollipop from child to child at the party table and tried not to let them see us cringe. My friend passed out party favors in the form of a little calendar marking the pox's incubation period. We waited.

Right on time, the girls got sick — but it wasn't the chicken pox. It was something awful and totally different, which Andrew and I came down with as well. To my knowledge, only one of the kids at the party successfully came down with chicken pox. I decided I had done my best and got the girls vaccinated. Blue was getting too old now to contract the disease safely and I couldn't swim against the tide any longer.

The egg business reliably met its own expenses, even though it wasn't yet creating enough profit to pay me a salary. The birds were supporting themselves and a percentage of the property's utility bills. Both of the girls were now in public school and the drive to town was becoming a significant obstacle. We joined the ballooning housing scramble and extended ourselves to buy one of the fast-appreciating condos in town that would give us access to a public school and a social life for the girls. That turned into a social life for me and we came, as a family, to the trailer for extended weekends. I came alone several times throughout the week to manage the poultry. Our lives changed profoundly, mostly driven by the growing needs of the girls.

We used range feeders and automatic waterers to care for the birds while we lived our townie lives. When the holiday season of December 2006 became the designated extended-family get-together in Reno, we made an effort to attend. This was the first time we'd planned to travel together since we had taken on the flock, and it was an exciting event. Our neighbor was willing to do the minimal care required on the flock and Rachel took up residence in a luxury dog kennel, complete with heated concrete flooring.

In Reno, we posed for family photos, got to know nieces and nephews, and had a lovely vacation together. We were planning to travel on to California to see Andrew's side of the family, but reports of a large storm system headed for Colorado began to fill the evening news. The biggest snow we had shaken down off our pen netting was seventeen inches. The snow load that had brought the netting down had been eight inches. I watched conservative early reports on this new storm from my parent's cozy home in Nevada with growing alarm.

I made the responsible decision and bailed on the family gathering. Christmas had already passed, so I would miss New Year's with my in-laws. I sent my regrets with Andrew and the girls as I went to the airport to catch anything flying in the direction of New Mexico. I kept second-guessing myself nervously until I reached Albuquerque and reclaimed my car from the long-term parking lot. The forecast had been for heavy snow in Colorado and had said nothing about northern New Mexico. When I drove onto clear roads through Albuquerque, I thought I had arrived in time, but I had not. The leading edge of the storm had already blanketed Santa Fe and closed roads leading north out of Albuquerque just hours before my plane landed.

Snow fell heavily all that night, as I waited in a hotel on Albuquerque's north side for the highway to open. The minute the road was clear, I scooted up I-25 in my two-wheel drive and almost didn't make it to Santa Fe. Enough other people were stuck to trigger another closing of the road, this time for days. In Santa Fe, I sat anxiously in the condo, waiting for roads to open so that I could get out to the property. Snow continued to fall. The storm stalled, spinning over the entire state, and continued to dump snow day and night.

Days passed. I called the kennel that was hosting Rachel and they reported that no dogs were going home that week. No one could get to them, but their power was holding and everyone was safe. Phones were down at our neighbors and so I had no news of conditions at the property. I went around and around in my mind, trying to figure out if the snow would have passed through the netting instead of collecting on top, because it was a much dryer snow, but there was just so much of it.

Finally, the storm moved into Texas and the snowplows cleared enough of the highway to open the roads. I drove anxiously toward the property, getting as close as I could before abandoning the car and walking the rest of the way. Plows had cleared the state and county roads, but private roads were the responsibility of the residents. Someone on cross-country skis had broken a trail along the last mile of road, but in places the snow was more than four feet deep.

With immense relief, I saw that the deep snow trail led all the way past our trailer and up to the pens. Someone had been to check on the birds. The netting was still up, but the snow was halfway up to the aviary roof. The good neighbor had dug out the gate enough for me to get through and I slipped inside. The snow was up to my waist in places. Feeders and waterers had been cleared, and pulled up to sit on top of the snow, but I saw no sign of the birds. Everything was utterly silent and white.

In the goose pen, the geese were in their own deep snow

well. They had been outside when the snow came down, and simply shook off the snow and tamped down their space as the storm progressed. Lofted snow surrounded them, climbing higher as the inches accumulated, and the geese held their position. They seemed happy enough, and their food had been uncovered as well. Their house was buried in snowdrifts to the roof.

I got busy scooping snow from every doorway and shelter that I could remember placing in the pen. I scooped out tunnels from the tree bases, and from under the chairs. I dug down to the straw bale shelter and made connecting passageways to the water and feed. Gradually the birds emerged. All were safe and healthy. They had sheltered under every space as the snow piled up, and waited out the storm in sealed snow caves.

Over the next several days, as phone service was restored, I discovered who it was that had made the incredible effort to break through to the bird pens and uncover the feed. One of the Guatemalan carpenters from Andrew's crew had become concerned as he saw the snow come down. Andrew had asked him to keep an eye on things at the property while we were gone, and he had taken the request seriously. When the snow began to come down, he persuaded his cousin who had a four-wheel-drive truck, to take them both out to check on our birds. He also had to convince the state police to allow him to travel over the closed roads a full day before they were opened to the public. The police were making exceptions only for people claiming to have stranded people or animals to care for, and who were obviously properly equipped. He had slogged by foot down the road, and broken the snow trail all the way to the pens. He had been the one to dig out the gates and feeders. Another neighbor had slogged, on foot, up our long driveway to check on our trailer, clearing the vents for the central heating so that the furnace could start automatically and prevent our pipes from freezing. Without their efforts, we would have had catastrophic losses from what turned out to be the biggest snowstorm in New Mexico history. Other people were not as lucky as we were. Livestock losses across the state were profound. We thanked our Good Samaritans profusely and sent them gifts. Because of them, we didn't lose a bird.

New Year's Day 2007 had passed under the smothering storm. As if plenty of snow were an introduction to plenty of luck and success, the year proved to be our best ever. Andrew's business fell into a cycle of completed jobs and profitable effort and we came very close to paying off our debt entirely. We were finally experiencing the kind of success we had planned on paper so many years earlier. It felt like our work was paying off.

The ice and snow packed down and refused to melt until early spring. By the time the birds could move around freely, unhampered by mud or slush, I realized that they were really starting to show their age. Their third laying season was unproductive by any standard. It became obvious that it was time to butcher them, but with my new busy life in town, I kept putting it off. I still was not a real poultry farmer. The birds were healthy enough, but there were clear signs of discomfort from what may have been arthritis in their feet and wings. When one of the Golden pheasant failed to move himself out of the path of a mild rainstorm, and instead rolled on his back and died in a puddle, I faced reality and scheduled a butchering day.

This butchering day was very different from our first attempt. We had our quick and humane rifle shot down to a fine science, and since we had been handling the birds constantly, they went with an absolute minimum of distress. Three paid helpers were set up in the workshop, ready to dry pluck the most beautiful feathers for my feather inventory. They looked at me as if I was crazy when I described how I needed them to pluck the birds. Perhaps it was my Spanish, or perhaps it was the idea of collecting and sorting what was usually a waste product in the butchering process.

Each feather had to be plucked one at a time and carefully sorted into paper bags by size and color. There was no question in my mind that it was worth it. After I put in many more hours of my time washing them and organically treating them to protect from bug predation, I knew I could sell them for enough to make the whole effort profitable. The workers plucked politely, humoring the eccentric *Patrona*, and each went home with a chicken for dinner and a bag of freshly chopped onion, celery and carrots to persuade them to make soup instead of trying to roast the tough old birds.

I encouraged the girls to participate in the butchering by telling them that these were life skills that were valuable to have. I told them that I wanted them to be able to both snag the high score on Wii and bring a chicken from the pen to table. It didn't take very much arm-twisting to get them to pay attention. Juno walked two severed chicken feet along the table edge in a macabre cabaret. Blue wanted to use the sharp knives instead of the safe butter knife we'd given her. They both turned out to be excellent feather workers, patiently plucking one feather at a time from the cooling bird. When they thought I wasn't looking, they inspected all the parts of the bird they had never been able to get close to before.

As I watched them work, I hoped that they were soaking up the skills and industrious atmosphere in a way that would prepare them well for their adult lives. I remembered some of the skills I had learned from my father. Dad was an exploration geologist, the kind that wasn't out looking for oil. He also enjoyed sailing. Our childhood vacations were spent in either abandoned gold mines in rural Australia or sailing through blue lagoons on the coasts of exotic islands in the southern hemisphere. I think he was trying to train his three daughters to crew his ship, but it didn't work out that way. Only my older sister had taken to it. I was a useless puker and my younger sister disappeared every time the boom came around. But he had also taught us to pan for gold and we spent many delighted afternoons on the banks of creeks and streams swirling handfuls of sediment in our very own pans. That skill had taken root and I was a pretty good gold panner. In retrospect, I realized that he was probably paying for those summer vacations with our panning efforts. That was the way to do it.

I had finally run out of cats after Not My Cat went back to her mysterious home and her adult offspring disappeared one by one. Because of my experience welcoming Not My Cat to the barn, I knew that not every missing cat was somebody's dinner for sure. It was remotely possible that the cat had moved on and was living the good life with one of the more distant neighbors. But I also knew that most of them were gone forever, feeding the wildlife that had called this place home long before we did. Owls were the biggest cat predators at our place. It was surprising, because these were not small cats. But the owls weren't small either and they had the advantage of silent flight. Domestic cats were the staple diet of owls, foxes, and coyotes throughout our area, and even in the heart of town. I always looked at the missing cat signs posted in town with a mix of optimism and despair. There was something so unreasonably hopeful about a flyer for a missing cat. But I knew the feeling. It wasn't always for *sure* that the cat was lunch. It was just really likely.

I once again worked hard to get another Mama Barn Cat, and found an overpopulated couple in town that were willing to trap a young mother with several of her own half-grown kittens. The new cats came in with such a virulent strain of ringworm that we were all slathered in anti-fungal cream for a month just from handling the cat carrier. Luckily, they were so feral that we were not tempted to snuggle them. New Mama Cat taught her brood well and the mouse population once again came under control. She was producing a litter a year, mostly males. One of her original kittens, Black Cat, became very friendly after he got used to his new home. His favorite pastime in cold weather months was to drop down from a workshop shelf into the hood of my down jacket when I was doing chores. He would ride around in the hood until I turned him out. This was kind of cute until the day when he jumped in with a half-dead mouse in his jaws. I didn't see him coming, but when he dropped the mouse down the back of my neck, I gave him a grand show. I kept my hood up after that.

In the spring of 2007, two years after I had done my first egg dance in the poultry pens, I got an order through my website that caused ripples of delight and excitement throughout my family. The *Martha Stewart* organization placed an order for a variety of blown eggs – and they needed them fast. Although I tried to fix a mask of professionalism and detachment over my smiling face, I couldn't hold it up. It was a hoot. We skipped around selecting the most perfect eggs and wrapped and packed and shipped them off express, then watched determinedly for the *Martha Stewart Show* with my eggs in it. I wasn't sure exactly which episode they would show up in, or if it was part of the crafts section. I had no information, but it wasn't a burden to be forced to watch the show. The staff had given me a date range in response to my enthusiasm at their order. I watched and watched, and learned a lot about how much better I could be keeping my linens. Finally, I saw them. They were sitting artfully innocuous in a nice bowl in the center of a table. Martha was behind the table talking to Lucy Liu. I was a big fan. I couldn't help the sizzle of glee I felt imagining that the eggs I had raised and sold were sitting so close to Lucy Liu.

My Santa Fe friends and I had a game I called Celebrity Poker. One of us would start it with a story about seeing a celebrity – of which there were plenty — around town. I had seen Ali MacGraw at a bookstore, but they claimed that was nothing. Everyone had seen Ali MacGraw. I tried to top myself with my conversation with Tommy Lee Jones at a restaurant in Tesuque. But when pressed, I had to admit that my part of the dialog was something like "ugh" and he was there with his hot young wife. Another friend who had actually given Melanie Griffith an hour-long massage won that particular round, but with my Martha eggs, I was ready for the next one.

For me, this order was the height of egging achievement. I had won no awards, no contests, no grants or special recognition. But I had sold to *Martha Stewart*, and that just made my day. With the Martha order in hand, I thought that my poultry adventure story was complete. Since the flock and the website were continuing into the future, I figured that this pinnacle of crafting achievement was a fitting place to close my book. While I was busy writing it up and weaving the threads of experience and tragedy into a readable tale, the world turned. Events were about to drop on everyone else's bathroom floor like a rotten egg. Our lives, and the lives of a whole lot of other people, were about to change.

2008 came down like a hammer on a crate of blown eggs, and our story took an unexpected direction.

Chapter Seventeen

*I*n the financial canyons of New York City and in the polished halls of Washington D.C., conditions were incubating that would change everything we were currently counting on. Our main income was from new construction and remodels done by people counting on the income and appreciation of their stock portfolios. Our condo had a fixed interest rate, but only because we had learned about variable interest rates the hard way with the purchase of our chicken property. We had purchased the condo with no money down and were counting on the steady appreciation it had shown in recent past years to be able to sell it if we needed to, or rent it with a lower refinanced mortgage.

Gas prices had been steadily climbing since I started my first flock. In March of 2004, gas was an average of $1.80 per gallon. One year later it was $2.19, and in March of 2006 it was $2.29. As long as the price stayed under $3.00 per gallon the issue seemed to stay out of the news, but in late 2007 gas prices hit $3.14 and climbed rapidly, sending any person or business dependent on gasoline (meaning everyone) into a frenzy of price adjustments and changed habits.

Our emergency backup plan was a low interest credit card we were holding with no balance. Despite the debt in the business, we were comfortably meeting all of our bills and had solid plans for paying it all off. But unforeseen nationwide financial events were on a countdown and we were positioned squarely in the worst way possible. We were making financially fatal mistakes while following what we thought was a sound plan. Our only eventual comfort would be that we weren't the only ones doing so. We went about our normal business, unaware of the storm that would break over our heads six months ahead.

January of 2008 slipped in quietly, with no hint of things that were to come. We were encouraged by our success and were making plans to continue along our same path. We felt we had a chance at paying off our debt in full with another good year like the last one. The egg business had enjoyed similar success through the just completed Christmas season and I was already planning for the Easter rush.

My website hit counter had logged almost 100,000 visits and I was considering starting a second flock. I had a good inventory from the first flock and could buy blown eggs for resale from farmers doing a similar backyard effort to mine, but it wasn't the same as raising the birds myself. I figured I could select all of the new birds for the beauty of their feathers and have an even greater range of feather inventory. I was beginning to market the feathers and they were selling regularly.

I missed my chickens. I imagined that the geese missed the chickens, but they showed no signs of even noticing that they were the sole poultry in the enormous pen. I had heard of an all-black duck, the Cayuga, that laid an all-black egg, and I knew that those would sell. I wanted to raise turkeys because their eggs and feathers and meat were all exceptional. We had a family meeting on the topic of a new flock.

"I could get turkeys," I began, "and we could have turkey dinner for Christmas and Thanksgiving."

"Like we planned to have goose dinner for Christmas and Thanksgiving?" Andrew asked innocently.

"I'm getting sick of ham," Blue offered (she was now ten years old).

"I like turkey!" Juno agreed, (she was now six).

"Well," I said, "we'd have to be a lot more dedicated to the dinner plan this time, but we could do it."

"I think we should have a new flock," Blue said, "because if we can't afford them, we can just eat them!"

And with that, I knew that at least some of the effort of the past years had been worth it. My babies were not suffering from my crippling urban guilt and had a comfortable practicality about where their food came from.

"Maybe we could try raising some rabbits for fur and for meat as well," I said, encouraged.

"Mommy, NO!" Blue and Juno cried in horrified unison.

We still had some distance to go.

So for the second time, I sat down with a hatchery catalog. The hatchery had changed with the times and their ordering process was more sophisticated, now online. I could enter the species I wanted and availability and delivery dates would pop up in response. My first choice of turkey breeds was the Standard Bronze, which was a heritage turkey breed – meaning less commercialized and less genetically modified. I learned to my great disappointment that they were not going to be available until late in the year. I wanted it for the spectacular color of its iridescent-tipped feathers. I settled for the Double-Breasted Bronze, and read the footnote that this breed of turkey, commercially popular for the amount of breast meat it yielded, could not be expected to reproduce on its own. I didn't plan to let the eggs hatch anyway so I accepted it. I also ordered some Bourbon Red turkeys, a straightforward heritage breed that had no footnotes.

I chose a wide variety of really beautiful chickens including some "top hat" varieties. My other choices all had elaborate and exciting names like Golden-Laced Wyandotte, Buff-Laced Polish, Blue Andalusian, Red-Laced Cornish. I was ordering early enough to get some Cuckoo Maran chickens, because I thought that the dark brown eggs they laid would sell like blown-egg hotcakes. The Cuckoo Maran only came in straight run, meaning a high likelihood of having roosters again, but because I was looking for feathers as much as for eggs, this was good news. Next to peacocks, roosters sport the most incredible feathers in the poultry world.

I was almost seduced by peacocks, but in the end I remembered the overwhelming work and learning effort from the first flock and ordered only about fifty birds: chickens, turkeys and ducks. Then, just to be a renegade, I threw in a request for Guinea Fowl. They wouldn't arrive until after the summer heat had abated. My flock was ordered and would arrive in six weeks.

Easter was a surprising bust for my website business. It was a sign of the impending crash that would begin to manifest soon in the nationwide economy, but I didn't realize it at the time. I was well stocked with blown eggs and had a wider variety of feathers ready than ever before, but sales were less than half of the previous year's total. Just as I was trying to tally up the disastrously small number of sales from the Easter 2008 egg-selling season, I received a surprising call on my home answering machine. A representative of the American Egg Board in Illinois wanted to know if I was interested in being New Mexico's State Egg Artist for 2009. I thought it was too oddly specific a call to be an advertisement or a prank, and frankly, I was excited about the idea. I had vaguely heard about the White House State Egg Collection from references within the egging community. I knew it was a huge honor to be selected to contribute a decorated egg on behalf of my state and immediately struggled with feelings of inadequacy. I'd never even submitted an egg to our own State Fair, or won any kind of egging contest. I hoped it wasn't a mistake but feared that it was.

Before I called her back, I looked up the American Egg Board on the Internet. It not only existed, but turned out to be a group funded by mandatory financial contributions from all egg producers over a certain size in the U.S. It was charged with lobbying Congress on behalf of chicken egg producers. The advertising campaign about "The Incredible Edible Egg" had come from them.

"I'd love to do the egg for New Mexico," I said, when I had the American Egg Board lady on the phone. "But I have to admit that I'm not in any egg-decorating clubs and I'm not really an established egg artist."

"Did you make the hinged eggs that you sell on your website?" she asked.

"Oh yes," I said. "I made them all."

"And that's not art?" she continued.

"Hold on," I said. "I want to tape this for my peanut gallery."

"Anyway," she went on, "we've selected different kinds of artists from New Mexico over the years, and you are totally qualified because you live in New Mexico and because I have chosen you."

"Isn't there some process that involves the State Fair or the Governor?" I asked.

"Not in New Mexico," she said. "Some states have their own selection process, but not yours."

"Then I'm in!" I said, delighted.

"Just a couple of cautions," she said, "we don't know if it is going to be held for sure because of the change in administration…"

"I understand," I said.

"And you can't do any publicity about it until after the presentation at the White House with the First Lady," she finished.

"White House?" I repeated. "First Lady?"

Was it actually possible that I was going to meet the First Lady as a result of my blown egg adventures? Was my life story truly going to be that wonderfully colorful? I might prefer getting my chance to pose for a picture with the First Spouse because of some kind of daring rescue, but I'd take the opportunity anyway. My little girls might see me invited to a ceremony at the White House because of a business I had started from scratch in our own backyard. That was something to be proud of.

The lady from the American Egg Board had seen my advertisement for my website *www.TheFeatheredEgg.com* in the International Egg Art Guild's quarterly journal while she was searching for artists. One egg from each state was presented in a collection to the First Lady at the White House each year near Easter, beginning in 1994. When the display was finished, the eggs went into permanent collections at the Presidential Libraries, under the care of the National Park Service. My little decorated egg could be rolling around the halls of Washington D.C. for decades to come. I made a mental note to put my name on it in some clear, distinct place.

I read the submission guidelines and deadlines carefully. The egg was due in November, but I marked my calendar a month in advance. I wasn't going to miss *this* deadline. It had to be a chicken egg, which explained the involvement of the American Egg Board. Their website described their mission "to promote the consumption of chicken eggs, egg products, and spent fowl." ("Spent fowl?") The egg had to be decorated in a way somehow representative of New Mexico. I started thinking aliens, dinosaurs, roasted chile, mesas, Indian tribes, smashing atoms, clouds in blue sky, covered wagons, conquistadors, and unspayed dogs.

There was a chance I'd be able to go to the unveiling ceremony, if there was one, and be photographed shaking hands with the First Lady. The Egg Board was clear that I'd have to pay my own way, but I could bring up to three

members of my immediate family. I mentioned to my mom
that I'd be tempted to sneak in some rabbit ear fingers during
the photo with the First Lady, because wouldn't that be funny,
and she mentioned in reply that she'd seriously disown me
if I tried to rabbit ear the First Lady. I gave up on the idea
after further reflecting that I'd probably get shot by the Secret
Service, and got to work decorating the egg.

Money was flowing from our income-producing efforts,
except for the Easter egg sales, but we had also stepped up
our lives to accommodate school, parties, ski trips to the
tantalizingly close Santa Fe ski basin, and dance lessons. We
were a more recognizable part of society now. We were still
carrying a typical American debt load, although we were close
to our goal of achieving zero. We had far too little savings,
but with the pitifully low interest rate savings accounts were
earning, it seemed far smarter to pay down our debt instead.
Life was busy and I felt more like a normal mom, only I
had a flock and a strange little almost-successful business. I
would consider it a success when it earned me a paycheck, so
while I waited for my new flock to arrive in the mail, I spent
the time attending free classes hosted by a city-funded small
business education service.

The chicken chicks, ducklings, and turkey poults arrived
within two days of each other at the end of March 2008. It
was right in the middle of the school Spring Break, and so
my excited little girls were able to go with me to collect the
peeping packages. Although it was not in the middle of the
night, we went in our pajamas to celebrate the moment. The
morning post office shift called just at the start of business

hours, and we were thumping the big red button on the loading dock door forty-five minutes later.

This time, we built brooders on the floor of the workshop so that the chicks would have more room. Andrew had constructed four square plywood boxes with hinged wire tops, and we hung the heat lamps on long chains from the ceiling. With about four inches of fresh clean woodchips, feeders and waterers ready to go, it looked like a cozy place to grow. The lids were covered with chicken wire, but the cats began to lie on the wire and dangle razor-loaded paws down into the chick spaces even before the birds arrived. We spent some additional time adding smaller gauge wire to the lids. For some reason, despite having set up the brooder in our cathouse of a workshop, we didn't see this coming. It brought back memories of our experience with our first flock, and all the last-minute construction emergencies. We thought we had finished with newbie-farmer mistakes with the construction of the chicken pen doorway too small to fit a wheelbarrow, but felt a new era of education coming on as we watched the cats loll on the wire under the heat lamps, blocking the warmth from the brooders below.

Thirty chicken chicks, ten ducklings, fifteen turkey poults, plus the inevitable extra chick or two in each order all made their way into their proper boxes and began to make a colossal mess of the furnishings. We had newspaper on top of the wood shavings for the first day, to encourage the birds to eat food and drink water instead of filling themselves with wood shavings. The Cayuga ducklings were indeed all-black. They were matte black, and fuzzy with their black down, so they absorbed light like black velvet and were difficult to examine under anything less than direct sunlight. We scooped them up and took them out of the shop to inspect them more closely.

The turkey poults looked much like the chicken chicks, only taller and more solid. The three different breeds, Double-Breasted Bronze, Blue Slate, and Bourbon Red, all had distinctly different personalities. I corralled the girls into helping me take some studio photos of the chicks on a makeshift table I had draped with a backdrop cloth. Juno was the chick catcher and Blue was the chick passer, as well as the shortstop, catching chicks that launched themselves from my set.

The different kinds of chicks were all very different in front of the camera. The ducks were a pain, as ducks always are, but they got away with it because they were so very cute. The Bourbon Red poults dozed off under the hot lights, but the Double-Breasted Bronze attacked the camera lens. The Blue Slate simply walked in circles like little wind-up toys.

I vividly remembered the last time I brooded up a bunch of chicks, and how I kept overheating them. The farmer's rule of thumb is that if the chicks are huddled together under the light, they are too cold, so hang the heat lamp closer to them. If they are all spread out in the corner of the brooder they are too hot, so raise it up. Just right is an even spacing of chicks everywhere under the light. I had hoped that with a bigger floor space I could simply hang the light and walk away. They could either get under it, or get far enough away when it was too hot. However the spring temperature range of our New Mexico March defeated me once again.

In the middle of the night, which dipped just below

freezing, they were piled under the hot spot so tightly they threatened to smother each other. In the middle of the clear sunny day, they were all climbing the plywood walls to escape the heat, or crowding under anything that made shade in the little brooder. So once again, I had to raise and lower the lights like a semaphore, fussing and worrying over chick dispersal night and day. Thinking I would outsmart the weather and the chicks, I put a thermometer in the brooder so that I could keep the temperature range on track based on this visual reference. That way, I could mark the height of the lamp when the thermometer read ninety to ninety-five degrees and create a standard placement based on the time of day. I was very pleased with myself for my technological solution.

The chicks promptly pooped on the thermometer and then fell asleep on it, which took care of technology, and I was back to checking on them day and night and waving lights around. Maybe farmer's rules of thumb work better for someone with farmer's hands.

During the first week after the chicks' arrival, in addition to photographing all of them one by one, I also cleaned brooders, replaced water (with electrolytes and terramycin for the ducks, who were sneezing), re-hung brooder lights, filled and cleaned feeders, unpasted the chick's bottoms, cleaned up boxes left to blow around the property while being "saved" for recycling, removed the leg bands from the ducks that marked them as females, washed a week's worth of dishes, put everything back in its place for the fourth time in twenty-four hours, fed the cats three times, fed the girls four times, moved three bags of feed, did the goose water, collected eggs, washed eggs, and yelled a lot (despite my vow to stop yelling).

One of the Mallard ducklings was impossibly small and perfect. She was half the size of the other tiny ducklings and wasn't eating. One of the turkey poults was motoring around like a little truck, just cruising figure eights in the brooder and also not eating. They expired, so the girls and I organized a funeral. We carried them in procession to the peace garden (named more poetically than The Pit, that hole in the ground which every poultry farm has). After the funeral, we all went back to the brooders to admire the remaining chicks. The hatchery had included two extra ducklings, so we were still well stocked with ducks, but Andrew was troubled over the death of the tiniest duckling.

"Can't you get your money back if a duckling dies within twenty-four hours?" he asked.

"Yes," I said. "But why would I ask for that when they already included two extra ducklings for free?"

"Because one died and it wasn't your fault," he said.

"But I ordered ten ducklings, and I got twelve ducklings and I still have eleven ducklings," I said.

"But maybe the one that died wasn't one of the free ones," he said.

"I really hope you are applying a different kind of logic with your construction clientele," I said.

He eventually turned out to be right. The duckling that died was one of the females, in an order where I had paid extra for all females. The two extra ducklings were male, although I couldn't tell that at the time. I still wasn't interested in hounding the hatchery for a refund, but it later dawned on me that Andrew's very strange logic processes regarding the ducks, and years ago, the geese, had all turned out to be correct - even though they had sounded outrageously strange at the time.

The feed store people knew me by now because I had been in every week buying enormous bags of expensive feed and causing them to adjust their weekly factory order upward.

"You have ducks, don't you?" asked the Feed Store Lady, one day soon after the chicks arrived.

"I do!" I said enthusiastically. "Mallard, and Rouen, and Cayuga. The Cayuga are totally black. All black, feet and faces and everything..." but she had glazed over.

"There's one duckling left for sale here," she said. "The other one died last night, and it's all alone."

Ah, I thought. An orphan duckling, possibly diseased. Another beak to feed.

"Is it female?" I asked, thinking of the egg sales.

"I don't know," she said. "I can give you a good deal."

I didn't look very happy.

"I can give it to you for free," she said.

Brimming full moon eyes peered up at me from somewhere around my waist. My daughters were listening to every word.

"Mommy!" whispered voices of compassionate innocence. "He's all *alone!*"

Dammit. I thought. He had better be a girl.

Andrew was just as pleased as I was.

"What's in that box?" he said,

"A duck," I said shortly, and turned up Britney's "You-Want-A-Piece-Of-Me?" on the stereo. The girls insisted on naming the duckling. It was a White Pekin. In its youth it was bright yellow, the yellow down would turn white once the feathers came in.

"Let's call it Mercy," I suggested, "because it was a pity duck, and we were merciful taking it home."

"We want to call him Lasty," said the girls, "because he was the Last!"

"I'm not calling him Lasty," I declared.

Andrew fiddled with the stereo and said he was looking for the new track from the band "Control Freak."

"All right," I said, irritably, "how about Mercy Lasty, and I'm not really asking, you dig?"

Mercy Lasty was gigantic. For one thing he, or she, was an old duckling having been in the feed store for three weeks before I came along. My other ducklings were not only younger, but all smaller breeds. Mercy Lasty was going to have to wait to be introduced to the other ducklings, giving them a chance to get bigger so he wouldn't hurt them. (I should say, at this time, that it is a patently bad idea to introduce a feed store duckling to a flock that came from a different hatchery due to the possible transmission of a book full of diseases. However, I did it, and it was fine.)

In the meantime, Mercy Lasty also grew…. enormously. A couple of weeks later, it was time to give Mercy Lasty some company. He had bravely suffered through his isolation, but could hear the other ducklings and spent most of his time at the brooder corner closest to the unseen companions. I scooped up six of the largest other ducklings and plopped them in with DuckZilla. The effect was immediate. Mercy Lasty rushed over to the other ducklings, brimming with delight and relief. The other ducklings stampeded away from him squawking with terror and revulsion. Round and round the brooder they went until I couldn't stand it anymore, and the girls and I reached in and held them all down. We gathered them together, scratching and bleating and wiggling away.

"They HATE him!" my daughters cried.

"It's like they are the Mean Girls," said my observant eldest. "They won't let him be in their club because he looks so different!"

And so it was. The Clique spent three days shunning Mercy Lasty, who tried and tried to join them. On the fourth day, we came up to the brooders to find Mercy Lasty blissing in a pile of sisterhood. They'd let him in, and it was good. The only better ending to Mercy's story would be if I could say he eventually laid an egg, and when he turned five months old, she did.

Chapter Eighteen

The turkey poults arrived within a week of the other chicks, in April of 2008. They acted very differently from the chicken chicks, even though they had initially looked similar. They slept together under the heat lamp with their long necks intertwined. As they got bigger, they began to run around the brooder in bursts of speed, triggered by nothing I could see. I knew that turkeys had a reputation for being stupid, but I was not willing to accept that as fact until I had observed it for myself. So I decided they must have a reason for suddenly running full speed into the side of the brooder. For instance, maybe they could sense that there was space between the atoms of the particleboard in the brooder walls. Maybe they just didn't yet know the limits of their growing bodies.

The darkly striped poults, which I decided were the Double-Breasted Bronze because they immediately grew twice as large as the others, seemed to spend a lot of time on their backs with legs paddling in the air. They were unable to roll over until I flipped them upright with a stick. I thought maybe they did that because the brooder was too hot and they were becoming disoriented, so I raised the light until they piled on top of each other in discomfort. I lowered the light, and over they went. Not all of them, just one or two at a time. It began to get annoying and I feared for the life of the flipped-over poults, and I couldn't understand why they couldn't get back on their feet. I put other chicks on their backs, and they twisted to the side and stood right up. I also noticed that it was only the Double-Breasted Bronze chicks that were having this problem.

The cats watched from lazy poses on the wire. They had learned by now to lie only at the edge of the turkey brooder because the turkeys were tall enough to reach the wire lid when standing on their waterers, which they did often enough to tip them over regularly. Turkeys don't have teeth, or even serrated beaks like geese, but they didn't need them. Their nips were enough to gain them a mouthful of cat, so there was a tension around the turkey brooder that was absent elsewhere. The cats, however, were in their element with chicks to watch, heat lamps to bask under, and mice attracted to the brooders in increasing numbers.

New Mama Cat had dropped her litter just a couple of weeks before the chicks arrived, so as I tended the brooders, she tended her kittens in a box high on a shelf near the ceiling. I climbed up to the cat nest to count the kittens. There were five, all little miniatures of their brother/fathers. They were nearing the time that she would bring them out and teach them to hunt. They hissed at me and arched their miniature backs. I noticed that there was a tiny unhappy live mouse in the nest, unwisely snuggled up to the rear end of a kitten. I climbed back down and tried to walk away. Not my problem, none of my business. This is how kittens learn to be barn cats, which is exactly what I wanted.

But I couldn't get to the door. I couldn't get the mouse out of my head. I felt far more identified with the mouse than I did with the kittens – he was in a jam and I was in a position to do something about it. Even though I knew that one mouse carried the ability to fill two acres with more mice in a very short period of time, I went back and let him go. My grand immediate reward was the opportunity to test more antifungal ointments on any part of my skin that had touched the kittens. The ringworm persisted through every effort I made to eradicate it. But I did it because it sucks to be the mouse.

Because of the turkey poult gymnastics, I began staying out at the trailer every day, instead of going back and forth from our home base in town. I timed my errands and bird feed runs to coincide with the end of school, so that I could pick up the girls at the end of the week and bring them home with me. Andrew would come a day later with his truck and tools, ready for a weekend of tuning up the pens for the chicks' eventual release. Each drive, I tried to interest the girls in telling me what they had learned in school that day.

"What did you learn in school today?" I asked Juno

"Can I take my shoes off, Mama?" Juno replied.

"I'd rather you kept them on," I answered, "because you will need them when we get to the trailer."

"But my feet are HOT, Mama!" Juno cried. "They are burning OFF!"

"All right then," I caved. "Take them off."

"Hey!" I exclaimed, a minute later. "What's that smell?

Your feet are stinky!"

Juno was silent for a moment, wriggling her bare toes in delight.

"Deal widdit mo-ther!" she suddenly shouted. "Deal wid my FEET!"

"And is that what you learned in school today?" I demanded, aghast.

"Smell it!" Juno crowed. "Smell my FEET!"

"Kindergarten," said Blue in disgust, "they teach them terrible stuff."

When we got home, we found another dark-striped turkey poult flipped over under the heat lamp. I trained the girls to push it over with a long stick. I now had a routine of going up to the pens every two hours to flip the chicks back over and felt that I couldn't leave the brooders for even half a day. It was becoming ridiculous, and I wondered if something was wrong with my brooder space. It finally occurred to me that it might be the same little turkey flipping over each time, so I got a permanent marker and drew an X on the belly of the next one I found turtled. Then I flipped it and returned to my daily chores. The next time I went up to the brooders, it was over again, legs waving and big black X mark clearly visible. It was the same chick.

The girls and I flipped him over four more times that evening, an acceleration of his instability, and I expected he'd be dead by morning. I had ordered fifteen turkeys because that was the minimum required by the hatchery, even though I didn't really want fifteen turkeys — especially not with their projected seventy-five pounds of feed in their four to one conversion ratio over eighteen weeks to a market weight of twenty-five to thirty pounds. But I still didn't like losing chicks, even the defective ones. Their little deaths littered the avenues of my heart.

I went to the Internet and searched for any information on baby turkeys falling over and not being able to get up. As I read, I began to see that other turkey farmers were experiencing the same thing. One thread suggested it was related to the heat lamp, but I had already experimented with that and almost killed the chicks by making the brooder too cold. There was another suggestion that it was caused by delayed leg coordination on one side, or more time needed in the incubator after hatching, or too slippery a brooder surface, or too high a protein in the feed causing too fast growth and lack of coordination. I could feel that I was close, but just needed the proper keywords to solve the mystery. I typed and typed as the girls slept.

"Turkey fell over and can't get up," (Nothing from the Oracle that was Google's search engine)

"Turkey baby on its back," (zip)

"Turkey poult feet in the air," (A little movement on the word *Poult*)

"Poult flipped on its back, can't get up" A hit! The words "poult" and "flip" brought me into some scientific-looking weird sites full of tiny text. I searched for those two words in the tiny text and found a reference to EPF, so I went back to the search engine.

"What is EPF?" I typed, and there it was: "Early Poult Flipover disease." It was a disease.

I was shocked. A disease that led to this silly and life-threatening behavior? I finally found an article that answered my questions, even though it took an hour of hard reading. It was a dense thesis authored by a committee funded through an agricultural research grant and destined for a readership deep inside the commercial poultry industry. I discovered that my problem with my turkey poult was also a problem for large-scale turkey growers using commercially enhanced turkey breeds, like the Double Breasted Bronze or its' non-bronze double-breasted white-feathered cousin. The disease was never seen in the heritage turkey breeds. The thickly worded thesis suggested that the problem was deep inside the DNA of the turkeys.

Apparently, the problem showed up in commercial turkey breeds a while ago, was genetically linked, and proved difficult to breed out of the lines because it appears along with the biggest, fastest growing, commercially attractive turkeys. A stopgap measure by the turkey industry was to hire a bunch of guys with sticks to go several times a day through the turkey poults and flip them back over on their feet. In flipping our turkey poults several times a day, my girls were actually training for a real job.

The article cited studies that indicated a one-in-three chance that a chick exhibiting EPF would spontaneously expire as an older bird, with no apparent cause of death (perhaps except that its' DNA was in the shape of a four-leaf clover instead of a spiral?). The treatise ended with a paragraph claiming that a solution for breeding EPF out of the genetic lines of commercial turkeys would be greeted with great appreciation. In the meantime, I guessed "Turkey Poult Flipper Backer Over-er" would remain an industry job description.

I was not pleased. The only reason I had settled for these Double-Breasted Bronze turkey chicks was because the heritage version of the breed, the Standard Bronze, was sold out. It was becoming more obvious by the week why it was sold out. The one commercial turkey breed I had settled for was already costing me more time and concern than the heritage turkey breeds.

The flipping little chick seemed happy enough. Then he died, problem solved, heart sore. We made another procession to the peace garden.

In the first week of May, the weather was warm during the day and often below freezing at night. Storms rolling through were mild. I needed to be out at the property every day to care for the chicks and with gas prices at almost four dollars a gallon, I couldn't afford to drive back and forth to the family. I was torn between my responsibilities to my girls and Andrew, and my preoccupation with conditions in the brooders. When the much-needed rains came in, I acquired another obstacle to joining my family in town.

Two or three days in a row of rain were certain to create the worst conditions on the funky little road that led to our home. Andrew and I had been trying to convince the neighbors that we could all work together to fix it, but only one or two were interested. It was not enough to make the road better. The road had never been properly constructed and there were now triple the number of neighbors in the area. It had started as a couple of tire tracks that led from the county road to the first populated house two decades ago. Since then, as the traffic increased, the tire tracks had deepened and widened until the lowest and widest spot in the area collected rainwater like a fishpond. The hard-packed dirt turned into fudge-soft mud with a surprisingly small amount of rain. It was a classic Northern New Mexico road, and I drove it like a classic Northern New Mexican, fast and with a lot of Hail Marys in a two-wheel-drive car.

The key to getting through was to go into it with enough forward momentum so that the deep ruts acted like the rails for a train, compensating for the lack of steering. But if the mud was too soft, I would run the risk of getting high-centered in my low clearance car and so I had to try to hydroplane over the mud, which was also a function of speed. Overall, safe passage depended on having the guts to go at it with recklessly high velocity and successfully manage the crazy fishtailing.

At the beginning of the road, drivers had to make a quick decision between right and left because a pole sat in the middle of the track for no reason at all. When the rains came, I had to choose between a side with a water-filled mud hole in the middle, or the high center adventure to the right. One day I tried to choose the adventure because the water-filled pool was bigger than my whole car. But I went into an unexpected slide and lost all my momentum. I slid to a stop facing the wrong way for anything. I sat a moment, reflecting on how many times I had fought with this road; how much effort we had put into trying to convince the neighbors to pool funds to fix it. Only two of them had chipped in and it hadn't been enough to do the whole road. I was getting mad and that was good because I was going to need to let it all hang out to get my car home from here.

My first task was to get the car headed in another direction, any other direction. So I gunned the motor while I held the emergency brake and threw my body weight against my door. Because the car was small and I was large, this was tremendously effective and I managed to slide the car back until it pointed in the right direction. The engine whine was earsplitting and I knew that the neighbors, who had all decided that the road was fine the way it was, would be gathering at their windows to watch the show. I was finally lined up and now rim deep in the soft mud.

I started rocking, first/reverse plus a butt shimmy in my seat because it actually did make a difference. I walked the tires to the right, then to the left, trying to catch any traction hidden in the mud. Two dogs from the closest house took this opportunity to start barking at my window, which was at their chest level by that time. I watched with satisfaction as I hosed them with a particularly good mud rooster-tail. A tire shimmied up over the edge of the rut and onto a bush.

With more engine whining and tire spinning, I hooked my front bumper on a rock, and then spun until I stalled the engine. But with that pivot point, I was able to restart the car and swing with more tire-spinning and engine-gunning until another tire was up on the edge of the rut. It was all about not giving up and trying not to count the cost to the transmission.

Finally, I got over the rock and onto the weedy median, then abandoned the road and bumped overland until I reached the properly graded section that we had paid to fix. That part was perfectly dry and safe despite exposure to the same weather as the rest of the track. I went triumphantly home with enough mud in my undercarriage to affect the alignment. There were also mud clots on the handles on every door and I had to sluice off the windshield with buckets of water.

Most people in our area either didn't drive in weather like this, or invested in a four-wheel-drive vehicle. But I had chicks to look after and only the small passenger car to do it in, so I was the one braving the road most frequently. The new ruts I had dug into the bad road exacerbated the whole issue. After this legendary experience, I stopped trying to commute to my family, and started to do my mothering by phone.

Back in the brooders, the chicks were getting big, the turkeys were getting restless, and the ducks were already out. I had decided to let the ducks out early because they could take it and because they were so messy. They had spent their brooder time playing in their water, sleeping in their feed, and using their torpedo-shaped rear ends to great effect at regular intervals. Ducks tend to stampede without provocation, and these girls were no exception. On their first day out, three of them failed to make the turn around the chicken house and went beak-first into the wire, where they stayed. There was some delay in freeing them because I was laughing so hard I almost hurt myself.

I was pet-sitting that week, so one guest dog created a threesome when added to my own dog plus the neighbor dog. I walked to the workshop from the trailer in a knee-slamming pack, and I felt like She-Who-Walks-With-Wolves. They were all quite well behaved because I was now on my seventh dog, having had each one for its whole life (although some of those lives were heart-breakingly short), and I had figured out how to manage myself in the pack. This consisted of tolerating no goofy stuff at all, something I had yet to apply to human parenting. But then again, I got more mileage out of being firm and consistent with the dogs than I did with the kids because I could employ methods with the dogs that were somewhat illegal with the kids.

The newest kittens were down from their nest, getting used to their suddenly long legs, and were piled in the cat bed under their own heat lamp. This new bed was supposed to encourage them not to sleep on the chick brooders and block the heat lamps. The dog pack faced off with the cat herd and there was lots of posturing and noise, but anyone getting aggressive got a feed bag between the eyes, so it was all dancing, like an animal version of West Side Story.

I started to feel like Mother Earth incarnate, surrounded by the purring, licking, padding, wagging, bumping, hugging, cheeping activities of all these different species. I enjoyed the moment. It was precious and precarious and impermanent and hard-won. A moment of simple pleasure in a life that was not simple at all to achieve, only simple to enjoy.

Chapter Nineteen

$\mathcal{B}$y the end of May, after several weeks of staying at the trailer and avoiding the road, it was time to put all of the chicks into the big pen. I waited until the whole family was home, then we carried them in one by one. The turkeys were now big enough that Juno couldn't carry one on her own. We put the chicks down in the chicken house, intending that they would first learn where the shelter was and then explore the large covered pen. For several evenings after that, I went out and herded them into the chicken house at dusk until they started to go in on their own.

The turkeys refused to sleep under shelter, and the heritage Bourbon Red and Blue Slate breeds got surprisingly far up on the wooden posts and tree branches to roost for the night, revealing that they were competent flyers. The release went well and the chickens and turkeys ignored each other completely. There were no fights and they all looked healthy and happy. The chicks we suspected were roosters began to crow immediately, sounding a little immature and strangled, but triumphant.

One week after all of the birds were out of the brooder, the turkeys went back in. I had seen some foamy yellow poo in the pen and traced it to the turkeys. Because I was raising my turkeys with my chickens, I lived in dutiful fear of Coccidosis, also known as Blackhead Disease. Almost everyone I knew out here who had poultry was raising chickens and turkeys together, but I seemed to be the only one freaking on the fear of disease. Poultry literature is unanimous on the subject of keeping chickens and turkeys together on the farm. It is a resounding "Don't." The advice is so dire and serious; you'd think that chickens and turkeys, when mixed, spontaneously ignite into balls of roasting fire.

The reason behind the furor is a protozoa, Histamonosis, which causes Blackhead. Chickens carry the bug and turkeys die of the disease. The best cure for Blackhead used to be wicked cool drugs with names like dimetridazole, furazolidone, or nifursol. These were very effective but are all now emphatically banned for use in the U.S. Considering what I know about animal husbandry practices in our food industry, they must have been very heinous substances indeed.

Being an internet-trained poultry farmer with no practical hands-on experience with turkeys, I watched my poults poo the most spectacularly sloppy, frothy, imaginative poos and wondered if I was witnessing Blackhead disease. While the birds did not have many of the actual symptoms of Blackhead, like depression, lack of appetite, stunted growth, or blue heads, I also didn't know what turkey poo was supposed to look like. In my opinion, it looked awful.

My organic farmer neighbor friend suggested a dose of healing clay, mixed to a soupy sludge so the turkey didn't choke. He swore by it. I just swore. I don't know how much the clay helped in the end, but I decided that if it was this hard to get it down the turkey's gullet, then the turkeys couldn't be that sick. A real diagnosis of Blackhead disease would have required me to kill and gut one of my birds and inspect the liver for lesions, but this did not gel with my zero fatality goals. Also, I am not an Augur or a soothsayer and didn't that go out with the Roman gods anyway? I called my local vet with the foamy poo story and he wanted to help.

"But I'm really more of a horse man than a chicken man," he said.

"I think I have to do something, man," I said.

"Well," he said, thinking out loud, "Flagyl is a broad spectrum worm killer, so it might help, and it probably wouldn't hurt."

I confined the turkeys back in their brooder with waterers full of flagyl for five days. Their poos improved, but their mood didn't. They were much too big for the brooder spaces now and were showing proof of their direct ancestry to Tyrannosaurs by the time I released them back into the main pen.

Back in the pen, the alarming poos returned, so I dosed everyone with a broad-spectrum antibiotic, throwing my organic mission off track in favor of retaining the birds for future organic lives. It was sort of like fishing with dynamite. I never knew if I really was fighting Blackhead, but all of the birds perked up with the tetracycline. Except for one hen, that died. There always seemed to be one.

Summer drove away the cold nights and all of the new

birds settled happily into the pens. There was far less trouble than we had experienced with our first flock, mainly because we had fewer birds and only three species. The ducks lived with the geese. We had initially been apprehensive that the geese would hurt the ducks due to competition for food, but the ducks took over the pen immediately. The geese were relegated to whatever portion of the large space the ducks didn't want at the time.

The turkeys grew quickly, but the Double-Breasted Bronze turkeys grew extraordinarily quickly. The tom turkey was enormous and staggered around doing his best to stay upright. Watching him struggle just to live, I voodoo'd the people responsible for mucking with this poor bird's DNA and wished them a return life spent as a Double-Breasted Bronze Turkey. That seemed fair. In the meantime, there was nothing I could do for him. The tom turkey walked on broken toes, injuries he incurred just by walking around the rocky pen. His toes would heal eventually and crookedly and he would probably break them again. He was simply too big and too clumsy.

As soon as he approached maturity, he began to try and mount the Double-Breasted Bronze hens. He probably tried to mount all the hens, but only the Double-Breasted Bronze hens were too slow to get out of his lumbering way. One hen suffered spinal damage from his attentions and we had to euthanize her. It was beyond frustrating and also difficult since she was also huge. Someone had failed to alert these turkeys of their catalog footnote, the one that foretold their inability to reproduce on their own. They may not be ultimately successful, but they still gave it a try, and that was the source of more injuries.

In contrast, the heritage turkeys danced around like ballerinas, flew like fighter jets with bad control modules, and played like cranes. They were beautiful, athletic, sociable (though I suspected their willingness to get close to me involved a plot to pluck out my eyes), and fascinating. Side-by-side with the Double-Breasted, the differences were glaringly obvious. They were one-third the bulk of the Bronze, and could take care of themselves much more effectively. I vowed to never again settle for a commercial breed, but in the meantime, I was stuck with my unfortunate Double-Breasted Bronze turkeys.

As soon as I began to feel overwhelmed by my farming tasks, a feeling that coincided with the beginning of my farming tasks, I immediately understood why farming families have so many children. It isn't about philosophy or religion, or even a historically high attrition rate in rural infants; it's because children are tools.

I contemplated agricultural expansion on my two little acres and found myself wishing, for the first and last time in my life, that I'd had more children. It was too late anyway, I'd had myself spayed, but how handy three or four more would be! Especially when trying to compare the rising price of feed to the availability of natural forage. I tried to figure out how to range the geese on the riparian plenty growing down by the edge of the river, outside the pens. Somebody would have to continually watch over them, for their safety and to keep them in the area. Goose Girl, I understood the concept now.

My girls were expert chicken-catchers by this time, but as the chickens were also expert girl-evaders, it still took a while to move the birds between the pens when I was trying to segregate the turkeys for more doses of poo de-foamer. The girls had their favorite chickens and they were the first to point out the fact that the Golden Wyandotte hens pecked like roosters. Those hens had better not BE roosters, because I had ordered all hens in that species. The Polish chickens were so helpless under their veil of feathers, largely blinded but apparently deafened too, that they spent most of their time being played with like dolls. Unable to run away in a straight line, they were the easiest to catch and therefore had to put up with it.

When there were birds to be caught or herded, or eggs to be collected, the girls were put to work. Blue very impressively cleaned out the floor brooders almost on her own, which was a significant job: twenty square feet of soiled wood chips scraped a shovel-full at a time into the waiting compost cans. True, it was a consequence (we called them consequences, rather than punishments, because we subscribed to several parenting magazines and followed the advice in the side bars), as I had caught her watching television when she was supposed to be idyllically playing outside in the ninety-eight degree summer heat of a Saturday, but still, she did a good job.

Juno, during the great butchering of last year, had turned out to be a great feather plucker. She was willing to stop poking at a dead chicken's head and tongue long enough to delicately pluck feathers as directed. She didn't seem to balk over the task like more experienced chicken butchers did, and was able to sort the feathers at a pretty good rate of speed. Both girls were gaining proficiency in all the routine household tasks like making my bed (as well as their own, of course).

The girls were in the long school slide toward summer. Field trips, parties, and performances punctuated their school days. Andrew had been taking care of their evening routine for so long that I was out of practice, but he was working longer and longer hours to try and bring in the same amount of income, and I had bedtime duty now. My version of a bath was dipping them like teabags in hot water, but they were thriving.

June 2008 and the end of the school year arrived with record high gas prices. At $4.14 a gallon, everything we paid money for was going up. I had originally intended to sell some of the turkeys once they were out of the brooders, and so I did. Because feed prices were the highest I had ever seen them, I decided to sell most of them, keeping only a core group of Bourbon Reds and the disastrous Bronze. I was determined to stay within my planned budget with the bird business this time around. I hadn't planned for gas prices like this or for all of the other price hikes that came with it. With great regret, I cancelled my order for Guinea Fowl chicks.

The news media began to report stories of people having to choose between filling their gas tanks and paying their bills. Stock prices took such dramatic tumbles that it was the main topic of conversation, even among those of us who didn't fully understand the far reaching implications of a 4% fall in a single day. We also didn't understand the consequences of the failure of some of the biggest mortgage lenders in the industry, The Federal National Mortgage Association (FNMA) Fannie Mae and Freddie Mac.

The economic crumble was beginning, but these indicators were not obvious enough for us to fully realize what was happening. We adjusted our lives in response, but a cold knot of misgiving took up residence in my stomach. It was costing me $15 round-trip each time I drove out to the trailer from our home base in town, and so we split our time as a family between the two locations. Andrew's work was primarily in town. I kept the girls with me on the property to care for the birds and dog. We adjusted our priorities and changed our habits. As gas prices began to affect our grocery bill and anything we were buying retail, we began to buy less. Andrew had to adjust his bids for the skyrocketing cost of fuel and supplies. The cost of concrete more than tripled, and the bids began to get rejected at a higher rate. Andrew's clients began to wave their tumbling stock statements at him as they regretfully pulled their request for a bid or simply backed out of the contracts.

Sales on my website slowed to a trickle, but they often did in the summer as all the crafters went outside to play. As the chickens approached their magical fifth month and the beginning of their first laying season, the girls and I prepared, against all reason, for a road trip to visit both sets of grandparents. The trip had been planned the previous winter and the grandparents were paying the fuel bill, arguing that it was still less expensive than trying to fly when aviation fuel costs were also skyrocketing. Andrew would stay behind to work and care for the flock. We drove away in our air-conditioned car as July brought in the full summer heat.

I had promised the girls that we would break up the long drive by stopping at all of the concrete dinosaurs that ranged I-40 on the way to California and Nevada. By the first evening of our road trip, we realized that the dinosaurs had gone through a second mass extinction. They were gone. The pay-for-entry park that built them out of concrete and rebar was out of business and dismantled. The girls were heartbroken. We chose our motel in the small mid-plains town of Holbrook because there was a graffiti-covered concrete tyrannosaurus morosely standing on a chipped stegosaurus in a field across the road. We were standing mournfully at the fence looking at the dinosaurs when a truck pulled up to the gate nearby.

"Do you want to see it?" called out a man in a cowboy hat at the wheel.

"Definitely!" I said, immediately hopping back in my car as he opened the gate and pulled forward. We slid in behind him.

"MOM!" Blue hissed in my ear.

"What? What?" I said.

"He's a Stranger!" she said.

"Yes," I admitted, "but he's a stranger with a dinosaur!"

"Mom!" Juno joined in, but distractedly, as she was getting her shoes on.

"You are right to be cautious," I told Blue, "but I think it'll be all right." I parked in the field and the girls ran full tilt to the dinosaurs.

"Do you own the dinosaur now?" I asked the man, helping him swing the gate back over a cattle grate.

"No," he said. "They just needed a place to put it while they figured out what to do, so I let them put it in my field."

He was about to latch the gate again when suddenly three more kid-filled cars materialized in front of the fence.

"Where did they come from?" I said, astonished. There had been nobody around when we had driven through.

"Happens every time," the man said, and opened the gate wide again.

The dinosaurs were quickly surrounded by as big a crowd as we had ever seen at an I-40 roadside attraction. It was hard to get a good photo of the girls, who wanted to pretend to have fallen back in time. They posed in positions of terror under the concrete monsters.

"You can take the poky bits out of the picture, right mom?" Blue asked, pointing to some protruding rebar.

"And the bad words, wight?" Juno said.

"How do you know they're bad words?" I asked, trying to decipher them myself, then wishing I hadn't.

"Blue tol' me," Juno said, despite dramatic attempts by Blue to hush her up.

"Stop using your reading powers for evil," I told Blue, but they had both disappeared again, behind a profanity-laced tail section.

We snapped plenty of pictures then pulled away, thanking the man in the truck. He was patiently parked in the shadow of a billboard while more people posed with the dinosaur. He had rescued our road trip theme.

I was frankly relieved to be on the road and headed toward some built-in babysitting. We hadn't seen any of our family members since the previous Easter and the girls had many skills and accomplishments they wanted to show off. It wasn't anywhere near Easter now, in late summer, but because we had the egg business, Easter was our favorite holiday. We were bringing a belated Easter-In-A-Box to this family gathering. The girls had decorated eggs and created new Easter baskets for the grandparents in anticipation.

The previous visit had gone pretty well, so I had optimistic hopes for this one.

Andrew called us on our second night on the road to report the first chicken egg, and we all danced in our seats doing seventy-five miles an hour in the direction away from the chicken. Once again, the chickens were two weeks shy of their twenty week birthday and already laying. My rooster fears were realized. We had expected five at the most, but Andrew reported nine confirmed roosters. One of the Red-Laced Cornish was a rooster, which was disappointing at first, but he eventually grew the most amazing hackle feathers to make up for it. Andrew reported that the nine roosters were crowing just before dawn and I thought of my neighbor, whose bedroom window was much closer to the pens than my own. Andrew went on to say that the roosters were crowing at dawn, then in the mid-morning, and again at noon. They crowed in the early afternoon, at happy hour, and in the early evening. When they also began to crow in the middle of the night, he realized that rooster stew was going to be our favorite summer dish.

His last message, before we entered our destination town and heavy traffic, was that a Cayuga hen laid the first duck egg of the season, and it was indeed black. Until she rolled it around in the straw for a while, and the black rubbed off. It turned out to be a fragile coating over an otherwise normal white egg, and Andrew saw that we were going to have to struggle to keep the black eggs saleable. But saleable they were. I listed them over the Internet while we were still on our trip and Andrew did the blowing and packing.

The news on the motel TV was all about rescuing mortgage lenders and banks, and vilification of high-risk, low-income borrowers. I didn't hear anybody linking the failure of the lower middle class to pay their mortgages with the astronomical rise in gas prices over the last three years. With gas creeping up on $5 a gallon, even the regular middle class was starting to talk about having to make choices between filling the car and buying food. We had seen a 20 percent increase in expenses even with our retail shopping decrease and every debt statement that came to us in the mail had a bigger bottom line than before. News reports were doom-filled and I was looking forward to the temporary relief of our extended family.

While we were away, Andrew was supposed to be able to focus even more of his time on drumming up new leads for work. Although it was the height of the summer, he wasn't getting as many calls as in previous years, and the calls he was getting weren't resulting in successful bids. He seemed distracted when I called him from the road and I began to get annoyed that I couldn't keep his attention. I had hours of excellent cell service on three states worth of I-40, but he wasn't in the mood to chat. I felt the beginnings of unease regarding his business.

The girls were sporting a fresh case of ringworm contracted from a pair of shop kittens who had been abandoned by their mother. We had bottle-reared them, and then shifted them to the lap of another bleeding-heart lady who promised to find them a home. The cat mother, herself one of a shop-born litter, had disappeared, either tragically or irresponsibly once she figured out that the kittens weren't going to feed themselves.

The girls had been feeding them every couple of hours for weeks until the kittens looked like tennis balls with legs, and the girls looked, well, spotty.

"When we get to Grandma's house, don't tell them you have ringworm," I said, as we made it into the home stretch.

"Okay," said Blue, nodding wisely.

"Why not?" asked Juno.

"Because it sounds yucky," I said. "Say you have itchy bites."

"Itchy bites," Juno repeated.

"You better!" Blue said, squeezing Juno's arm.

"MOM!" Juno howled, as we pulled into the grandparental driveway.

Family poured out of the front door to welcome us and I felt a load drop from my shoulders. It was truly great to see them. Juno and Blue jumped down from the car and flung themselves into the loving waiting arms, red heads meeting fellow red heads with smiles all around. I breathed in relief as if starved of oxygen, just as Juno leaned back from a gigantic grandparent hug.

"I don't have wingworm!" she shouted.

"JUNO!" Blue and I groaned in unison.

"Well, you said not to tell them!" Juno retorted, almost in tears, "and so I said I *didn't.*"

The grandparents took a step back and I resigned myself to the realities of a family visit. The glory we would cover ourselves in wasn't the kind of glory I aspired to.

Chapter Twenty

$\mathscr{A}$ couple of weeks into the trip, Andrew stopped answering or returning my calls and I, in a less-than-attractive moment, accused him of treating his beloved contracting business like a mistress. I claimed he was giving it his best attention and all his passion. I was sending him about five emails to his one response.

"I'm here at YOUR parents' house," I wrote, "and you not only don't call me, but I can't get you to answer when I call. It's embarrassing!" and I sent him a digital photograph of my fully clothed rear end. I was entering a time in my life that I am not proud of.

In late August 2008, we started the drive home after our successful family visits and observed that gas prices had finally started to fall away from their $4 a gallon or more peak. But the damage was already done. More companies were failing, more stock accounts were tanking, and the concept of a business being "too big to fail" in a capitalist system was something I marveled over. Andrew greeted us as we pulled into the driveway. He looked a lot older to my eyes than the time away warranted. When our conversation inevitably turned to how the business was doing, as in how our sole means of support was faring, he told me with tired pride that he had a job in hand that was big enough to cover our bills. For at least a while.

"That's great!" I said. "We need to be careful to put the client deposit in a separate account, right?"

"Well," Andrew said. "There isn't actually a deposit."

"So the contract covers that issue then?" I asked.

"Um," Andrew said. "There isn't actually a contract."

"When is the first payment then?" I asked. "Don't tell me it's one of those thirty-day billing cycles."

"Actually," Andrew said. "I would get paid about sixty days after the first thirty-day regular inspection has been cleared."

I didn't say anything about this three-month delay before the first check would arrive and he started to look even older.

"There will be some up-front fees," he admitted. "I'm figuring that out."

"And a few interstate shipping insurance issues that I'm supposed to cover," he continued.

"This job sounds like a…"

"Don't say it!" he interrupted. "Think of the children."

Over several more reluctant conversations, Andrew revealed that his silence during the road trip was caused by his being overwhelmed at having every current contracting job on his books fall through; either stopped mid-work or canceled before it began. New bids were not being accepted, projects were being pulled from consideration, and by the time summer ended he had only one possible income source at hand: the job I did not like.

We had never seen this kind of collapse. We'd had years where we went one job at a time, scratching for the next contract, but never a year when there was no next contract. Andrew started marketing efforts he had never done before and although he received friendly responses, he received no work. A cascade effect of realtors, architects, subcontractors, and designers having no work to pass on had begun. Many contractors reported that they were working their last job in sight and asked, in return, if Andrew had any job leads.

By September, my weekly feed bill topped $75 a month and I faced the fact that I had to reduce the number of birds in the pens. The geese were first on my list, but I couldn't stand the idea of butchering them. It was hard enough to accept that they had to go, I just couldn't kill them. Not only would butchering be hard work and traumatic for both the birds and for me, but I also didn't think I could handle nine goose carcasses destined for soups and stews. I didn't like stewed goose that much. I turned to Craig's List and posted an ad for "A Flock of Super Loud Geese, Really. Really. Loud."

I could only hope to find someone who didn't want them for dinner, but would keep them the same way I had, for eggs and feathers. I imagined they would be useful as watch geese, or as weeder geese, or to keep some lonely horse company. My daydreams about their future could not keep pace with my nightmares. I worried that finding a home for a flock of hostile geese wasn't going to be easy, especially as most cities had laws banning them because they really were uncomfortably loud.

But within two days, I had an email from a man in New York who was relocating after retirement to New Mexico. He had fond memories of geese from his childhood and wanted them as watch geese, since he didn't want another dog and his current dog was the size of a block of cheese. It was a perfect match.

When the day came to put the geese one by one into the giant dog kennel he had in the back of his Jeep Wagoneer, I was feeling more upset than I let on. The geese were going to a home that might even turn out to be better than mine. Maybe they would have more room, or real pasture to graze. It was better than being butchered, but I still felt sad. I knew when I got them that I was unlikely to have them for their entire lives. They were livestock and in demand as a food animal, as well as home alarm system or feather factory. But there had been geese in our area since we'd moved in, fifteen years earlier. Our closest neighbor had kept a gaggle of geese for nearly ten years before he moved away. I started my flock soon after. Now there would be no goose calls echoing against the mesa. No pre-dawn bugle to announce the presence of a predator at the wire. I would miss them more than I wanted to admit, but at least they were getting a chance at a longer life.

Encouraged, I listed the ducks. Andrew said that he liked roast duck, or stewed duck, or duck soup, but he had no time to butcher them. He was busy chasing the illusion of the job he thought was real and I argued was not. The ghost job with the promise of phantom money.

The Mallard and Cayuga duck breeds were in high demand and I got several emails on my posting. I chose a guy doing permaculture near Santa Fe. He already had some ducks and I worried that my ducks might not assimilate immediately into his existing flock. When I delivered the ducks, I stayed to make sure they were all right. There was a fight, but it was a duck fight, and hard to take seriously. The two flocks were eventually seamlessly united.

A neighbor several miles down the road was interested in taking half the chickens and most of the remaining turkeys. He had a free-range by day, secure by night, chicken system and I was curious to find out how the birds would do in that situation. All the money we had spent making our pens totally secure was again weighing on my mind and I wondered how much of it was strictly necessary. All of the heritage turkeys went to him and most of the chickens, including one rooster. He wouldn't take more roosters, although I tried. I kept a dozen chickens and all of the lumbering Bronze turkeys. They were not suited to a free-range life.

October 2008 dawned on eight crowing roosters and the sounds of knives being sharpened. Roosters that crow are roosters that ambush, and the pens were no longer safe for our little girls. They weren't safe for us either. One day I walked into the pen to a frontal assault. A rooster was doing a Bruce Lee in front of me. As I walked by, he launched himself, spurs forward, at knee height and opened up a long gash in my pants. Another day, I was crouching down in the hen house, collecting eggs from a particularly inaccessible corner of the floor when a whoosh of feathers kicked straw and dirt up into my face. When the dust cleared, I realized that a rooster had tried to attack my face but had been clotheslined by the doorway. His spurs waved an inch away from my face, where they would have done significant damage. It was obviously past time to butcher the roosters.

The turkey hens had begun to lay in late summer, about two to three eggs each week. Big Tom had decided to be a standup guy and set the eggs for his ladies. Only Big Tom was pretty much crippled by his gigantic size and was a major klutz, so he was setting a wad of scrambled egg yolk, straw, and poo. I asked him to please give it up, for the sake of my profit and loss statement, but he was dedicated. The only eggs I was able to collect after he began his mission of fatherhood were ones I could get to before he did. Everything else went straight into the compost. He was living on borrowed time as we set our sights on truly following through with a Thanksgiving Turkey Dinner this year.

I started strafing our bills as our checking account balance stagnated. Our financial situation was becoming critical. I cancelled our health insurance because we simply didn't have the cash to pay the premium. That was a cold moment. We had been self-insured for ten years, paying individual policy premiums that got bigger every year. We were now totally uninsured and it felt like a weird kind of nakedness. In order to afford the premiums at all we'd had high deductibles and limited coverage, but it was at least something. The income Andrew was counting on from the job he was still courting got pushed back as it was delayed. He was now completely finished with all of his past jobs and his crew faced unemployment until he found another builder who could take them on temporarily. His crew all had families as well. We had a fast dwindling reserve of cash and I didn't see a way it was going to get replenished. Andrew tried to be more optimistic about jobs coming his way, but I was stridently practical about already being past the point of no return.

We began a breath-hitching bellyache of what got paid, what got cancelled, and what got postponed: dance lessons, aftercare, subscriptions, and future appointments of all kinds. We started selling furniture, camera equipment, specialty tools, and spare tires, but it wasn't enough. Every passing week racked up more of a balance on the credit cards and bank loan as the contracting business leaned on us with its full crushing weight.

The girls had gone back to school and we were spending most of our time in town to cover that schedule. I finally got the public school bus system worked out, and the girls now took the bus to school from our condo. I tried to follow the bus by car on the first day but it was too fast. I arrived at school after the girls had already disembarked. They arrived early enough to get the free breakfast the school was offering as an incentive to get kids to school on time. At our school, ninety percent of students were brought to school by private car, so the tardiness issue was really due to the parents. The free breakfast helped us a lot, but didn't seem to help the tardiness numbers very much. Maybe they should have offered free coffee.

One of Andrew's jobs that should have been finished by now was instead causing him no end of headaches. He had taken the client's money and put a massive down payment on their choice of custom windows, but the custom window company had failed, and the money was not returned. The client had hired a lawyer who had Andrew's number on speed dial. I began searching for a job, a bankruptcy attorney, and the address of the welfare office in town. Andrew was so opposed to all of those ideas that he wouldn't even discuss the issue.

There was a small job that slipped away. A man had a stove hood that was too low and asked Andrew for a bid on raising it in an attractive way. He chose to wait, because his stock portfolio was down. The same man had a beam in his outdoor room that was sagging because it was not up to code and he was worried a big snow would take the roof down. He decided to take his chances. Another man had a drainage issue threatening his house if heavy rains brought flood. He chose to wait because his home equity loan got adjusted down and he had flood insurance. All of the large remodel or custom home building projects Andrew had been working on were also cancelled. Two that were still pending were waiting on the sale of homes in other states and my hope that they would come through was gone. In such a short time we had gone from carrying a lot of debt but managing it and seeing the payoff potential on the horizon to being completely broke.

I finished the decorated egg for the White House collection, and mailed it off. In the chaos and horror of our spectacular slow motion crash, I had been sorely tempted to make a tiny clay dinosaur with his middle finger waving in the air to let the President know what I thought of his management style. But of course, the egg wasn't destined for the current president, who seemed to be looking at the end of his term with palpable relief. It would be part of the next administration's collection, as yet un-elected. So I stuck to safe New Mexico symbols like green chile, the Zia symbol, and the state colors of red and green. I did make it a hinged egg, because those were my specialty. I used a brown egg, to mimic the adobe of Santa Fe-style architecture. It was an egg that my own chicken had laid, so it was New Mexican in every respect.

I'd done my usual research before coming up with a decorating plan, and found some hilariously scathing reviews of past State egg submissions. There was a fan club of sorts on the Internet who watched with glee every time the National Park Service posted each year's photographs of the State eggs. I laughed out loud at some of the reviews, but they made me nervous. I wasn't sure how my own egg would hold up to the scrutiny. At least it was finished on time.

The Easter 2008 sales slump in my egg business had continued into the summer. What was normally a slow season had turned into a complete standstill. My pre-Christmas season began in September, but I was not seeing the usual increase in activity. By the end of September, gas prices were still high ($3.88 a gallon) and my website was collecting about 500 hits a day. This was a good hit rate, but it was no longer resulting in very many sales.

I gathered my blown egg statistics and discovered that this second flock had been much less productive than the first. Primarily it was because I had chosen chickens for their colorful feathers and then just expected them to produce copious numbers of eggs. The fancy breeds turned out to be much less productive, as any chicken expert could have told me. The productive chickens were bred specifically to be productive and many of those breeds wore less spectacular feathers. The White Leghorn, Black Australorp, Rhode Island Red, and Buff Orpington chickens were tremendous layers. Their feathers were often beautiful and useful, but the laced, spangled, barred, frosted, grizzled, or variegated feathers were something altogether different. This second flock had boosted my feather inventory at the cost of the egg inventory. Another lesson learned; there were chickens for feathers and chickens for eggs and they were rarely the same bird.

Another possible reason for the lower egg production was our early brush with possible blackhead disease. Although I still wasn't sure that the turkeys had been suffering from that specifically, the chickens were exhibiting mildly bloody stool at the same time, which was also a symptom. One of the long-term ramifications of chickens recovering successfully from Coccidosis was reduced production. I had made it through, but it was possible that my adventure in raising chickens and turkeys together had cost me down the road in reduced egg inventory.

The whole economy was constricting, and not just for us. Now it was obvious that the entire country was suffering, first through failing mortgages, then through chain reaction spending reductions. We were on the front lines of something nobody had seen since the Great Depression. We weren't the only ones who hadn't seen it coming and were not well positioned for it. I felt like we'd been caught in an awful game of freeze tag where everyone was forced to stand in place with only what they had in hand at the time, or as though we were caught naked in the bathtub; exposed and holding nothing useful.

But it turned out to be more complicated for Andrew. His business was more to him than just an income activity. He had identified with it on a deep level. Every critique I expressed about its productivity was, to him, a deep personal attack. When I suggested loudly, firmly, and repetitively, that it was time to close the business and consider bankruptcy, he heard me saying that he was a failure and a loser, and he fought back accordingly. My suggestions that I go out and get a job, preferably immediately, he perceived as betrayal and a vote of no confidence in his leadership.

Contractors who were well capitalized and not carrying a big debt were still doing work, but they didn't have many jobs lined up for the future. He felt that my insistence that his business close was implied criticism of his abilities.

"You think this disaster is all my fault," he said.

"No," I said. "But I think we have to respond to it and not stand around hoping it's going to get better."

"You've never liked my business," he said.

"That's true," I agreed. "It's too hard, and too exposed financially, and with the effort you've put in, you should have seen a greater return by now."

"I don't have any idea what I'll do next," he said. "This is how I make a living!"

"But it ISN'T making a living," I said. "Not anymore, and you have to do something about it, you can't just keep going under these conditions."

"These conditions could change any day," he insisted. "Nobody knows where this is going."

"It's already too late," I said. "We are past the point of no return. It's over."

"You don't get to say when it's over!" he shouted.

"The hell I don't!" I shouted back. "I signed the debt papers same as you! That gives me a say!"

"You think this is all my fault!" he shouted.

"You are such a flipping child!" I shouted, and it went downhill from there, at volume, and at regular intervals.

We were as far from each other as we had ever been in our relationship. I firmly believed we needed to file for bankruptcy, put the condo up for sale, live full time again in the trailer on the property far from town, and put me to work outside the home. Andrew insisted that we just needed to hang in there and stay positive. I knew from experience that shouting matches were distinctly audible to the upstairs neighbors in our complex and our upstairs neighbor was an older lady who never went out. She was likely catching every word. Now that we were shouting every night, I felt an even more urgent need to return to the trailer. I was sure that we were disturbing her, and it was also acutely embarrassing. The embarrassment was mine alone, however; Andrew was utterly immune. He claimed that she probably wouldn't even remember it one morning to the next, since her mental deterioration was beginning to show. She had recently begun introducing everyone in the block to her new cat, Tiger, which was obviously a small dog.

The fighting was taking a toll on the children. Blue's grades had slipped, and I called for a special conference with the teacher to explain our position. The teacher suggested giving Blue access to the school counselor during class time and submitted us for the free lunch program at the school cafeteria. Juno gave Blue the finger one afternoon, claiming she had learned it from kids at school. During class one day, Juno gleefully ripped her pant leg from hip to knee because she thought it looked cool. Instead of calling me to come and pick her up for violating school dress code, the school counselor redressed her from the donated clothes box. It made me sad to see this evidence of stress in my girls, and it made me even sadder to see how much this effort on the part of the school helped us. We were that far down our dark hole, and desperately-optimistic Andrew was still digging.

"Don't you think," I said, trying not to shout this time, "that if we find ourselves in a deep dark hole, the first thing we should do is stop digging?"

"I don't want to stop," Andrew said quietly.

"I know," I said, matching his tone and looking him straight in the eyes. "I understand that you don't want to. But you have to. It's time."

"I don't want to fight about it anymore," Andrew said.

"I don't either," I agreed. "But here is the bottom line. I'm going to get a job and you are going to close your business."

"It just breaks my heart," he admitted. "It makes me sick to my stomach."

"But you still have us!" I said, getting on the edge of loudness again. "It frustrates me that you don't look for what's best for *us*!"

"It's really difficult to grow up like that," he said, turning the conversation finally into the light. "It's really hard to put the emotion aside and take a practical approach."

"I understand," I said.

"No," he corrected, "you actually don't. You're the practical one, you've been the grown-up in this."

"True," I said. "You've been a thorough Peter Pan."

"Be nice," he bristled. "I'm making an effort here."

"I call you Peter Pan in the nicest possible way," I said.

"And so who are you?" he asked, "are you my Wendy? All practical mother energy?"

"Definitely not Wendy," I said, thinking of the finite limits of my nurturing self, "and I don't think I'm Tinker Bell either."

"So who are you?" he asked again.

"Actually," I said, more and more sure about it. "I think I'm Captain Hook."

"Tick Tock," said the checking account.

Chapter Twenty-One

*N*ear the end of that very long September, Andrew and I had finally reached a truce emotionally. We agreed that I'd stop referring to his business as a bloated corpse and he would stop objecting to my efforts to find a job. He still would not consider bankruptcy because he felt that the phantom job (I wasn't supposed to use the word phantom) was going to come through and see him through this rocky time. We were still pretty far from united, though. What he considered a rocky time, I considered a direct hit by a rock the size of Texas; rocky time versus extinction event. Regardless, it was time for me to get a job.

I dug around and found my old résumé. I'd been a stay-at-home mom for so long that my last job, and therefore my last work reference, was back in 1998. That was almost eleven years earlier, actually in the previous century. So I wrote my résumé in a different way and instead of listing past employment, I listed skills. All my computer skills, all my Internet skills, everything I'd learned in building my egg business. The fact was I was a much better employee now than

I had been eleven years earlier. Now I was used to serving everyone else, doing what was needed in a cost-effective manner, and packing an astonishing number of tasks into a single day. I could butcher a chicken and keep my small child from choking on a toy with one hand tied behind my back, but I thought I should leave the word "butcher" off my résumé.

I marched down to the local temp agency, ready for part-time temporary work. I chose the Kelly agency because I had fond memories of working for them back in college.

"I used to be a Kelly Girl," I said cheerfully to the woman at the main desk.

"We aren't Kelly Girl," she said firmly. "We are Kelly Services."

"Oh," I said. "I guess I can see the reason for that change."

"What are you looking for?" she said, looking somewhere past me.

"Temporary part-time work," I announced firmly.

"We have full-time temporary work," she said, "and we have part-time permanent work."

"Okay," I said.

"But we have no part-time temporary work," she concluded.

"But there must be somebody who needs a worker part-time for a short time," I protested.

"Not here," she said.

"Well, why don't you take my résumé anyway," I suggested, and she mutely handed me the application form.

I waited for her to indicate where I should go to sit down,

but she turned her attention to her computer and I was on my own. I settled down with a form that seemed to be nothing but requests for examples of recent past employment and tried not to feel discouraged. I came to a box asking me if I'd ever received food stamps from the state, and I hesitated. I was planning to apply for food stamps, but was that going to be a barrier to getting a job through this agency? The very next question asked if I had ever been convicted of a felony. There was no check box for "not yet." I went back over to the woman who looked at me with impatience.

"What happens if I answer yes to this food stamp question?" I asked.

"We get special funding if we put people to work who are on state aid," she said, as she typed into her computer and ignored a ringing phone simultaneously.

"Oh well, that's a good thing then!" I said, relieved.

She said nothing.

"But you really shouldn't put it next to this box about felony convictions," I continued, "because that is a bad thing, it's really kind of an unfortunate placement of boxed responses."

She paused in her typing.

"Are you finished with the form?" she said, and finally picked up the phone before I could answer her question.

I thought I was finished, but quickly found out that next was the automated computer testing, and by the time that was done I had some more suggestions for improvements to the Kelly system. My word processing score was lower than I had expected due to software version issues. I had a bone to pick with the spreadsheet portion of the exam, which had blindsided me with an auto-fill formula question. I waited while she finished another call, shamelessly eavesdropping from right in front of her desk. I learned that there were plenty of jobs at $10 an hour doing all night banquet work at the local casinos, if you had your own transportation.

"You have a car?" she asked, ignoring my protests and stapling my test results to my application.

"Yes," I said, in my only positive response of the entire experience.

"We'll call you if we have something," she said.

I walked out of there feeling deflated, but my phone rang before I even got home.

"I've got a temporary full-time job to put your résumé down on," the Kelly Services woman said.

"But I need part-time temporary work," I said. She called the next day.

"I've got a permanent part-time job to put you in for," she said and named a wage less than half what I had put down on my application as my target salary. I stood firm.

It was gut roiling to stick to my salary level, which I had already listed much lower than I really wanted. I needed to get a job, but I also needed to use my time properly. I privately set myself a deadline to call her back about the low-paying banquet work if something didn't come through soon. Finally, a better call came through.

"This one is a permanent part-time job," she said, "but it really matches your résumé, so why don't you go in and see for yourself what they want."

"Okay!" I said, encouraged. I was a little surprised that she had made such a helpful suggestion, but after thinking it through, I realized that this employment agency, and basically all of them, was really in the business of putting people into the jobs that were listed with them. They made their money as a portion of their employee's hourly wage, so if I was working zero hours, they made zero money. It probably wouldn't hurt a bit for me to go interview for a job and then spring the news that I could make no promises for sticking around permanently. With the reported unemployment numbers rising daily and the number of layoffs nationwide, I privately doubted that any of the jobs listed with the service were really permanent anyway.

I washed my shoes with bleach, decked myself out in the one nice outfit I owned, and went to my first interview in a decade. Sure enough, their version of permanent was satisfied by my assurance that I would work at least the next nine months, and I got the job. I was now managing a database for a non-profit health services clinic, and our food and gas income was secure. It was an enormous relief. I spent our last cash reserve on a set of three office-friendly outfits and got ready to wear them over and over again for the next nine months.

By mid-October 2008, gas prices had finally come down under $3 a gallon and for us, that relief was critical. We tried to list the condo for sale, but so many other condos were already listed that the market was flooded. Many of those condos were offered for sale at prices so far below the price we needed that selling became out of the question. We turned to the idea of renting out the condo, leaving us to go back to living full time at the trailer far out of town. We discovered that a whole mess of other condos were already listed for rent at prices well below our mortgage payment. We were obviously not the only ones struggling and we entered the renting war with a listing that was $25 below the lowest comparable competition. Then, we waited.

When I had my first paycheck in hand, I prepared myself for the first visit to a state aid office in my entire life. Andrew was not happy about my intentions.

"We aren't the kind of people who go on state aid," he said.

"We are now," I said.

I didn't know where to go to get started. I didn't even know what the state aid office was called in the yellow pages. So I asked a hippie at Whole Foods, and instead of taking offense, she gave me directions. Even with that help, it took me two afternoons to find it, because the office had moved. When I finally arrived in the right place, there was no line, perhaps because nobody else could find it, either. An armed security guard at the entrance told me how to put my name on the sign-up sheet. There was a notice on the wall directing me to sign up on the sheet. Writing my name on the sign-up sheet put me in line for filling out a form that was six pages long. It asked for every possible number I could come up with, including income and expenses, and documentation that proved the numbers correct.

Once I filled out the form, I got to see a caseworker right away. She spent a lot of time filling out more papers by hand and poking at a handheld calculator. She had to push her computer out of the way to do that, and I wondered why the computer couldn't be cajoled to do that work for her — but

I didn't make any suggestions. I figured the less I said in this office, the better. I had prepared for my quest by collecting every piece of family documentation I could think of. I had copies of bills, statements, pay stubs (from the job I had just gotten), children's birth certificates, credit card agreements, and profit and loss statements. But I didn't have the two pieces of paper the caseworker wanted. Some kind of verification of the work Andrew did not have, and two more pay stubs for weeks I had not yet worked at my new job.

I tried to be patient and see it as a process like the birth process, or like the death process, or a whole lot like the fermentation process. It seemed to me that a person had to be both dedicated and organized to negotiate these aid offices and applications. The people I was in line with at this office did not strike me as dedicated or organized. Batshit maybe, organized, no. Some of them appeared to be quite drunk.

I decided that I probably needed to simply give the caseworker exactly what she asked for and no more. I could only fill out the forms to the best of my ability and see what happened. I applied for everything. I asked the caseworker if there were any more boxes to check and she said there were none that I qualified for. I pressed her and she got a little testy. Since I was not, as far as she could tell, sitting in my own urine and homeless, the other programs were not designed for me. I thought that I could probably swing the urine thing, but it really was time to go home.

In the end, I did receive some state assistance. It took about two weeks for all of my information to filter through the system and I got all my answers through the mail. I did not qualify for food stamps, but I did receive the little credit card-looking thing that I would have used to buy food with the food stamps that I didn't get. I did get a one-time $120 credit on my power bill for the winter, sent directly to my power company. I learned I was also eligible for a $10 reduction on my phone bill for a month. Andrew and I did not qualify for state medical insurance, but the children did, so for one year they were covered. That was a huge relief. I would have been eligible if I had been pregnant, but since I was now in my early forties, post tubal ligation and not looking so fondly at Andrew most of the time, it seemed unlikely.

On the day I applied for aid, I was close to tears by the time I was through. It was a low point in a series of low points that had hit me in succession ever since we had returned from our road trip. I was tired and discouraged, and even my birds were mostly gone. I had a job, but I also had to work the job, and there were so few sales coming in through my website that I feared my little business was going away as well. It was an awful time.

"I am going to be a princess for Halloween," Blue announced and proceeded to slather on pink eye shadow.

"Not scary," Juno pronounced.

"So I'll be a dead princess then," Blue amended, and added some black grease pencil to her eyelids.

"What are you going to be, Mommy?" Juno asked me.

"I'm going as myself," I said tiredly.

"You can't go as yourself," Blue said, hand on hip, giving me a black blink.

"Not scary," Juno pronounced.

"Yes it is," Andrew corrected, "it's terrifying."

We had just finished our final argument about his contracting business and he was feeling bruised. The job he had been counting on had been pushed back for the third time, and it was already a job with a built-in three month delay on any payments for materials and labor. At my "urging," he agreed to cancel his participation in the job. Since there was no contract or deposit, it was a simple phone call. We both hesitated when he picked up the phone. There are some actions in life we take knowing full well that once we do them, we can't take them back. Words we can't un-say. A hatchet blow we can't undo. This was one of those moments. Even though I felt strongly about it being the right and only thing to do, I still couldn't listen to Andrew while he made the irrevocable call that cancelled his involvement with the phantom job. We both felt sick.

"How did it go?" I said, afterwards.

"I spoke to the office manager," Andrew said.

"And?" I prompted.

"And she'll pass the message to the project manager," he said.

The project manager never called Andrew back.

"Probably he's pissed that he has to find another patsy," I said later.

"Do you have to be so much like how you are?" Andrew said.

Andrew had finally agreed to make an appointment with a bankruptcy attorney. It had been a bitter discussion, but he was finally letting go of everything. He was closing doors that he'd held open through force of optimism alone. He had ended the living legal entity that was his business. His crew was now officially unemployed and all of the business debt reverted to us personally.

Twelve months previously, we were on track to pay all of our debts to zero with one more year of profitable jobs. Within that time, our debt had ballooned as we tried to keep the business alive without clients and without realizing that it was far more than a temporary couple of slow months. Giving up on any recovery in the custom home-building business had been the most difficult action of our lives. The bankruptcy process was our only option now. We had no possibility of financial recovery with the business debt burden now in our hands.

The bankruptcy lawyer was in Albuquerque, an hour's drive south. All of the Santa Fe bankruptcy attorneys were booked solidly into the next year. We drove to the appointment during the school day and sat together uncomfortably in the lawyer's meeting room. Bill came in and held out his hand for us to shake. His hand was huge. It engulfed my own with ease and I am not a small person. But Bill was one of those large people who did not seem large. He was graceful and self-assured. He did not seem to be in dire straits and I had a moment of seriously regretting that I had not become a bankruptcy attorney. He asked us some questions, gave us some answers, and then announced that if we chose to declare, he would be able to represent us. I guess I must have relaxed a little with that pronouncement.

"I'm glad to see you smiling finally!" he said to me.

"This isn't where I want to be," I said, as gracefully as I could.

"Never is," he boomed, and gestured to the meeting room, "Even though I try to make it nice."

At the lawyer's direction, Andrew called the bank and offered to surrender his tools for repossession before they could call him with the demand. The bank seemed confused by his action. They said that it didn't usually work that way. Usually it was an adversarial process involving police presence. Andrew delivered all but a basic set of heirloom tools to a warehouse filled with the trappings of other dead businesses. These items would all be sold at auction.

The bankruptcy attorney gave us a four page list of documents and information he would need in order to process our case. He suggested that we stop paying any minimum payments on our debts, and not to answer any creditor calls. The calls began immediately. Andrew's phone was ringing almost constantly. We set every phone to silent, and I would have cut my service completely, but the phone service contract was long term and unbreakable.

It took us weeks to finish the application, and in the end, we turned in a ten-pound, three-ring binder of information. The lawyer was pleased with our thorough approach, but his paralegal assistant was definitely not. She let us know that even with our hand drawn index, the binder was unwieldy. We let her complaints go to the same non-committal voice mail as the creditor calls.

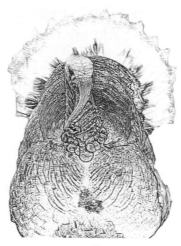

Chapter Twenty-Two

We celebrated the dark day of turning in our bankruptcy application by preparing Big Turkey Tom for Thanksgiving dinner. He was suffering more than we were. He had broken several toes again, stumbling around under his colossal weight. Letting him live any longer seemed crueler than butchering him and since we were feeling numb from the difficulty of the last months, we were up to the task. He was now the size of a wheelbarrow and our humane air rifle method was not going to work. Andrew sharpened the long-handled axe and we wrestled him out to the butcher block. Even the cone method wasn't going to work for a bird this size, and we were left with no option other than the most direct. We tied him up, gave him our sincerest thanks, and chopped off his head.

It was brutal. It was a fitting punctuation to our horrible year. We probably should have tied his feet. When he finally stopped running around, at greater speeds than he had ever achieved with his head attached, we got to work plucking and cleaning. The girls were right there with us, hollering in horror when his head rolled, hooting in pursuit when he ran away. Exclaiming in awe at his amazing weight. Even I had less trouble with the killing part this time because he had been so valiantly miserable. Despite his size, he had been low in the pecking order, and in the last weeks had gotten no rest. The smallest chicken would peck his tail ragged. When I tried to sequester him alone, to give him a chance to recover his torn and broken feathers, he scrambled against the wire in a desperate attempt to rejoin the flock. This was how he had broken one toe, hanging it up in the wire trying to get back to his abusive wives.

After all of our efforts to secure the feathers of a Bronze Turkey, we were finally defeated. Only one in ten feathers was salvageable and his tail fan was broken. As Andrew cleaned the body cavity, he exclaimed in disgusted surprise. Big Turkey Tom's heart was the size of a regular turkey and his lungs were tiny, much too small for his enormous size. This explained his distress after any kind of exertion. We probably could have chased him around the pen to kill him, instead of the gothic horror show we'd just gone through.

Big Turkey Tom's meat-boosting genetic manipulation had resulted in a turkey that weighed in at a post-butchering weight of thirty-seven pounds. It was the largest turkey I had ever seen, much less tried to cook. He didn't fit in the oven bag, so I wrapped him in aluminum foil. He didn't fit in the oven. It took both of us to lift the jury-rigged foil drip pan I had fashioned for roasting him, and we squeezed him in – pressing hard against all sides and top of the oven. The door didn't quite close and I sealed the gap with more aluminum foil. I expected that the escaping heat from the oven would heat the trailer all by itself, but we had to light a fire in the woodstove anyway. The roasting turkey was soaking up all the heat the oven was putting out until the last hour, which is how I figured the turkey was done.

Where the turkey had touched the sides and top of the oven, the meat was a deep ebony roast; kind of crunchy and overdone, but not ruined. The drumstick meat was much darker than any store bought turkey leg I'd ever seen, but flavorful and tender. The breast meat was perfectly cooked and perfectly flavored. It was really good and it filled two of the biggest foil pans completely. He truly was double breasted. The biggest turkey I had ever cooked before had filled one foil pan with meat after I had pulled it all off the bone, but this bird filled two pans with just his breast meat. It suddenly occurred to me that I should have had a neighborhood Thanksgiving party to share this harvest. I had been so deeply mired in our trouble that it had never crossed my mind, and while the area was not a close community, there were some neighbors I could have happily invited over. Now I had more roast turkey than my family could eat in a month.

The lawyer filed our bankruptcy on a Monday and the calls stopped by the end of the week. One credit card company didn't seem to get the memo until midway through the following week. We had listed a loan from my father in our application. He copied us on the paperwork so we were able to see the kind of notifications our creditors were getting during the process. It was a letter Dad claimed he had hoped never to get with my name on it, but then he reflected that it was better than something from the U.S. Marshals.

Our creditors were notified of a meeting called the "Meeting of Creditors" scheduled for mid-January where they would have the opportunity to show up in person and object to our attempt to jettison our debt to them. Our lawyer said that he'd never had a creditor show up at that meeting in his years of handling bankruptcies. But, he continued, all bets were off with us. We were currently his smallest case and his biggest pain in the ass because of all our questions and nervous bellyaching. I found him a bit sarcastic. He said we needed to chill out, but I didn't think that a bankruptcy process was a good place to begin a new habit of chilling out.

After we had filed, we successfully rented the condo, but not for the amount of the mortgage. Andrew's family helped pay that monthly gap and we moved back out to the trailer, forty-five minutes from town and the girls' school. Because the girls had been at that school for several years they were able to continue attendance, but we had to get up very early in the morning to be there in time. This kept me from being late to work so it was a good combination.

Andrew still had his company logo emblazoned all over his truck and trailer. Since those were his personal vehicles and not truly business infrastructure, I insisted that he take them off. He had the company logo on my car as well, which had seemed a good idea at the time for additional advertising around the town. The logos were made of colorful vinyl lettering; they were supposed to stay on in all weather conditions and come off easily at any time. But Andrew had put off removing them, like a band-aid glued to an exceptionally hairy body part. I wanted him to rip them off quickly, suck it up and take the pain. He couldn't bring himself to do it until I pitched yet another fit. He finally went grimly out on a cold morning in late November and came back an hour later with a sad little pile of wiggly acrylic bits in the company colors and ceremoniously put them into the fire.

"Did they come off completely?" I asked,

"Well, the paint underneath hasn't been exposed to the sun as much as the paint around it," he explained.

"You *promised*," I said, reasonably loudly, "that the logos would just peel off!"

"They did," he assured me, "they peeled right off."

"Did they leave a mark on the car door?" I persisted.

Andrew stirred the fire.

"Seriously," I said, getting irritated yet again, "you told me with doe-eyed innocence that those logos would come right off."

"Doe-eyed?" he said. "I think that's the nicest thing you've called me in months."

"The car isn't going to be the only thing with a scar around here," I said, and wrapped up to go inspect my polluted car door for myself.

"This whole process is leaving a mark," he said, poking the fire, "on a lot more than just the car door."

December 2008 began for me with a strange sense of suspended calm. We had watched the presidential election together as a family on TV and the glow, the amazement, of watching our own choice for President successfully elected had not faded. Andrew and I had both voted and at our little polling station; the girls had been allowed to watch – although not allowed to touch the ballots or the ballot boxes. There was a quiet to our lives at the trailer in comparison to the national noise preceding the election and our personal chaos preceding the action of filing for bankruptcy. We relied on my job, the girls went to school, and Andrew continued to clean up everything, including things lying in the yard.

I hit my turkey and rooster food wall in the middle of the month. I just couldn't eat them anymore, not in any form. I realized with sudden clarity that I was going to have to seriously improve my cooking skills if I was going to be living off what I raised on my own land. I was thankful for a freezer full of high quality, home-raised meat, but I could also understand why cultures with centuries-old traditions of living off their land came up with fiery and exotic spice mixtures. I started to prepare a separate dinner plate for myself, loaded up with hot green chile, flash-frozen from the autumn New Mexico chile roast. I experimented with deeply rich curry sauces, and Mexican molé. The girls had turkey spaghetti, rooster-noodle soup, and mystery meat with rice. It wasn't much of a mystery though.

Christmas approached and I tried to prepare the girls for a smaller celebration this year. I reminded them of all the nice toys they already had, like the electronic gaming system they had received last Christmas, after I had decided that they needed to learn some basic video game skills. Blue had become proficient at setting up the system and giving her sister a control unit so that they could play together, a happy scene until I looked closer.

"Did you just blow up your sister?" I asked.

"Shush Mom!" Blue said, neatly avoiding her own land mines and running for the prize.

"How long have you been doing this?' I pressed.

"Mom!" Blue protested, still scooping up blinking prizes on screen. "You're giving it away! She's still playing happily enough."

"I'm gonna WIN!" Juno crowed, cranking on her joystick, unaware that it was controlling nothing on the screen.

"Not okay," I said.

"She gets in the way!" Blue complained.

"That's the whole point of playing together!" I said.

"I win!" Juno announced, her controller pointing completely the wrong way in her hand.

"No blowing up of sisters," I announced. "New rule.'

"MOM!" they both cried in unison, Juno clueless to the fine print but sensitive to the injustice of a new rule.

We made a point of including the girls in our discussions of new financial habit-building as we tried to repair the damage of our months of angry fighting. We went through the grocery store making a running tally of the costs of items in the basket, mainly for their education but also to stay in budget with the money we had in hand. New habits and new beginnings were all in the planning stages. We didn't really know what our position would be once the bankruptcy was settled, or when that would happen. It was a limbo Christmas and I tried hard to be cheerful.

The school invited us to participate in a program for low-income families and I accepted. I sent Andrew to the function. I couldn't face the school staff and felt it was only fair considering I had done all the other programs on our behalf. He managed to have a genuinely good time, in typical Andrew style, and came home with two wrapped presents each for the girls, selected from items donated to the program from local businesses.

Our families sent presents in big boxes by mail, and the pile under our Christmas tree (cut from our land that year) grew to surprising dimensions. My lectures to the girls about the scarcity of money for Christmas this year had worried them, but the pile underneath the tree delighted them. I overheard them talking in their playroom one morning close to Christmas day and realized that I was almost, but not quite, getting through.

"What would you do if you had a million dollars?" asked Blue.

"I'd buy a million bucks!" said Juno.

"But you'd already have a million bucks," said Blue.

"So I'd buy a million more!" sang Juno.

"You don't buy a million dollars with a million bucks," Blue said. "It doesn't help you that way."

"Then I'd buy a bathtub!" said Juno, and fell over laughing.

In the previous December, I had been frantically busy with my egg business during the weeks before Christmas. I had worried, when I took my job, about how I would manage the orders and my work schedule. I had been teaching Andrew my system in preparation, but very few orders came in. The Easter sales slowdown had been remarkable, but the

Christmas drop was pushing 80 percent. Customers simply did not need pre-blown eggs or natural feathers and were choosing to save their money for essentials. As big name companies filed for bankruptcy, I watched news reports of equally dire drops in retail spending across all industries. I decided, with deep sadness, that the hinged eggs had to go. They were labor-intensive and although they had previously sold in plentiful quantities, I had to make changes in my business. I would hold on to the blown egg inventory for the coming Easter season, as I was sure I could sell them, but I wasn't getting very many eggs from the fourteen-bird flock in the pens.

The birds were spending their days under a heat lamp in their straw-filled house, looking comfortable despite the cold, and kicking out the occasional small white egg. I still had feathers to process from the big rooster reduction, and so I listed more of those than I had before, but business did not pick up. I felt sad, but unsurprised, that my egg business would probably have to close as well. The overhead was low enough that I could keep it online until next Easter, but past that time, I wasn't sure.

We heated the trailer exclusively with wood scavenged from the lumber piles in the yard. Andrew stayed warm chopping and cutting the wood to fit the stove, then hauling it down to the trailer to burn. Propane prices had followed gasoline prices to astounding heights, and the previous winter we had seen more than $800 dollars a month in propane heating bills. This year we gave the propane company a "do not fill" notice and took our chances the old fashioned way. It worked well as long as one of us was home to stoke the fire all day, but when we were all in town, it made for a cold evening. The girls slept hidden under piles of blankets and comforters and I got up nervously throughout the night to check on them. But the bill was zero, and we had enough wood trash to heat the house all winter, cleaning up the property in the process.

We had a white Christmas, to the girls' delight, one of the first snowfalls of the winter that the girls were able to enjoy at home. They ran for the snow pants I had unearthed from the workshop and quickly pulled them on. The snow pants came to their knees. Both girls looked at each other, and at me in shock; they had grown that much since last winter. We covered the gap with socks and sweat pants, and they went out to play.

"It's a nice day for Christmas," I said to Andrew, who was slowly getting his own gear on to go out and play with the girls.

"It is," he agreed, "and I'm really glad to be seeing the end of THIS year."

"But it's not over," I said, "until it's over."

"Yeah," he sighed, "and it's not going to be over soon."

"What do you know?" I asked, suspicious.

"I'll tell you after Christmas," he said.

"Tell me now," I said. "I'm a Grinch anyway. Easter is my favorite celebration because there's more chocolate."

"We got a letter from a creditor," he said, "objecting to the filing."

"Didn't they all object to the filing?" I asked.

"I mean officially," he said. "The bankruptcy isn't going

to be a complete discharge."

"Well!" I swore.

"But the lawyer is on it," he added, "he says we can pay him to fight it."

"Merry Christmas, lawyer," I said.

"One day," Andrew said, "this *will* be over."

Chapter Twenty-Three

*I*n January of 2009, I received a significant email. It wasn't very long and it didn't come in with any flashing lights or media coverage, but it was a life-changing email all the same. It was from the *Martha Stewart* people and it said that they were planning to mention my website in their April issue, in the supply section. Was I still in business? I immediately stopped my frantic efforts to dismember and sell my egg business piece by piece. I emailed back that yes, I was still in business, and thank you for the heads up. Then I sat back in stunned amazement. My first thought, so mature, was how cool this was going to make me look to my sisters' friends.

I got to work right away, reversing the destruction of my egg business and unpacking the bulk lots I had created from most of the products. I left the hinged eggs in their bulk packaging. I still didn't have enough time to pursue that product along with my part-time job. The blown eggs lined up in well-behaved rows and the feathers preened, getting ready for their close up. I crawled through every page of my website and tuned it all up. I didn't know how much business might be generated by a mention in the back of the Easter issue of *Martha Stewart Living* magazine, but I thought it might be at least something.

In March of 2009, the April issue of *Martha Stewart Living* came to me in the mail. I eagerly opened it, flipped through the pages, and then almost fell over in shock. My website was not only listed twice in the supply page in the back of the magazine, it was also listed on the crafts page in the center of the magazine. Every page of the magazine featured beautifully decorated eggs, some of which I recognized as coming from my stock. Those past sales to *Martha Stewart* were all roosting in this one magazine. I shivered. This was a huge placement. It was so much more than I had expected that I knew I wasn't going to have enough eggs. The orders started to roll in that night.

My hit counter, which had been registering about a thousand hits a week, jumped immediately to a thousand hits a day and I was flooded with requests for blown eggs. My statistical best had been about twenty orders in a week prior to mention in the magazine. This wave started at ten orders a day, climbing up from there. I went into ultra-efficiency mode and enlisted the help of the whole family. The orders kept coming in and everything on the site was selling. It was gloriously stressful.

As I ran out of chicken eggs, I started to reach out in my rural community to neighbors who also had chickens. Andrew began an egg roundup, driving up every local driveway we suspected hosted chickens and coming away with more eggs, all laid in accordance with our mission of organic (uncertified), domestic, and humane. Country chickens leading happy lives didn't lay as many eggs as factory chickens living miserable lives, but when we collected from multiple farms, it was enough to fill my orders for a while. When I ran out of eggs that nobody else raised, like pheasant eggs, I faced a business dilemma. I knew that there were other online egg sellers out there who had excellent business ethics and sold eggs collected from well-raised birds, but their prices were generally lower than mine. Either they had a more efficient way of blowing their eggs, or lower cost overheads, but I had never been able to produce my eggs for prices matching theirs. I considered referring my magazine customers to these websites when I ran out of inventory, thus satisfying the customers' needs and sharing the bonanza of my lucky placement. It was a pivotal moment. My instinct was to clutch my customers close to my website and not let them go. I also knew that giving was a better way to live and giving other businesses access to some of the good fortune that had come my way was never going to be a mistake. I posted each sold-out egg with a link to another egging source and the orders continued to pour in.

The wave of egg-selling success continued as Easter grew closer and I began to count on Easter day as a goal. I achieved the online business milestone of selling to every state in the Union when an order from the state of Alaska finally came in. When I started notifying customers that express shipping in time for Easter day was no longer possible, since it was now the day before Easter, I learned the difference between secular Easter and Greek Orthodox Easter. It turned out I had another week to go and the sales continued.

Once all of the Easters were over, I went facedown in a

pillow and stayed there in satisfaction. It was transformative. The egg business was here to stay, at least as far as I could see. While most of the earnings from the Easter rush went to business overhead, it was still extraordinarily helpful to our budget. That overhead would have otherwise come from money we simply didn't have. In the quiet following Easter, I reflected on my windfall. I had been named in *Martha Stewart Living* magazine, The Easter Edition. That was huge. In the middle of our worst time had come the best egg thing ever, at least from my point of view.

This was even bigger than being the State Egg Artist of 2009. That thought took a little of the Martha glow away temporarily as we had recently learned that the White House State Egg presentation had been postponed.

Throughout the crazed build-up to Easter and the rush of orders, we had been desperately contacting the American Egg Board to find out when the State Egg presentation was going to be held. We needed to figure out if we could go. Since we obviously couldn't afford the trip, I had written a letter to the Governor asking for help with travel expenses but he had responded with a reciprocal request for campaign support. He claimed to be broke as well. Andrew had made it his personal mission to acquire the funding through a benefactor. He had boldly asked for help with the trip's travel expenses from a local philanthropist. He filled out a grant request in great detail and submitted it to the philanthropist's charitable organization and his request was granted. We were over the moon with joy and relief and gratitude. Andrew's success in securing the trip was his biggest validation and success of the entire year. I had achieved the distinction of being selected and Andrew had worked a miracle to secure the funding, but now it looked like the event itself had been called off.

The new administration, after confirming that the event would take place, now wasn't talking to the American Egg Board and the whole event was in peril. The annual Easter Egg roll on the White House lawn had taken place on time, but it was changed from the Washington D.C. exclusive it had once been. The new First Family had opened the event up to the nation via lottery. It seemed that there was no room in the schedule for the State Eggs. We were all disappointed, but Andrew was the most affected by the cancellation. I was secretly relieved because I had nothing to wear and all of the clothes available in my size looked like tablecloths.

Even though the event didn't take place, that didn't change the fact that I had submitted the egg for 2009. And it didn't change my website's listing in the April copy of Martha's magazine. And my hit counter was still clicking away with visitors from all over the world. I had achieved much more than I thought I would with this idea of selling a variety of blown eggs from my own birds, ordered out of a hatchery catalog. My business strategy of being almost organic, definitely domestic, and completely humane had struck a chord with my customers. As we went into the last stages of our bankruptcy process, I kept those truths with me like a tiny glowing light. No matter what happened next, those things remained true.

Gas prices in spring of 2009 fell below two dollars a gallon and that helped everything look better. Memories of the $5 a gallon gas prices in some cities were fading already. With media sources trying desperately to make the economic crash of 2008 look like a thing of the past while it was still in full flow, I made notes about what we had gone through. It would be too easy to forget, or allow selective memory to rule, under the onslaught of the nation's informational spin-doctors. News reporters started using the term "lower climb than expected" to describe rising unemployment numbers. I thought this was a masterful piece of propaganda writing. We got ready for our meeting of creditors.

We went to the Federal Building in Santa Fe and met a stranger at the door to the meeting room who claimed to be our lawyer. Our actual lawyer was too busy to come up to Santa Fe that day, but our new lawyer assured us that it was a routine process, so long as we didn't say anything unexpected. He showed us a paper taped to the wall outside the meeting room that was filled with three columns of names. These were people who also had their meeting today. Too many people to be seen in one day, but he said that it was double and triple-booked to compensate for the numbers of people who would fail to show up on time. Each name was paired with a lawyer's name and many listed the same guy. Our lawyer claimed that the many-times listed lawyer was a hack who processed bankruptcies like he was on an assembly line. He was cheaper than our lawyer, but he did less, too. I looked in horrified fascination at this list of names that contained our own.

"Is this evidence of more people filing for bankruptcy than in past months?" I asked our lawyer.

"Well, it's a little higher," he said.

"Are you seeing a rise in your business?" Andrew asked.

"We are definitely seeing more people come in for the free consult," our lawyer replied, "but we haven't seen more business yet. Guys like that are seeing their business skyrocket," he gestured to the lawyer he had called a hack.

"So I guess even the business of bankruptcy law has to deal with cheaper competitors," I said, looking at Andrew.

"Maybe they need tighter pants," Andrew mused.

The lawyer interrupted to remind us to answer only "yes" or "no" to the questions asked, and to refer everything else to him. We didn't have any tricky or shady areas. Ours was a very straightforward bankruptcy case, but I suspected the lawyer had been warned about Andrew's tendency to tell his life history when given an audience. Not me, of course. I was like a safe, un-crackable. We went inside to wait for our turn in the mismatched chairs that littered the small space around a single table.

The person in charge, called the "Trustee," was a woman named Yolanda. She eyed Andrew's cargo of file boxes and binders with misgiving and punched the start button on a tape recorder. She asked our names and the name of our lawyer. We deferred to him to answer since we had both forgotten it by that time. We showed our identification and she riffled through sheaves of paper, asking yes or no questions.

"What about this Toyota truck?" she said. "Couldn't it be sold to satisfy some of the debt?" We looked to the lawyer.

"If you choose to order it," he said.

"Although it has more than 200,000 miles on it," I added, glaring at him.

"Never mind, then," the trustee said.

"Are there any creditors present for the case under review?" she announced, without looking up.

"Yes!" said a voice from the back of the room and everybody jumped in surprise, including our own lawyer. The trustee waved him over and we all looked at him in horror. He was from the bank and he looked supremely uncomfortable, as if this process was as unusual for him as having a creditor actually show up seemed to be for the trustee.

"We want to ask about the valuation of the tools that were surrendered for repossession," the bank man said.

"Did you sell the tools at auction?" asked the trustee.

"Yes," the man affirmed. "We had extended a loan of sixty thousand dollars for the tools in Andrew's business."

"And how much did you get for the sale of the tools?" asked the trustee.

"Two thousand dollars," the man replied.

"*What?*" Andrew and I both exclaimed simultaneously, triggering our lawyer into paroxysms of shushing motions.

"Two thousand?" I exclaimed. "No freakin' *way!*"

"Way," the bank man said sadly.

"And what is your question?" the trustee said.

"We'd like Andrew to explain the difference between that number and the amount he valued the tools at," the man replied. Everyone in the room looked at Andrew.

"I don't know what to tell you," Andrew said slowly. "That's what I paid for the tools and you're selling used tools in a down market." Everyone continued to stare at him.

"It's the law of supply and demand," he concluded. "I'm sorry it went that way, man."

The trustee concluded our case soon afterwards and our lawyer bulldozed us out into the hall, as far away from the bank man as he could get. We asked him how he thought it went and he was vaguely reassuring. "You shouldn't say sorry," he said. "It can be construed as an admission of guilt."

"Guilt in what?" Andrew demanded. "Guilt in failing at something I worked at harder than ever before in my whole life?"

"Never mind," the lawyer said, looking at his watch. "It's done now, and we should hear soon."

He promised to email us within the next several days and when we didn't hear from him we got nervous. But it turned out to be a delay caused by a record number of bankruptcy filings flooding the Santa Fe courts and we soon got word that the trustee had closed our case. She declared us without assets, recommended the bankruptcy be awarded, and washed her hands of our case number. Other than the now *two* creditors who had sued to be excluded from our filing, we were in line for an end to our process in March. The other two issues were still in the hands of our lawyer who assured us that he would work out a settlement. We should work as hard as we could and save towards the day we had to pay the settlement.

We completed our credit-counseling course that was court-mandated before any bankruptcy discharge. We did it online and I suspected that the "live" coach was a robot. It was a polite and encouraging robot and the course material was actually useful. We got our bankruptcy discharge in March of 2009, and were finished with the settlement issues by August. With the help of family, we paid it all and had a debt load (and a credit rating) of zero by the end of summer. Well, except for the car that we were still paying on, and the condo, that was still rented for less than the mortgage. Both properties were precariously almost supporting themselves and we were perched in the trailer by the road. We had carved a little time and space out of the chaos and settled in to make some decisions.

Andrew had small, short-term carpentry jobs and I had my database work, and it kept us eating but was a very low-income lifestyle and hard to get used to. We slid farther down the economic ladder and into the level where we qualified for state medical coverage. At least we now had some kind of health insurance, but it was a very strange achievement to celebrate.

People who needed Andrew's contractor skills simply didn't have the money to pay him, and barter moved into our lives surprisingly quickly. The gymnastics school owner needed a fence built and the girls wanted gymnastics lessons, so that worked well. We needed some drip irrigation line for our gardening plans and the nursery owner needed some roofing fixed, so that fell into place. Andrew was busy reinventing the Middle Ages.

Summer began for us when school ended and I quit my part-time job to stay home and care for the girls. This let Andrew pursue any work options, which were still not flowing steadily. He did carpentry work, handyman work, and small construction jobs, anything that came his way. I told the girls it was going to be an old-fashioned summer, outside in the yard with a hose. After three weeks of getting used to an unstructured life, they began to enjoy it. Juno expanded her tree-climbing skills in a huge piñon that grew outside the trailer. The girls named it Mother Tree and clambered around it like monkeys until Juno did a George-of-the-Jungle down the trunk and grated off an expanse of skin. When she stopped howling long enough for me to hear myself speak, I told her to be proud of her tree-climbing scars. They were badges of success and experience.

We went down to the banks of the Pecos River every afternoon and ran the knee-deep rapids. We planted a garden and watched as the seedlings came up. One garden, as a test, went in unprotected from rabbits or ground squirrels and we were amazed to see that the only thing successfully growing after a month was corn, beans, and squash: the three sisters of Southwestern food traditions.

As spring arrived, the two remaining turkey hens and twelve chicken hens all proved their happy adjustment to a life without men and began to lay regularly. They still didn't match the production levels of my first flock, but it was something. My feed bill had stabilized at about $12 a month and these hens were safe for now. Without their tom turkey, the turkey hens developed a strange series of behaviors aimed at my feet. They vocalized almost constantly when I was in the pen and reminded me strongly of a pair of yappy dogs.

I kept in touch with the neighbor who had taken the turkeys and chickens that I could no longer feed. He had steadily lost birds to natural daytime predators and domestic dogs. A bobcat took the final turkey hens in broad daylight before summer's end. This answered my question regarding my overbuilt pens. In my region of New Mexico, if I wanted my birds to live more than a year, I did have to keep them in the bombproof covered aviary-style pens that we had built. New Mexico was the true Wild West and, although we didn't usually see them, the predators were keeping us in mind.

Our process of blowing the eggs and sluicing the contents down the sink had bothered everyone, including us. Our friend Tom, a talented engineer, came to visit during the summer with his daughter, Iris. Tom built us a glorious machine of PVC and a ball-point pen part that sped up our process and captured the contents of the egg. Iris played magnificently with the girls from dawn to dusk. Over a celebratory dinner of scrambled egg and chicken stew, we christened the machine "The Egg-Sucking Dawg," and asked Tom to sign it. Our septic tank would have to do without the egg from now on.

When my first chicks arrived in 2004, I had started a process of learning by doing that proved to be marginally effective and totally hilarious in hindsight. The days of struggling to properly care for more than 100 little creatures, all struggling equally hard to pursue their own agendas, had left their mark deep in my psyche. In retrospect, I had done most of it wrong, but it had been a success overall anyway. Maybe not for the pheasant roosters who lost in armed combat, or the hens that helplessly laid themselves to death, or the turkeys with the twisted genome, but overall, it was a success. Poultry raising turned out to be an endeavor that can take a lot of stumbling around in the dark and still turn out okay.

One of the hardest elements of raising the birds was the culling. In fact, I never did become comfortable with that aspect. We live in a society where individual lives are precious and tremendous resources are expended to save a single life. Even a life that is compromised by illness or disability, and even when the attempt puts other lives at risk. Moving from that cultural standard to a farmer's point of view in managing animals for optimal health and productivity was my biggest obstacle in this experience. A farmer or a breeder has to be willing to put the welfare of the flock or breed first and sacrifice an individual life in the process. Helping a badly injured bird to live turned out to be cruel when the other members of the flock turned on it. Birds don't seem to have the same altruistic attitudes as we do — to them survival of the fittest is a daily mantra. We all got along better once I finally understood that.

When I began raising my birds, there wasn't nearly as much information on the Internet as there is now. In just five years, the amount of valuable advice and expertise on poultry and game birds has exploded. I don't know if that is because the search engines are better or if people have posted more, but it's there. It is now easier and cheaper than ever to make a website, and all of that can be learned through self-study on the Internet as well.

The beginning of this project was hard because everything was new for me and there was so much to learn. I wasn't used to the routine and I didn't know what I was doing. I enjoyed some of the element of surprise that began every day with my new birds, but there were nasty surprises as well. It was hard to be new at something, but that passed.

Experience set in and changed everything. The middle of this project was hard because that was where follow-through was needed. Once the blush of new adventure turned into a daily grind, I had to reach down for some discipline to keep going. Somewhere in the middle of our chicken project, I found a kind of rhythm to the days. I started to feel competent and I liked how the birds kept me in touch with the seasons. Seasons are everything to poultry. But there were many times in the middle of all this wonder and chaos that I wanted to stop and think it over, or wondered why I'd ever pursued the idea in the first place. The middle was where most of life took place. That's where hard work and monotony lived. Ending this project was hard because change is both alluring and frightening. Endings can be mixed with relief and grief, but mostly they are full of decision points. Transitioning from the follow-through and routine of the middle of a project to planning how it would end took up enormous mental space. Then there was the action of ending, which quickly turned into a new beginning, and beginnings are hard.

I've decided that learning-by-doing is a good way to accomplish a great deal in a short amount of time, but it is also painful and expensive. Knowing what I do now, I would not try to raise male pheasant in a mixed species pen. I probably won't mix my chickens and turkeys in the same pen next time round, and I will definitely stick to heritage breeds forever more. Our grand house rental plan turned out well in the end, but we keep expecting to win an academy award for the drama. Now, however, we follow the advice of the landlording books.

The contracting industry is not as forgiving of mistakes as poultry raising turned out to be. We went down in a historically bad economic downturn, and without that collapse we might not have failed so spectacularly, but we also realized that we never had a plan for failure, and that was our biggest mistake. We had all kinds of plans for expansion and success and none at all for setback or collapse. This aspect of learning-by-doing was perhaps the most instructive of all. Now we make back-up plans and exit strategies. We have personal mile markers to let us know when something isn't working and needs to be reconsidered. Overall, it was worth doing and it made quite a story, one that isn't at an end. We are not finished with our poultry project; we are making new plans.

I'm thinking of trying a new-fangled approach of planning and education for my next adventure. Writing up a detailed plan and going out and talking with people involved in the activity already, or creating a model of supply and demand for a new product I have in mind and thinking through all the possible markets. It's a revolutionary idea that I'm considering applying to a journey into Ostrich, Emu, and Rhea. These are big birds with big eggs and a big market for their products and I have an idea.

I don't know anything about handling birds large enough to take my head off, but how hard can it be?

The Reference Section

"When you write your book," my sister said one day, *"include a quick reference section so that I can learn all I need to know without reading the whole thing."*

"But I want you to read the whole thing!" I said.

"I will," she promised, *"but I really am planning to get some chickens and I have no idea where to start. I need the info fast."*

When we were growing up, I noticed that my sister always skipped to the end of a book to see how the story ended.

"You could put the quick reference sections at the back," my sister suggested.

"I suppose I could," I said, and I did. But before I did, I asked my family to read a draft copy with all the reference information interleaved between each chapter. Their reaction was heartwarming but they were all in accord with my sister.

"Put it in the back," they said.

"In my own defense," my sister said, after faithfully reading the entire draft, *"I honestly didn't know that you were a good shot."*

"It's okay," I said.

"And Mom thinks she's been misquoted," she finished.

Contents

Brooding Chicks

All chicks have basically the same needs regardless of species: warmth, water, food, ground cover, and protection. The brooder space itself can be anywhere that works for both the farmer and the chicks. It has to have confining walls to keep the chicks from straying too far from the heater and to protect them from drafts. It's better if the walls are curved, with no right angles, so that the chicks can't pile up in the corners and suffocate each other – but I've had right angles in every brooder so far without piling problems. The top has to be covered if the space is vulnerable to predators, including mice. Barns and garages are great settings for brooders, but I did have temperature challenges even there. The easiest place I ever brooded chicks was my laundry room. Easy temperature control, easy clean up. But the stink permeated the entire house by the time they were grown. The birds take four to six weeks to grow big enough to live in an outside setting, so wherever the brooder is, that should be a major consideration. A box in the bathroom, as long as the vent fan works, for three chicks from the feed store is a fine solution.

The general guide is to provide a hot spot of ninety to ninety-five degrees Fahrenheit, and access to space elsewhere in the brooder that is cooler. The chicks can then choose their most comfortable zone. My trouble with temperature came up when, because of outside temperature influences, the entire brooder space was either over ninety-five degrees, or significantly under. Ideally, the chicks should be evenly dispersed throughout the space, not lined up along the outside wall or piled in the center under the warmest spot.

Any heat source can be used as a brooder – the term farmers use to refer to the actual heater. It can be an incandescent bulb in a socket, or a kerosene powered burner. Professional brooder lights are usually red to reduce light stress on the chicks, which can manifest as harmful pecking at each other. The brooder stays on all the time, primarily for heat, but also providing light so that the chicks can see where the water and food are.

The water should be ambient temperature, not cold. Chicken chicks were the easiest to raise, mostly because as long as their water source was set higher than their rear-ends, it stayed clean and drinkable. They drank easily and didn't knock the waterer over until it was almost empty. Dipping a chick's beak in the water when placing it in the brooder helps trigger the instinct to drink. Quail chicks are notorious for not starting to drink, even though the water is right in front of them, and dying from dehydration. Quail chicks can drown in even the smallest waterers, so it's a good idea to fill the water dish with pebbles or marbles. Enough water is available between the pebbles to drink from, but they can't get in there. Turkey chicks like to get up on top of the waterer, knocking it over and flooding the brooder. Ducklings and goslings love to paddle around in the water, or splash it around with their bills. They have to do some splashing to eat and drink, but they often manage to transform their surroundings into a swamp in anything other than a professional hatchery brooder setup, which has the food and water in troughs outside the cage. Hatcheries offer mixes of vitamins and electrolytes in water-soluble, easy-to-measure packets for the chick's first days. I did use them, as well as the newer green gel substance that provides food and water together, with good effect. The key is to encourage the chicks to eat and drink right away. Feed stores sell a grain mix designed for brooding chicks. It is usually already a "crumble," very small grains of food instead of a pellet, and is called "Chick Starter." If the chicks are small, like partridge or quail, you may have to grind the crumble in a food processor so that they can eat it comfortably. Feed used to come pre-medicated, but there's been some real progress in the industry toward making simple, clean poultry food readily available. I prefer to medicate the chicks separately, and only if they need it. A dose of antibiotic in the water can clear up a host of common chick ailments, but it is not considered organic. The antibiotic solutions are available at the feed stores and come with dosage instructions.

The litter in the brooder should be covered for the first day to prevent the chicks from confusing the litter with the food and eating it. Litter soaks up droppings and gives the chicks a safe surface to walk around on. If the brooder surface is slippery, the chicks can develop spraddle – even chicken chicks. "Spraddle" is an injury or improper growth pattern in the legs or hips that cripples the chick. Ducklings are particularly vulnerable to spraddle. Those are the two most important considerations for litter. Some farmers use straw, wood chips (not cedar), or shredded paper. Newspaper is generally too slippery and the inks aren't great, but I've used it for the first day. I used feed store wood chips last time, but that got expensive in the small volumes I was buying it.

Overall, brooding chicks is not that hard – once they have what they need. Chickens are the easiest chicks to brood and quail are the most difficult. Ducks are the cutest but also the messiest. Pheasant mature the fastest but turkeys grow in size more quickly than any of the others. There is also the option of letting a hen hatch up a fertile clutch and do the brooding work. Most hens will kill chicks that they did not hatch themselves, but using a broody hen to raise day-old chicks has been done successfully at times. This makes the whole thing easier from our point of view. The hen will need her own space, with feeders and waterers that are low to the ground so that the chicks can reach them, but she comes already equipped with everything else.

Choosing Chicks

With so many poultry breeds and species within reach, how do we choose? Ordering chicks from the hatchery late in the season and at the last minute makes the process simpler. In that case, it's whatever is available. But given time to plan and ponder, certain critical considerations help narrow down the choices: purpose, budget, location, and climate.

What is the primary purpose for the poultry? Meat, eggs, breeding, weeders, feathers? All of the birds are edible, but if meat is the main purpose, there are specific breeds of all the species, including pheasant, for superior meat production. Hens that excel as layers may not be the same breeds as meat birds, but all hens will lay eggs. Egg-producing specialty breeds just lay more. Breeder birds will cost more and require more specialized housing to promote fertility. Weeder birds are often crossbreeds and available at a discount and in bulk. I found that birds I chose specifically for their feathers did not produce as many eggs or as much meat as other breeds, but again, all of the birds yield meat, eggs, and feathers in differing amounts and qualities.

Budget can make the selection process easier. There are a lot of great deals through the hatcheries for shipments of chicks at reduced rates if the hatchery is allowed to choose the breed or the species. This enables them to place chicks and gives you a great deal. It's an excellent way of stocking a farm if your purpose is just having poultry in general. The chick's health and vigor is the same as a special order. On the other hand, if your budget is big enough, there are wonderfully specialized breeders outside the hatcheries producing beautiful heritage birds for those who are interested. Regional poultry clubs are the best way to find those sources.

Climate and location are important considerations. Chicken's combs are vulnerable to frostbite. The rose comb breeds are supposed to fare better in deep winter cold, although my rose comb chickens still had some frost bite spots. The rose comb is a flat, bumpy comb that doesn't stand up tall like a single comb. All of the chickens will grow a winter plumage of thick, furry underfeathers, but heavy-bodied chickens do better in cold temperatures. Small backyard locations are perfect for bantam breeds, which are often just a smaller version of classic breeds. All chickens make noise, but roosters are specifically banned in most urban locations for good reason.

With over sixty breeds to choose from, chicken raising can be a full-time passion. Then again, there is always the local feed store on chick day, and taking what comes. Either way, no matter the breed, chickens are rewarding and easy. Even the plainest breeds are beautiful and useful.

For my next flock, I'm going to choose some heavy meat breeds as well as some production egg breeds. Then I'll select one or two of the most dramatic feathered breeds for my feather inventory. I'll do turkeys again, but only heritage breeds, and I'll raise them far away from my chickens. This way, all of my desired product needs should be happily met. And since I got a compost turner and started cycling my stagnating compost pile through it, the one thing all poultry breeds produce the most of will be turned to gold every twenty-one days. My garden will flourish.

Pen Construction

Chicken pens are necessary primarily to keep predators out. Game bird pens are necessary to both keep the birds in and the predators out, because game birds can fly. Even in areas that don't seem prime wild animal habitat, a secure pen is a necessity. Dogs and cats are the leading urban predators but bobcats with bus passes are city culprits too. Wire pen walls are nice and secure; it's the top and bottom boundaries of the wire that need work. If the ground is too rocky or hard to dig into, you can lay a wide strip of wire at the base of the fence and weight it with rocks. Predators can start digging under, but it takes them so long to get into the pen that you should be able to see the intrusion before it's successful. The doorway is the spot most vulnerable to intrusion because doors are not usually sunk into the ground. A wire or concrete pad at the doorway is important.

Overhead coverage protects against owls, raptors, and wily climbing coyotes. Chickens can also fly short distances. They do generally return to their chicken house voluntarily to roost for the night, but they are vulnerable while they are out. I know some farmers who weigh the cost of protection against the cost of losing a few birds and let some details go. In my area any exposure or free ranging resulted in 100% losses over time. Completely enclosed pens were the only option.

The best pen design depends on your physical location, climate, budget, and the birds it will house. If you have a wide-open, flat space, there are dozens of good pen plans on the Internet that provide the best space for the least money.

We were building around trees, rocks, and arroyos and had to design accordingly, which was more expensive and difficult. Chicken tractors, which are movable pens with built-in nest boxes, are wonderful for pasture. They don't work at all in rocky, forested terrain. It's very useful to design the pen to be separated. Chickens that are all the same age can live together as a flock, but when it's time to integrate a new brood of younger birds, you have to wait until they are all the same size. Older chickens will kill smaller, younger chickens.

The hen house should be a sturdy, well-ventilated building with nest boxes and roosting bars. Chickens prefer to sleep on branches or wooden rods. These should be placed so that anything being expelled from the chicken during the night doesn't fall on another chicken, or on the eggs. We found that when we elevated the water and food off the ground, keeping them at beak height, we had fewer rodent issues. The mice still came to eat the fallen food, but they no longer held parties in the feeders themselves, or drowned in the buckets. Both food and water will benefit from being in the shade. There are a wide variety of automatic waterers and range feeders that make flock maintenance much easier.

Security and comfort are the most important design elements in building a pen. The actual materials can be whatever is at hand, assembled in whatever way works, but it does help if the doorways are built wide enough to accommodate a wheelbarrow.

About Eggs

There are an amazing number of different kinds of eggs in the world and yet the egg itself tastes largely the same. There are small differences based on how large the yolk is compared to the amount of white. Duck and turkey eggs are very "eggy" because of their large yolk ratios. Goose eggs taste lighter and sweeter because of their large white ratio. But nutritional differences are minor. Size, shape, shell thickness, and shell appearance are where all the variety occurs.

All eggs are edible, but wild bird eggs must be left undisturbed by law. Some food philosophies consider fertile eggs more nutritious than infertile, but the real difference is only obvious if the fertile egg is left sitting around in a warm place for too long. Raw egg is not dangerous unless it contains the salmonella bacteria, which can be destroyed by cooking. Cooking also makes more of the egg's natural protein digestible and therefore available for our bodies to use.

What the bird eats does affect the flavor of the egg. Onion and garlic are not harmful to backyard chicken flocks, but farmers are discouraged from feeding those vegetables to poultry because of the odor that can be imparted to the egg once the hen eats them. Fish-eating hens will produce fishy tasting eggs.

There is almost no nutritional difference between white and brown eggs. The breed of the bird determines the shell color. Any measurable difference in proteins or fats may have more to do with the bird's diet than the color of the eggshell. The color of the yolk is entirely dependent on the diet of the hen which is why farmyard free-range hens lay eggs with vividly colored yolks.

Eggs really are a wonder food and they are a huge part of our American diet. Commercial egg production is laden with some of the worst industry practices of all, so it is a good place to start consumer-driven demand for change. We must first be willing to pay more for our eggs. Cost and production volume are the driving forces behind the bad practices. Labeled certifications like "humanely raised" are as important to the hens as "organic" is to us.

Eggs are basically growth machines. They are intended to grow a chick. None of the commonly recognizable parts of the egg are the actual chick. When the egg is fertile, there is a small circular white spot on the yolk called the blastodisc. The blastodisc, or germ, will develop into the chick. The chick will use the yolk and white as it grows. The blood spot occasionally seen on the yolk is not the germ; it's just a blood spot from the egg development inside the hen.

Fertile eggs can be detected by shining a bright light through the shell about five days after the egg was laid. Any darkness in the candled egg indicates something going on inside. Rotten eggs also show a dark spot during candling. If a network of veins and a dark spot show up through the shell, the egg is developing and should NOT be cracked into a bowl. Put you off omelets forever, that will.

In many ways, an egg is a perfect food. The issue of eggs and cholesterol had been long debated with stridency from groups representing both sides. As with any great food, moderation may be the key. It's not surprising that the better the food going into the hen, the better the egg coming out.

How to Tell If a Hen is Laying

Other than actually seeing the hen lay an egg, which is by far the best method to tell if a hen is laying or not, there are some other telltale signs. Provided the chicken is not one of those with a head covered by feathers, the comb will be full and healthy looking — not dried out or scaly or withered. Those words all sound so harsh — the difference in combs between laying and not laying hens is not actually that dramatic. The laying hen's comb just looks better, fuller, moister, and happier.

The hen may suddenly squat in front of the farmer, wings tucked away from her body, tail down. This is an invitation to join together and joyfully fertilize a new generation, so I'll euphemize the whole subject by calling the hen "more approachable." Laying hens are more approachable. Their hormones pimp them out.

Laying hens will also have a greater distance between the pelvic bones over the vent, but this can be difficult to determine if you didn't already know the distance before she started laying. Three finger width between the bones for laying; one finger width for not is the general rule. This is an external measurement, no euphemism required.

Depending on the breed, the lack of yellow color in the legs can indicate a laying hen. This is most useful for light colored hens that may have had yellow legs in the first place. It really doesn't work at all for black-legged chickens. The yellow pigment fades over the laying season as components of it are used up in egg production. After the August molt, the yellow may come back. Hens typically lay fewer or no eggs during their molt.

The vent of a laying hen should be moist, full and vibrant looking. If it is small and dry, the hen may not be using it for eggs. Ironically, the more raggedy a chicken hen looks during the laying season, the more eggs she may be producing. All of her energy is going into producing the eggs, not into the condition of her feathers. Laying hens will also molt later in the season than non-layers, so that pathetic-looking hen might be one of the best.

Knowing what color egg a specific breed of hen will lay helps in a mixed breed flock. If there is only one brown egg layer and brown eggs are showing up in the nest box, then that is a good clue to figuring out which hen is laying.

Seeing a hen in the laying box may seem like a good indicator, but is only really conclusive if you also see her lay an egg there. A non-productive hen might be in the nest box to eat the eggs the other hens just laid. Of course, hens that lay eggs may also be hens that eat eggs. Suffice it to say that just being in the nest box is not a good indicator.

Hens will eventually stop laying due to age, but can lay into their third or fourth year. They will stop laying during their molt, then pick back up again when ready, so when the eggs stop rolling, it might be temporary. Or it might not, and then it is handy to be able to tell which hens are laying.

About Geese

Most of my geese were African. This means that they originally came from China, like the White Chinese goose, but in long-ago Victorian England it was the fashion to name animals after exotic places and so this breed became African. The Toulouse Goose is from Toulouse, France. It has no knob on its head and is known for soft abundant feathers. The White Chinese does have a head knob, is all white, and is a very good watch goose. The African goose, also with a head knob, is one of the loudest of the goose breeds, something I learned after I had already established my flock.

On the ground, a bunch of geese is called a gaggle. In the air, they are called a wedge. The male is a gander, the female is a goose, and the babies are goslings. They are incredibly loud birds. Our gaggle would stretch out their necks and honk, bleat, and blart in the most ear-splitting way whenever we brought a new person out to the pens. They could not only tell the difference, they shouted about it. It was impossible to hold a conversation and was actually physically painful when they were really mad. When I went into the pens alone, they made much less noise, sometimes just passing a honk back and forth amongst themselves.

Domestic geese, like my breeds of African, Toulouse, and White Chinese, are all larger than wild geese and can't fly when they are mature. But as young birds, their wingspan is long enough that they can catch some air if they run fast enough and they tested the pen walls regularly. Their wings are formidable weapons and a goose attack is no joke. I learned to quickly catch the head and then pin the wings, but I didn't always get it right, and then it was my loss.

My geese would molt their wing feathers twice a year and I collected the feathers for use and for sale. The primary feathers are the most popular. These are the longest flight feathers, but the secondary feathers were nice as well. The geese were almost a year old before they laid any eggs and only produced for three months, starting January or February and ending in June. They are long lived and the heavy breeds can live for almost twenty years. The lighter geese live even longer; I've heard rumors of past fifty years.

I tried to tame my geese by hand feeding them when they were little and snuggling them every day. They would readily eat what I offered, but as they matured, hand feeding would often turn into hand attacking which escalated into arm biting and general beating. I was never sure what triggered an attack, other than my heartbeat, and finally gave up trying to give my geese a kiss. The children were at constant risk until they grew tall enough to give the goose second thoughts, or maybe the kids just learned to run fast enough. I loved my geese, but they did not love me.

About Ducks

Ducks have immensely complex political and social lives. This doesn't leave them a lot of time for bonding with their keeper. In fact, in duck society, the keeper is the lowest of the low, treated with equal parts disdain and fear. One duck alone makes a great pet. Many ducks together make a big mess. But ducks are wonderfully useful and productive. They lay more eggs than most chickens and eat bugs that would destroy garden crops. They can be used as weeders, depending on the crop, and are a fast-growing meat source. Their feathers are also useful.

A group of ducks is called a flock or a raft or a paddling. I called them my bevy, but that term can be applied to any group of birds. The male is a drake and the female is a duck or a hen. The babies are ducklings. My bevy did not produce well at all in their second or third years. The big egg bonanza was in the first year, with good numbers and strong shells. They started laying at five months of age and continued well into the cold season before they stopped. Mallard and Rouen breeds lay green tinted eggs (also known as blue eggs), which are in high demand as blown eggs. White Pekin ducks lay a large white egg, which is great for baking. The Cayuga breed is an all-black duck that lays a black egg. Actually, the eggshell is white but is covered with a dark pigmented coating that is very vulnerable to scratches. Over time Cayuga ducks will lay lighter and lighter tinted eggs until the egg just looks dirty rather than black. Inside the egg is the same.

Drakes will fight, but mine didn't significantly injure each other. New ducks will fight until they establish their social hierarchy, which is tremendously important to them. They spend a great deal of time bowing, dipping, tail waddling, and quacking to work it all out. They are terrible gossips and big jokers. A favorite pastime was to roll an egg in the mud, then place it carefully on the path to look like a rock. When I stepped on the egg and exclaimed in dismay, they blarted themselves into a frenzy over their success.

Some of the most popular duck breeds have been exposed to commercial breeding crimes that push them to get too big too fast. The White Pekin in particular is a good layer, but is also considered a meat breed and ours reached market weight in just four months. The cost of such fast growth is poor health, weak hearts, and crippling joint issues. Because the ducks suffered from these defects, I decided to avoid that breed whenever I could.

The ducks didn't make easy companions in a mixed pen because of their food and water requirements. The water had to be placed low enough for them to flush their beaks. The food also had to be low and they would wet the crumble into paste with their water habits. I managed this by setting out enough for them to eat, but not enough to spoil, although this practice did present complications for the other birds. They shared a pen with the geese, which worked well because ducks are bullies, while geese are tall. The ducks could stand up for themselves against goose aggression and the geese were able to rise above the ducks' provocation.

Waterfowl don't have to have ponds, but they enjoy them so much it seems a shame not to at least have a wading pool for them. However, they will foul the water.

About Chukar Partridge

Alectoris chukar is a member of the pheasant family and one in a huge group of partridge species. The bird is the size of a softball and dresses like Robin Hood in war paint riding a zebra. A group of partridge is called a covey. The male is a cock or a rooster and the female is a hen. Chukar Partridge are native to India, Pakistan and Afghanistan, but have successfully colonized most of the western states of America. They are game birds, hunted for sport and because they are tasty, but considered a challenge because they are fast and live in steep rocky hillsides.

We also found them difficult to catch. They move in a group and one of their defense mechanisms is to burst up into flight all at once, known as "rising." It's an explosive, dirt strewn flapping nightmare in a pen, usually leaving us with grit in our eyes, mouth and hair. We called it "Chukar Face," because we always knew when the covey had risen based on what one of us looked like coming back from the pen.

It took them almost a year to begin laying, but then the chukar hens laid an egg a day for the entire season. The male chukar hold onto the hen's scalp feathers when breeding, and if there are too many males, the females can develop nasty wounds on their heads as the feathers pull out but the males continue to peck and grab. Male chukar are identically feathered to female, but their heads are larger and their spur bumps more pronounced. The hens have a feminine look to their heads and legs that is obvious when compared side by side with the male.

They were brutal to each other in the brooder and in

the early stages of their lives, but they were not aggressive to other bird species. Nor were other birds aggressive to them, even the serial killer pheasant that hunted everything else to extinction. Chukar are fierce fighters and the males routinely went at it, but never to the death. I think the chukar got along with all the other birds in our pens simply because chukar are scary birds. Nobody messes with chukar. Looking closely, I could see their mad, red-rimmed gaze sizzle on everything within their range — just before I was blinded by dust and grit with Chukar Face.

Brooding them was not difficult, but they were bitter about my overcrowding and prone to piling in the corners when I reached in to change the water. The chukar were the worst feather pickers of any species I raised, but they did all grow fresh healthy feathers when the cold weather set in. They were very hardy in the snow and rarely sheltered under a roof but seemed comfortable despite the deep cold. They weren't very long lived, and in their fourth year began to die naturally of old age. The males went first, having exhausted themselves fighting, romancing, and pealing out their beautiful call, chuck-chuck-chukar!

About Ringneck Pheasant

The Ringneck Pheasant, *Phasianus colchicus*, is a sub-species of the Common Pheasant. I think that these chicks were included in my hatchery collection of exotic pheasant to round out the numbers, but they turned out to be some of the most beautiful pheasant in my pens. The male Ringneck developed a series of bronze, green, cream, white, red, yellow, and green feathers that were truly eye-popping. The feathers got better as he matured, an amazing color palette that got even more complex in his second and third years of life. The male is called a cock, the female is a hen, and two or more together are called a brace.

The pheasant hen's appearance was more subdued, but her feather detail was exquisitely beautiful close-up. She's born to blend into the grass and nest and he's born to catch her attention. Ringneck Pheasant are easily available through hatcheries or game bird farms and are simple to raise, if you follow the rules pheasant live by. They are very hardy in the cold. We gave them heat lamps, but they ignored them. The few times they got saturated by rain and storm, they quickly shook off and preened themselves into beauty once again. The only real issue with Ringneck, which is true for all but a few pheasant species, is that the males have to be separated during the mating season or they will kill each other.

One cock to three hens is a good ratio. Some game bird farmers make long, narrow pens that give the birds room to fly. They also provide plenty of ground cover to hide in and the pheasant thrive. Many farmers raise pheasant on wire to protect from parasites and disease, but I preferred to give them natural ground because they enjoyed it so much. I also raised them in a very dry climate with a deep-freezing winter, which reduced the risk. There are some climates where wire is really necessary. The pens should have sight barriers between them, like a sheet of plywood, to keep the cocks from fighting through the wire. They can exhaust and injure themselves through their constant posturing and reduce their mating success. Outside of the mating season, they can live in a flock if they have enough room.

Pheasant can fly short distances and it is a treat to see them take to the air. All of their wing and tail feathers align in flight and I loved the opportunity to see them all in action. Ringneck are not aggressive with their keepers, but they have sharp leg spurs and long claws, so handling them takes attention and care. Pheasant, like all game birds, require a higher protein percentage in their feed. Most feed stores carry a game bird formula, so it isn't difficult to meet this nutritional requirement.

The birds are native to Asia but took to England nicely, where they live and breed in the wild. In the U.S., North and South Dakota have the largest wild pheasant populations and the birds are not endangered. Pheasant is the world's most hunted bird. It yields dark meat that is flavorful and not as gamey as other wild birds. It is not a fatty meat at all and I had to take care not to dry it out in the cooking. I didn't try to hang my pheasant, to let the meat age and "improve," because I didn't know what I was doing and feared poisoning my family. It may be that it's even more delicious and tender after hanging. We did have to make an effort to tenderize the meat.

There are so many color variations to the Common Pheasant that I can't list them all here. I had Melanistic Mutant and White Pheasant along with my Ringnecks. The Melanistic Mutant is a true mutation that arose in wild populations in England more than a hundred years ago. The Mutant looks like an all-black bird until it wanders into the sun and then a rainbow of colors explodes into view.

My pheasant hens laid an egg about every third day. They did lay in nest boxes but would also scratch out a patch of bare earth and lay an egg out in the open. Some of the hens simply laid an egg wherever they happened to be at the time. The eggs were most often a uniform military green, but I occasionally got a blue egg, or light green, or almost white. The hens started laying after the last snow of spring. They had an uncanny ability to predict when the last snow would be, and for as long as I had them in the pens, they were right. They stopped laying as summer turned into fall.

Pheasant are truly rewarding birds to raise, provided they get what they need. It's no wonder that the word "pheasant" itself conveys an exotic air, because even the Common Pheasant are not common at all.

About Silver Pheasant

Wolves of the pheasant world; Silver Pheasant are intense. They appear innocuous as chicks, with dull brown down and bright red legs. It's the red legs that give them away. Only Silver Pheasant, *Lophura nycthemera*, have red legs as chicks. Even young, our pheasants were curious and forthcoming. They were always at the front of the flock or hanging close by when we sat in the pens. But it wasn't affection; it was reconnaissance.

The hens retained their brown feathers, but the males slowly changed until they were utterly transformed. They grew massively complicated red face armor and snow white feathers penciled with iridescent black. Their chests and bellies were coated with blue-black feathers. The whole effect was stunning, which is just what they intended, because while we were stunned, they were creeping closer and closer.

The Silvers hunted in packs. They did plenty of mock fighting and posturing among themselves, but gave each other no injuries. The same was not true of other pheasant. They wasted no time in displays of dominance, they went in for the kill and they were fast. We finally separated them from the other flock, but not before they took out two other pheasant.

Their behavior was fascinating. They stood in our path and whirred their wings, while making a booming sound that we could more feel than hear. The males danced in circles around each other, wings outstretched. The females were haughty and cliquish. Every pheasant cock and chicken rooster in the pen was in love with them, but they didn't care.

It took more than a year for the males' mature plumage to come in, and along the way they battled for dominance with success reflected in their feathers. The most dominant male had the longest tail and most extensive white feathering. Lower caste males kept the brown feathers longer and had less of a tail display.

The hens began to lay after the final storms of the spring – when they were almost a year old. They used a nest box, but they were dedicated about eating as many eggs as they laid, so I had to be quick to collect the eggs for my purposes. The shell was a very light pastel pink, completely different from Common Pheasant eggs.

They did well together as a flock, but they were destruction incarnate for the rest of the birds once they reached maturity. Even outside of the laying season, I couldn't trust them; not even with the chickens. They were not safe around our small children. Their spurs were extremely sharp and they knew how to use them. Despite all of that, they are fascinating and beautiful birds. Rewarding, but not easy.

About Reeves Pheasant

The Reeves Pheasant, *Syrmaticus reevesii*, is a long-tailed pheasant. Although its body is about the same size as the Common Pheasant, the tail is truly tremendous. This pheasant species holds the record for longest tail feather in the world, up to eight feet long. Our male grew about three feet of gorgeous tail feathers before he broke them off by falling asleep on a winter day with his tail near the waterer. Water splashed out by the other birds froze his tail to the ground and when he woke up and ran off, it snapped in half. Some Reeves Pheasant farmers build special pens to prevent this from happening. The really long tail feathers are valuable and find an avid market. These pheasant do molt the tail feathers, so it isn't necessary to kill the bird to get these feathers. But they have been hunted into vulnerability as a species because of their tail.

In addition to his record tail feathers, the male Reeves Pheasant is known for killing other male pheasant during the mating season, and ours was no exception. He had the longest, sharpest spurs of any bird we raised. He stayed away from us, but was good at sneak attacks on unprotected jackets.

The female Reeves had very intricate feathers, which were beautiful in her own right, even if she looked more subdued than her flamboyant mate. She was very timid and if there was ground cover, she hid in it. She was a regular layer, and her eggs were a light green, easily distinguished from the Ringneck Pheasant eggs.

About Golden Pheasant

These boys were an utter delight. We had three males only, no females, and they were affectionate from the very beginning. When we opened the brooder, three delicate light-colored chicks were always at the front, ready to step onto our hands. As they grew gangly and effete, they ran circles around our feet. It wasn't until they came into their feathers that we realized that they were Golden Pheasant, *Chrysolophus pictus*. They come in a variety of color sub-species; ours were Yellow Golden. They had every shade of yellow feather imaginable, and at maturity grew a neck helmet of stiff, fan-shaped orange feathers. As those feathers came in, the birds looked like real aliens. The feathers were in sheaths as they emerged from the skin, and they all came in at once. Thick blunt needles covered the backs of their necks and then erupted all together in bright new feathers.

With their mating plumage in place, the Golden Boys set to work dancing in front of any pheasant or chicken hen, displaying fantastic steps and trilling songs. I could sit and watch them inexhaustibly. For some reason they thought the Silver Pheasant girls were the most desirable. The Goldens would cut them off and fan out their wings and tail in a sudden tilt. All of their flashiest feathers would be on show that way, with the crest feathers turning whichever way the hen was headed. It was impressive.

The Golden Pheasant never fought with malice. They dueled with each other, more of a dance than a fight, and although they had spurs, they didn't use them. We could mix these pheasant with all of the other birds successfully, but we did protect them from the more aggressive pheasant by putting them in with the chickens at mating season. Based on the fertile eggs we then got from the chickens, the Goldens did not discriminate between chickens and pheasant for their loving attentions.

These pheasant don't make very rewarding eating simply because their bodies are small. They are mostly leg and neck, but they are flavorful. Breeders in the U.S. have made them a readily available bird, but caution that many Golden Pheasant have been crossed with Lady Amherst Pheasant, so purebred lines are hard to find. The bird is native to China, and incredibly, their brilliant plumage makes them hard to see in their native habitat.

The Yellow Golden Pheasant are all about spirit. They are cheerful and interactive, although they draw the line at being touched. One of the males snuck into the segregated Silver Pheasant pen after posturing for months at the wire. It really seemed like he had something to prove. The Silvers thrashed him and would have killed him if I hadn't found him in time. Although I nursed him in the hospital brooder until his wounds healed, he never regained his cheerful good nature. He huddled in the corner of the pen and barely ate. When a big rainstorm came through, the wind knocked him upside down in a puddle and he just stayed there. He died three days later in the hospital brooder, of what I can only surmise was a broken spirit.

These were very easy pheasant to raise, hardy in the cold, and comfortable in the hot weather so long as they had access to deep shade. They were longer-lived than many of our other pheasant and brought joy to the pen.

About Chicken Breeds

Over the years we raised a variety of chicken breeds including: Buff Orpington, Silver Spangled Hamburg, Ancona, Blue Andalusian, Australorp, Red-Laced Cornish, Dominiques, White Leghorn, Buff Laced Polish, Silver Laced Polish, Gold Laced Wyandotte, Partridge Rock, Cuckoo Maran, Rhode Island Red, and Black Star.

All of them were dedicated layers, except for the Polish. Polish are "top hat" chickens, the ones with feathers growing out of their heads instead of combs. The feathers seemed to obscure their vision and their hearing. They were also unable to run in a straight line, but were very easy to catch due to their habit of zigzagging back into reach every time. When they did lay, they produced elongated small eggs that were useless for my blown egg sales. They were also small-bodied, so it took three of them to make a decent dinner. But they were pretty and weird and the girls loved them.

Cuckoo Maran are stripey black-and-gray chickens that lay a deep brown egg. Sometimes they lay a dark chocolate brown egg, much prized in the blown egg industry. Those are rare and it would take a whole flock of Cuckoo Maran to get a steady supply of the brown glories. The Cuckoo Maran are good layers. The roosters, however, are possessed by demons fresh from hell and thirsty for vengeance. They were by far the most aggressive and dangerous roosters we had, and made the pen a misery after they reached maturity. They continued their attitude at the dinner table by bringing a gamey fishy atmosphere to their stew.

Red-Laced Cornish might be my favorite chickens so

far. They really do look like griffins. Real life little griffins, filling my chicken pen. They are beautiful and lay a smallish white egg. The rooster's feathers are unique and robust, with top feathers having a hard shiny quality that's difficult to describe. The rooster's comb was vulnerable to frostbite in our climate, but he thrived anyway and the hen denied having any trouble at all.

Each of the more than sixty chicken breeds available through hatcheries and fanciers today is so well studied that we can accurately choose for the characteristics we want from the birds. I chose some chickens for their spectacular feathers, but took a hit in the egg inventory. They didn't lay as productively as the ones known for their egg production. Some of those have really beautiful feathers, too. Choosing heritage chickens is not as important as choosing heritage turkeys, but it is still a good philosophy. Our home-raised chickens were smaller and tougher than commercial chicken from the grocery store, even when we did butcher them at the right time instead of at the end of their laying life, but their flavor was intense and delightful.

Each of the breeds had something special to offer, even the Polish, who weren't much good for eggs or meat, but were good for a laugh.

About Turkeys

Around the same time that I decided, based on my own observations, that turkeys were not stupid, the scientific community announced the discovery of a direct link from Tyrannosaurus Rex to the modern-day turkey. It came as no surprise to me, because I had already seen the light. Turkeys are creatures with an ancient cold wisdom. They have very good reasons for doing the things they do. Even when some of the things they do don't make sense from our perspective.

I think Tyrannosaurs must have been gregarious and congenial creatures, despite their portrayal as lone engines of destruction. Turkeys interact with everything around them. They leave nothing uninvestigated. The Jurassic jungle must also have been a noisy place because turkeys can't be quiet to save their lives. They keep voicing a running commentary on everything.

The turkey pen is no place to fall unconscious. If the turkeys don't eat you alive, the chickens will. I learned the hard way that a turkey's inquisitive attention precedes a massively powerful pecking action. I lost two waterer o-rings and some knuckle to that lesson.

Even given these issues, I've decided that turkeys are delightful and delicious. They are not as easy to raise as chickens because of their susceptibility to disease, but the heritage breeds can be very hardy once mature. They can fly, so they can leave an untopped pen, and they have no real defenses against the predators aligned against them. They are no longer King Lizard in the jungle. They are a main course.

Heritage turkeys are the breeds that hold these joys and promises for the farmer. Commercial breed turkeys bring only a heap of hurt. I will never again raise a commercial turkey breed, which I can't say of chickens, ducks, or geese. Many of the commercial breeds in those other species are still hardy enough to live comfortable lives, but commercial turkeys have been bred beyond the bounds of common sense for meat production. They are so ungainly and crippled that it both horrified me and broke my heart. It wasn't worth the extra meat at butchering time. Even if an animal has a short life for our dietary benefit, it should still be a good life.

Turkeys also lay large numbers of eggs. My turkey hens laid an egg every two to three days during their season. The eggs are delicious and beautiful. They are large, twice the size of a chicken egg, and speckled with raised bumps on a beige shell. The heritage hens were expert nest hiders and may have brooded up their chicks if given the chance. They did well in the cold and might have had a decently long life span if they didn't taste so good. Maybe that's what really happened to the dinosaurs. Maybe it wasn't a meteor after all. Maybe it was because they tasted like chicken.

About Butchering

This is the part of poultry raising that completes the circle. We can do it in a respectful and mindful way, but we *have* to do it to fully realize the benefits of poultry farming. I have never become comfortable with it, but I feel that is because of my urban upbringing. Something I need to grow out of. And those times that I haven't butchered my birds, when I've let them live on, I can see that I didn't do them a favor. They begin to suffer from joint pain and old age discomforts. Even the heritage breed birds, with their lighter bodies and better health, are not destined to live long lives. These creatures are primary producers on the food chain and everything eats them. Nature's bargain, which I call *The Favor of the Wolf*, is that they will not have to suffer illness or old age. As soon as they slow down or falter, something will come and kill them quickly.

We have tried to transition the birds as quickly as we can from life to death. There is very little mess, provided a small child doesn't carry the headless carcass around the yard by the feet to show everyone. There are many good sources for step-by-step butchering instructions on the Internet, but outside of instructions, the only way to learn is to do it. The process doesn't take much room. Once you have a system for the butchering and have the equipment at hand, it can be a quick and routine process. The basic actions are not a mystery. We kill the bird, remove the feathers, take off the feet and wings, clean out the innards, then dispose of the parts we will not eat. Instructions for each of these steps are rife with good advice and tricks of the trade, so it's worth a little research even once we knew how to do it. People can be so innovative.

The innards of a chicken hold a universal secret. There is one key place at which the whole arrangement is attached to the rest of the bird. Sever that attachment and you can pull out all of the innards cleanly and quickly. It takes practice to find exactly the right cut point, but then out everything comes with a twist and a yank.

That mysterious attachment point is the anus.

It is the only place poultry are actually connected, the point that holds them all together. In retrospect, it explains a lot.

"It's true," Andrew says, unfortunately demonstrating, "you just reach in around the anus and give it a pull and the whole thing comes out!"

"There is something about that statement that is just so disturbing," I say.

"Except the lungs," Andrew amends, "those you have to kind of scrape out with a special tool called a Lung Puller."

"Lung Puller," I say, waving the tool in the air. "Sounds like a good name for a monster truck."

These are new moments in our long relationship. New opportunities to say things I never expected we would say to each other, for example:

"Please pass the lung puller."

Or my favorite so far:

"Shut up and reload."

About Farm Cooking

Apparently, a bad cook can get away with a lot using today's super-prepared grocery store ingredients. I didn't realize that I was a bad cook until I began using produce and meat I had grown myself, on my own land. It is pretty easy to make homegrown meat taste like a sponge simmered in hairball soup. It takes a little time to remove the spines from a zucchini. I didn't even know zucchini had spines.

Most commercial chickens intended for meat are butchered as soon as they reach market weight. They are far less than a year old and are kept from moving around very much during those short lives, in order to keep their meat tender. Even those few times that I butchered a chicken in the right time scale, my birds were tougher and leaner, but also more flavorful. Over time, supermarket chicken began to seem mushy and bland to our educated palates. Our chicken's flavor was almost as intense as bullion.

Far more often, our dinners were three-year old chickens. That is a soup chicken, no argument. Even after forty minutes of pressure-cooking, the meat was a chewing adventure. I cut it up into tiny tasty morsels that blended in with the chopped carrots, onion, and celery. If I let the meat cool in the cooking broth, I would get the nutritious gel that comes from the bone marrow and adds a super charge of goodness to the stock.

So much of the chicken or other poultry is left over that we were able to keep the dog and cats well fed also. No part of the bird has to go to waste. Even the plucked feathers can be composted using the right techniques. Not daring to give my dog the cooked chicken bones for fear of intestinal perforation, I pressure-cooked the bones a second time and ground them into paste in the food processor. It turned their kibble dinner from low nutrition mass-produced blah to a wonder food in an instant.

Basic chicken stock has onion, carrot, and celery. Basic chicken herbs are sage, rosemary, and thyme. From there, it is anybody's guess. Roosters find a way to be objectionable even when butchered early. They benefit from heavy spicing and lots of hot green chile; taste-killing hot. I could benefit from a cooking class, or a series of them. Then maybe I could branch out with my lovingly nurtured ingredients. In the meantime, it's a soup kitchen at our house around butchering time.

About Permits

Permits and licenses generally apply to game birds or specially protected species, like the Rio Grande Wild Turkey, or certain pigeon species. More often, depending on your location, restrictions or covenants are placed on owning birds. All cities have poultry laws, but a surprising number of them are in favor of having small backyard flocks (geese and roosters excepted). A county extension office is a good place to begin checking for restrictions in your area.

Each state has different regulations for game birds and even what is defined as a game bird. Generally permits, known as Game Bird Propagation Permits, are required but they are also usually easy to get and don't cost very much. It is the responsibility of the person getting the birds to get the permit; there are no red flags about it until Game & Fish is standing outside your pen asking to see the permit you didn't know you needed.

In New Mexico, I need a permit to keep and raise pheasant, partridge, grouse, quail, and Rio Grande Wild Turkey. It is a simple process that costs $10 a year. I called the New Mexico Department of Game & Fish and asked how I could get the permit. I was transferred to the Special Use Permits department and they sent out my application.

Game birds are not wild birds. All wild birds are protected. Migratory birds, like Canada geese and wild mallard ducks, have their own collection of state and federal laws. It is utterly illegal to collect eggs from the wild or to possess or to use feathers, even those from a road kill. The restrictions and consequences are fierce.

In my first year, my game bird license did not permit me to sell live adult birds, but my second and subsequent year permits specifically did. I listed disposal of the birds as butchered and consumed or died of natural causes and buried or burned. What they were really concerned about is that I did not release my birds to the wild on purpose. If I were raising my birds for hunters and intending to release them, I would need a different kind of permit and licensing.

In my New Mexico case, this propagation permit did not cover bringing the birds into the state from a hatchery. I would need an additional permit for that, as described in the fine print of the permit itself. Once again, Special Use Permits was the place to call. Anytime I sold a live bird, except for food, the person buying was responsible for their own permit, and I was supposed to tell them but not required to see the permit myself.

Pullorum Testing is generally not a legal requirement for the buyer or small flock farmer, but it is for a hatchery shipping out live chicks or hatching eggs. Pullorum is a bacterium of the Salmonella family that can be carried by live birds, including game birds, and can live in the eggs. The pullorum-free flock effort, through testing and treatment, is a nationwide movement by the USDA to reduce the presence of the salmonella bacteria in poultry flocks and therefore reduce outbreaks of the food-borne illness it causes.

Chickens and other more familiar poultry don't require special permits, but the paperwork for raising game birds shouldn't be a deterrent to owning these colorful and interesting species. It just takes a little time to stay within the law.

About The Darkling Beetle

Mealworms are such an excellent source of food and entertainment for game birds or chickens that they are worth raising. The mealworm isn't actually a worm; it's the larva of the Darkling Beetle, *Tenebrio*. (As if larvae were less creepy than worms.) They are really more like a caterpillar than a worm, from a scientific point of view. But from a poultry farmer point of view, it's all about how to get more mealworms.

One jar of mealworms from a pet store can provide a wriggly treat for a flock of poultry for about fifteen minutes, but that same jar of mealworms can form the foundation of a year-round bonanza of protein-packed fun. All the beetles need is the proper farming approach to their room and board. The basic phases of their life cycle are mealworm (larva), pupa, beetle, and egg. The beetle lays the eggs, which hatch into the larva, which turns into the pupa, which becomes the beetle.

Three large containers with more surface area than depth are perfect for an ongoing mealworm farm. I recommend lids with small holes for air because those beetles are active and ugly. Each container should be filled with bran, available at the feed store in bulk, mixed with chick starter. The dust at the bottom of the feeder after the chickens are done with it is perfect for mealworm feed. Every week, an apple, potato, carrot, or cabbage should go into the containers for additional food and moisture. Keep the containers warm (above seventy degrees Fahrenheit) and pour mealworms into each bin at one-month intervals to start. They'll go through their life cycle and keep you worming. Warmth speeds the process. Use the mealworms from one container until they are mostly gone, then clean out the box and leave the survivors alone while you harvest from the next box. The first box should re-stock itself into a mealworm city within three months.

The mealworms can take thirty to ninety days to turn into pupa. Once they are pupa, they don't eat or drink until they hatch out into beetles, about ten to twenty days. The beetles party for about ten days, then begin to lay eggs. They may live and lay for a couple of months, then die. The eggs hatch into larva in about two weeks, and the larva eat and molt and grow for thirty to ninety days. The more nutrition provided to the mealworms, the more nutritious they will be, so add things like skim milk powder and wheat germ to the bran.

As the larva and beetles consume the vegetables, bran, and chick starter, they mix it all into the bran. The vegetables will also mold unless carefully managed and the beetles lay their eggs in the potato as it dries out. This makes the container unappetizing for keeping in the kitchen. Any warm dry place with good ventilation is a fine place to keep the worm farm. Maintain the containers by periodically sifting out the bran from the worm castings and setting the whole thing up again. The waste can go into the compost for a nice boost. When you get tired of worm farming, you can toss the entire colony to the birds. Then, when you get to missing them, you can do it all over again.

The Truth About Mobile Homes

The one thing we wished we had known before rehabilitating an old mobile home was the cost and politics of moving it. Almost every mobile home transaction on the level we were dealing with includes the reality that the monster has to be moved. Many homes in mobile home parks can be bought and sold without being moved, but we were dealing with singlewides that were much more distressed than those. We were looking for a mobile home that was basically sound but otherwise heinously dilapidated, because we planned to gut it anyway. There are plenty of those in every state and they can often be bought for very little – because the seller needs to have it moved.

It's a good idea to talk first to a mobile home transport company for an estimate of the moving costs and concerns involved in your target location. One critical issue is always the axles and tires on the distressed mobile home. They are often missing and that's an important negotiation point because the seller, buyer, or transport company is going to have to come up with some before the deal is sealed.

Construction throughout these trailers is basically conventional. The exception is the floor, which is most often particleboard and extremely vulnerable to water damage. A leaky roof can compromise the structural integrity of the whole floor by allowing water to flow inside the walls. This isn't an impossible fix, but it adds to the rehab cost. The windows always leak and so rebuilding them is also a standard cost.

In northern climates, the pipes of the mobile home will

almost certainly have frozen and burst sometime during its abandonment. The plumbing is not only a probable total loss, but it's the source of so many potential leaks that it makes sense to replace it all. Even if the electrical works, it's a good idea to run new electrical that is modern, up to code, and sound.

The outside skin of the home may also need some attention, again for leak control. Once the roof is tight, the outside walls fixed, and the windows well installed, the trailer will be well protected. Then you can do whatever you like to the inside. We painted our interior "Sundawn," a color that I chose for cheerfulness and everyone else ungraciously referred to as orange. It may not have been the best color choice, but it was consistent throughout the trailer walls, ceiling and floors, which tied the whole place together nicely.

Trailers are surprisingly easy to heat, because of the low ceilings and small spaces, and any added insulation helps. We had a wood stove, properly installed and shielded, which provided immensely comforting warmth but also some lost hours of sleep for me as I checked and doubled checked for embers or danger. We had several window-mounted air conditioners for the summer and we were able to ice that trailer *down*!

Summer cooling was not all that costly in electrical power, again because of the small size of the space. Insulation and weather stripping counts as much in trailers as any other kind of home. The better the insulation, the lower the costs for heating and cooling.

All in all, a trailer can be very comfortable once someone has finished beavering it all out and replacing practically everything. But the key point in getting one is figuring the cost and effort involved in moving it. It's the *mobile* part of mobile home that makes all the difference.

Debts Not Helped
By Bankruptcy

Chapter 7 bankruptcy is personal bankruptcy. All debts discharged, no payback plan, and no reorganization. Some personal possessions, like house and car and iPod, are exempted (which means you keep them) within certain value limits. There is a certain income bracket (poverty requirement) that has to be met. There are other kinds of bankruptcy that may apply to a person's situation when Chapter 7 doesn't, and the laws vary by state. Even with a Chapter 7 Bankruptcy, there are some debts that are not dischargeable. Examples include debts for most taxes, debts incurred to pay taxes, debts that are domestic support obligations, debts for most student loans, debts for most fines, penalties, or criminal restitution obligations, debts for personal injuries or death caused by the debtor's DWI, and some debts that were not properly listed by the debtor

Debts that the bankruptcy court specifically has decided, or will decide in the bankruptcy, are not discharged

Debts for which the debtor has given up discharge protections by signing the proper reaffirmation agreement with the creditor.

Debts owed to certain pension, profit sharing, stock bonus, other retirement plans or to the Thrift Savings Plan for federal employees for certain types of loans from these plans.

Translation to all this: *Get A Lawyer*

About Bankruptcy

Should I file for bankruptcy? Will I even be eligible? How much will it cost? Where will I get the money? What will my friends and family think? Will I lose my house? What about my credit rating?

Those were nauseating questions for us, and the only answers I have are the ones that pertain to us specifically, but I do have some general information – the stuff I wish I'd had when I was trying to make the decision.

I originally thought that going to see an attorney was a good first step in answering the question, but it turns out that the action of going to see a bankruptcy attorney, even if you decide not to file, can have consequences in the outcome of the bankruptcy. Some creditors construe the act of making an appointment with a bankruptcy attorney as evidence of intent to file and therefore consider any credit card or credit line use after that appointment to be fraud; charges incurred that the debtor had no intention of paying. Do go talk to an attorney: just don't use your credit cards afterwards.

Those bitter stay-awake nights of trying to make the decision and worrying about the outcome do end. The good news is that the chaos preceding the decision, the process of deciding, and the preparation for the application are the worst parts. I can't even begin to touch the ethics of bankruptcy, as I simply no longer know how I feel about the law itself. Our custom home-building business was managing the debt load until it tanked catastrophically, and then no job in the world was going to earn enough to carry us through to paying that debt off. The business debt reverted to us personally, and there we were, with an additional personal debt burden as well.

Basically, bankruptcy is supposed to be a tool of last resort for people who have been scratching around at the poverty level for the last year and are living in a modest house with personal possessions that don't amount to much. The spirit of the law is to relieve the debt burden from a person, enabling them to rejoin society as a productive tax-paying wage earner. The process is not supposed to take your house, your car, or the basic tools you need to earn a living. Bankruptcy abuses and creditor lobbying during the Bush administration changed the definitions of all those terms: debt burden, house, car, and basic tools. The new laws added the poverty level earnings issue and guaranteed the necessity of a bankruptcy lawyer to make sense of it all.

If you can sell a bunch of possessions, downscale your house, tighten your belt, and work off your debt in a few years of concentrated effort, then do it. The bankruptcy process might result in forcing you to do that anyway while taking away your credit rating at the end of it. If there is absolutely no hope of paying it off and your income has evaporated and your heirloom collection of Hello Kitty rubber stamps isn't selling on eBay even with free shipping... then you might consider it.

If you are trying to decide whether to declare bankruptcy or to go for credit counseling, do the credit counseling. It is a requirement of the bankruptcy process anyway. The credit card companies fund the credit counseling agencies and they are dedicated to making it possible for you to pay off your debt. It is, however, a good idea to consult a bankruptcy lawyer before making an agreement with the credit counselors so that you are completely informed.

If you are struggling under the burden of a court-ordered settlement to an old lady you ran over while driving drunk on your way to mail a bad check on your delinquent student loan, then don't bother to file for bankruptcy. None of those debts are dischargeable. And neither are unpaid taxes.

A lawyer who does all the work and patiently answers all your nervous questions costs plenty. A lawyer who only fills out the form based on information you have provided and shows up with you at the courthouse costs less. But either way, in our state in 2009, costs ranged between $1500 to $7000, depending on everything. The first thing a lawyer may recommend that you do is stop paying all the bills outside of car payment, house payment and living expenses, and to not talk to any of your creditors. All the funds you were spending on minimum payments are then available for the lawyer's fee which may be one reason the lawyer's suggestion. It is a first step in the process, but you don't have to be in default to file for bankruptcy.

Assuming friends and family aren't in line ahead of you filing for their own bankruptcy, it's a toss-up what they'll think. The social stigma of a bankruptcy is definitely less in 2009 than it was many years ago. The most common cause of bankruptcy is a medical emergency. Even with health insurance, many people are forced to declare after going through a serious health crisis or accident because our health insurance industry is a crock.

Family members that are ethically opposed on moral grounds can often change their tune rapidly when you suggest moving in to live with them as an alternative to filing for bankruptcy.

You aren't supposed to lose your house in a bankruptcy – the exemptions are supposed to allow you to retain your house and your basic possessions. But if you live in a mansion surrounded by jet skis and gold-plated motorbikes, you are probably going to lose your house, and your jet skis, and your gold-plated motorbikes. There are several different kinds of bankruptcy and gold-plated motorbike owners may have to choose reorganization over discharge.

Having bad credit is not actually the end of the world, as a distressingly large percentage of the American population has found out. Bankruptcy lowers your credit score for seven years, and it stays on your credit report for ten years. It does mean that it will be harder to get loans, but that could turn out to be a good thing if it encourages one to build a life of paid-in-full assets. Recently, personal credit ratings have become an unwanted evaluation of our character and in that way, bankruptcy sucks. I had great credit before the bankruptcy and I intend to go to job interviews with proof of prior credit, my explanation, and a cheerful disposition.

Coming to the realization that you might have to declare bankruptcy, dealing with creditors if you are already in default, making the decision, and filing out the form prior to filing is an awful time. Filing, paying the lawyer, and living the limbo while the case is decided is much less stressful. The horror and fear of the collapse was worse. The truth is, having a bankruptcy on your record does not cut off all access to credit. There are lenders who solicit the newly bankrupt because they can demand exorbitantly high interest and because the debtor will not be able to file another discharge for seven years.

Once the process is over, the debtor has to grow new habits, or the problem can get worse. Bankruptcy is not a total solution, it is only a tool.

Acknowledgments

Thank you Andrew and Blue and Juno. Thank you Mr. and Mrs. Tippett. Thank you Faith Hisey and Suellen Knopick. Thank you Sue Tippett. Thank you Sue Waterman. Thank you John and June Hunt. Thank you Tom Berto and Iris and Monica. Thank you Annette. Thank you Sonya and David. Thank you Stacey. Thank you Mari and Stephanie. Thank you Diane, and Sara, and Mia. Thank you Nancy, and Katy, and Marla, and Marilyn, and Trish. Thank you Stuart, and Aimee, and Karen, and Michael Motley. Thank you Dr. Leland Hayes, and Gary LeMaster, and Jodi McDonald (Chinese Blue-Breasted Quail, not Chinese Painted Quail, and all mis-named as Button Quail), and Dr. Michael Callahan. Thank you everyone who has read, listened to, discussed, or been promised this book for so very long. Thank you anyone who has posted to community forums or maintained blogs on writing and publishing and poultry farming. Thank you Rachel, and Luka, and thank you animals.